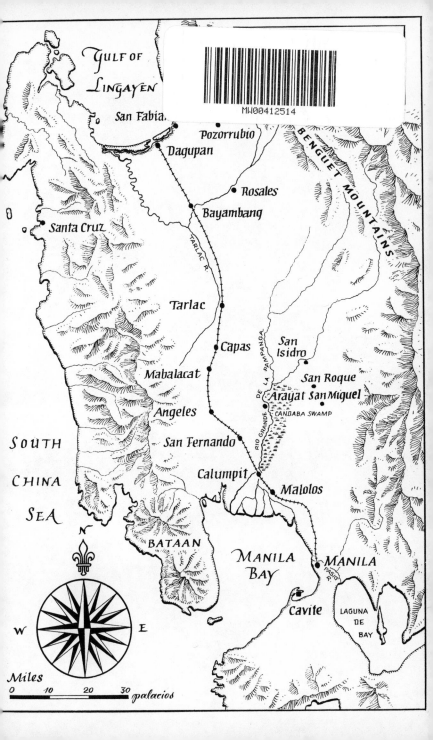

LITTLE
BROWN
BROTHER

by Leon Wolff

LITTLE
BROWN
BROTHER

HOW THE UNITED STATES PURCHASED

AND PACIFIED THE PHILIPPINES

ILLUSTRATED WITH 32 PAGES OF PHOTOGRAPHS

SINGAPORE
OXFORD UNIVERSITY PRESS
OXFORD NEW YORK
1991

Oxford University Press

Oxford New York Toronto
Delhi Bombay Calcutta Madras Karachi
Petaling Jaya Singapore Hong Kong Tokyo
Nairobi Dar es Salaam Cape Town
Melbourne Auckland
and associated companies in
Berlin Ibadan

Oxford is a trade mark of Oxford University Press

First published in the United Kingdom by
Longmans, Green and Co. Ltd., London, 1960 and in
the United States of America by
Doubleday & Company, Inc., New York, 1961

First issued as an Oxford University Press paperback 1991

This edition is published by arrangement
with Leon Wolff and Longman Group UK Limited, London

ISBN 0 19 588986 X

Printed in Malaysia by Peter Chong Printers Sdn. Bhd.
Published by Oxford University Press Pte. Ltd.,
Unit 221, Ubi Avenue 4, Singapore 1440

To My Mother and Father

ACKNOWLEDGMENTS

All photographs from the collections of the National Archives and the Library of Congress, except those of General Gregorio del Pilar and General Antonio Luna or where otherwise noted.

Acknowledgment is hereby gratefully made to the following publishers and copyright holders for permission to reprint quotations from the sources listed below:

Appleton-Century-Crofts, Inc. for *The Case for the Filipinos* by Maximo Kalaw.

Thomas Y. Crowell Company for *The Imperial Years*. Copyright 1956 by the author, Foster Rhea Dulles. Thomas Y. Crowell Company, New York.

Farrar, Straus & Cudahy, Inc. for *The Philippine Story*. Copyright 1947 by David Bernstein. Reprinted by permission of Franz Horch Associates for David Bernstein.

Houghton Mifflin Company for *The Martial Spirit* by Walter Millis.

Kansas State Historical Society for "Oh, Dewy Was the Morning" by Eugene F. Ware.

G. P. Putnam's Sons for *American Occupation of the Philippines* by James H. Blount, and *The Conquest of the Philippines by the United States* by Moorfield Storey and Marcial P. Lichauco.

San Francisco *Examiner* for "Casey at the Bat" by Ernest Lawrence Thayer.

Charles Scribner's Sons for *Memories of Two Wars* by Frederick Funston; *Our Times: The United States, 1900–1925*, Volume I, "The Turn of the Century" by Mark Sullivan; and *The Relations of the U.S. and Spain* by French E. Chadwick.

Robert Speller & Sons, Publishers, Inc. for *A Second Look at America* by Emilio Aguinaldo and Vincente Albano Pacis.

Stackpole Company for *Soldiers in the Sun* by William T. Sexton, published by The Military Service Publishing Company, Harrisburg, Pa.

CONTENTS

1

EXPANSION
AND
INSURRECTION

At 8:30 P.M., FEBRUARY 4, 1899, PRIVATE WILLIAM W. Grayson of Company B, 1st Nebraska Volunteers, was patrolling his regimental outpost near Santa Mesa, a desolate, scrubby suburb of Manila, in the Philippine Islands. We shall investigate later how he happened to be there, but for the moment it is sufficient to say that the large and obsolescent Civil War .45 Springfield rifle which he carried on his shoulder was loaded and cocked and that the young man was somewhat more nervous than usual. In theory he and the Filipinos were allies in the war against Spain, but that conflict was over, for all practical purposes, and lately new tensions had been building up between the erstwhile friends. The patrol of which Grayson was a unit had orders, in fact, to shoot any Filipino soldier who might try to enter the neutral area which separated the two armies. Only two days ago Brigadier General Arthur MacArthur had warned Colonel San Miguel in unmistakable terms concerning such boundary violations, and the Philippine officer had promised to restrain his troops. This sort of thing had been going on for some months, however, with both sides violating the zone freely. The Nebraskans had been exchanging particularly acrid insults with the Filipino insurgents, for the American camp and outposts protruded sharply into the bend of the San Juan River and were surrounded on three sides by the native army.

The evening was warm, silent, and pitch-dark. Accompanied by Private Miller, Private Grayson had cautiously worked his way into the advance area as far as the San Juan Bridge when he heard a Filipino signal-whistle on his left. It was answered by another from the right. Directly ahead, from the native blockhouse designated as Number Seven, a red lantern unaccountably flashed. The two Americans froze. Four Filipinos loomed up on the dirt road. "Halt!" Grayson shouted.

They stopped. Their lieutenant replied, *"Halto!"*—either derisively or because he was under orders similar to Grayson's. The Filipinos moved up to within fifteen feet. Grayson again yelled, "Halt!"

"Halto, halto!" snapped the native lieutenant. After a moment's deliberation, Grayson fired and dropped him. When two of the other natives sprang forward, Private Miller killed one and Grayson the other. Their marksmanship was astonishing; in total darkness they had wiped out three men with three bullets. They ran back to rejoin their patrol. "Line up, fellows," Grayson called out. "The niggers are in here all through these yards."

Within a few minutes a general engagement was in progress along a ten-mile front, the rattle of Mausers, Springfields, and Krag-Jorgensens blending into a roar that floated into Manila from the north and east. The metropolis panicked. Quickly the crowded Saturday-night cafés and theatres were emptied. Streets and parks full of promenading Americans, Filipinos, and Spaniards were left deserted. U.S. enlisted troops rushed to their barracks from all over town. In the Binondo district, Colonel Frederick Funston of the 20th

Kansas was half-asleep when someone pounded on his bedroom door and shouted, "Come out here, Colonel. The ball has begun."

Calling out excitedly, people ran toward their homes. Doors and windows were slammed shut. Soon the silence of the city was that of a tomb, except for the occasional clatter of hooves as an American officer galloped to his field headquarters. Four miles distant, the fire of massed rifles, already punctuated by the dull crash of artillery, was like continuous surf against a faraway shore. The ball had indeed begun. It was to be a dance of death for two hundred thousand souls.

II

With Private William Grayson killing Filipinos ten thousand miles from his home, the proverbial man from Mars might well have inquired what United States interests were thereby being served, and how two such diverse nations had ever managed to come to blows in the first place. From a Filipino's standpoint, the answer was simple: he was resisting annexation because he assumed that America's rule would be about as intolerable as Spain's had been, and because he saw no earthly reason why his countrymen should not govern themselves. To him the charge that they were incapable of doing so was preposterous. The words of Richard Cobden concerning India apply verbatim to the Philippines: "Its people will prefer to be ruled badly—according to our notions—by its own colour, kith, and kin, than to submit to the humiliation of being better governed by a succession of transient intruders . . ." Thus the native reaction (for this and other reasons with which our narrative will deal) was obvious and predictable.

The same apparently cannot be said for the motives of the United States of America, a democracy which itself had rebelled against foreign vassalage not many decades ago. If any theme in its philosophy could be singled out as predominant it was that all nations were entitled to self-determination. As a corollary, activities in the foreign sphere had been negligible since 1783. Except for a major rupture with adjacent Mexico at mid-century and its attendant flurry of land-greed, America's international conduct generally consisted of minding her own business; the outright acquisition by force of an African or an Asian or even a South American country was close to inconceivable. All these principles were suddenly and spectacularly violated by the Philippine embroilment.

While the shift was scarcely as abrupt as it appeared, it is not the purpose of this narrative to examine in much detail the factors which brought it about. It is enough to say that the drive toward war and the urge to expand had been some years in the making, especially since 1876, when for the first time a favorable balance of trade had come into being. By 1895 foreign business had approached the two-billion-dollar mark, and every thinking statesman had noted that the export of manufactured goods was increasing fastest of all. Years before Private Grayson disposed of his first two Filipinos, a further expansion of foreign markets had been clearly in the cards; as the *Overland Review* bluntly remarked: "The subjugation of a continent was sufficient to keep the American people busy at home for a century . . . but now that the continent is subdued, we are looking for fresh worlds to conquer . . ." Sketched by Captain Alfred Mahan of the United States Navy, young Theodore Roosevelt, who in the early 1890's was cooling his heels as U. S. Civil Service Commissioner in a run-down bureau at Eighth and E Streets, and Senator Henry Cabot Lodge of Massachusetts, the outline of the future gradually took form. Having defeated Bryan in 1896, to the immense relief of most commercial interests, William McKinley dwelt in the White House—a portly, amiable man who kept his ear to the ground and followed the popular will.

Opinions differ as to his strength of purpose and willingness to lead, but in general the traditional picture of McKinley is probably more accurate than otherwise—a good president but a weak one, sound but easily influenced. A current joke ran: "Why is McKinley's mind like a bed? Because it has to be made up for him every time he wants to use it." Could such a man halt the drift toward imperialism and war? It was said that while men would not die for William McKinley they would at least vote for him. Could it be that thousands would soon die for him?

Early in this decade fissures appeared in the wall of historic continentalism, though in no case was the physical territory of the nation increased. The pressures to play at imperialism were manifold, and a major cause was the remarkable increase in U.S. manufactured goods. But was it only economic determinism that drew us into global adventure? It is true that there were material considerations, but something more than the scent of business was in the wind. The aggressive nationalism that gripped the nation in the 1890's derived, perhaps, from a century of almost neurotic self-preoccupation. First there had been the revolution which, in its agony, had created the state; then generations of consolidation and westward expansion; then the bloodiest civil war in world history; finally years of convalescence. In the 1890's the nation raised its head and looked about. Certain fetishes developed concerning the flag. A new group of symbolisms regulated the songs, the verbal declarations of devotion to the clan—all these in such rigidity and complexity as would have astounded an African medicine man. Even the *Journal of Commerce* noted in surprise "this remarkable fashion of hanging the flag over every schoolhouse and of giving the boys military drill."

The rank of ambassador was created by Congress in 1893 —no longer would paltry ministers do. In 1895 Senator Shelby M. Cullom of Illinois exclaimed, "It is time that someone woke up and realized the necessity of annexing some property." World trade was beckoning more and more insist-

ently. There were interesting islands in various oceans. Other
great nations were on the move. At last America, too—a bit
timidly and self-consciously—stepped into the limelight.

Samoa was carved up into a protectorate under this country, Germany, and Great Britain. A seal-hunting dispute in
the Bering Sea almost brought us and England to blows. After
two of our sailors were killed in a Valparaiso brawl, a U.S.-
Chile war was narrowly averted. We nearly went to war with
Italy when, after the lynching of eleven Italians by a mob in
New Orleans, that nation demanded indemnities. Again
(1895) we challenged Britain, this time over a border dispute
between Venezuela and British Guiana, the position taken by
Downing Street having struck President Cleveland as a violation of the Monroe Doctrine. "WAR IF NECESSARY" thundered
the New York *Sun,* and the stock market tumbled to the tune
of half a billion dollars.

Meanwhile the business panic which had begun in 1893
continued. Each time the nation's economy showed signs of
recuperating, another war scare set it back momentarily. The
buying public became jittery, commodity exchanges sagged,
financial and commercial interests marked time. But the expansionists waxed more outward-looking, more confident
than ever that America's future called for an end to isolationism. Concerning the risks attendant to such policy, Captain Mahan was reassuring: "War now not only occurs more
rarely, but has rather the character of an occasional excess,
from which recovery is easy." It was not only good clean fun
but, in the opinion of Roosevelt, essential therapy: "The
clamor of the peace faction has convinced me that the country needs a war."

Yet the God-fearing, benign Republican who walked into
the White House with his equally pious wife early in 1897
was anything but an adventurer. As a former congressman
and governor of Ohio, McKinley had ignored foreign issues.
His specialties had always been money regulation and the
tariff. Coming into office during a severe depression, his main

concern was to get the country back on its feet. The last thing he wanted was a war or a tropical island. There would not be any jingo nonsense under his administration, he assured Carl Schurz; and in his inaugural address he torpedoed his party's entire foreign policy plank: "We want no wars of conquest; we must avoid the temptation of territorial aggression."

And always there was the Hawaiian problem. Ninety-nine per cent of the islands' exports sailed to the United States, and by the 1890's it appeared that their future would soon be linked to this country by bonds far stronger than mere reciprocity treaties. Beyond Hawaii beckoned another prize —China—where 400,000,000 prospective customers lived, inexcusably ignorant of the wonders of Yankee commerce. In 1896 trade with China had amounted to less than 1 per cent of total U.S. exports. On the other hand, the figure doubled next year. Could the trend continue? Unfortunately China had been defeated by Japan in 1895, following which England, Russia, France, and Germany—after shoving the outraged Japanese aside—descended like vultures upon the mainland for spheres of influence. "The various powers," piteously complained Empress Dowager Tzu Hsi, "cast upon us looks of tiger-like voracity, hustling each other in their endeavors to seize upon our innermost territories." In America consternation struck home like a dagger, and the State Department was besieged with cries from commercial interests to do something about our plain rights in the Far East.

Among people interested in foreign developments there was also an undercurrent of anxious talk about Cuba, where a violent revolution against Spanish misrule had just erupted. Times had been bad there since 1893, and when America then proceeded to raise the tariff on Cuban sugar the bottom had fallen out of that wretched economy completely. Our Cuban trade, which had exceeded a hundred million dollars yearly, dwindled to nearly nothing. Yet most Americans were forced to applaud the natives in their revolt against exploitation.

16 LITTLE BROWN BROTHER

Had we not done the same? And could a state of war, disruption of American trade, Old World suppression of Western Hemispheric freedom, be countenanced only a few miles from our coastline? Even Grover Cleveland, as his term of office drew to a close, had become annoyed by that cruel conflict just off the Florida Keys. Might we have to intervene after all? He was constrained to remark in his final message to Congress that "the United States is not a nation to which peace is a necessity." Since America had been at war with other nations, or with itself, or with Indians, or at the brink of war, ever since 1775, the Spaniards must have realized that the president's words were uncomfortably accurate.

Worse yet for Queen-Regent Christina and her boy king, another colonial revolt had just broken out against their Most Benevolent and Catholic Highnesses. The newly infected land was halfway around the world, and its ungrateful inhabitants were called Filipinos.

III

For nearly four centuries after being discovered by Magellan, the Philippine Islands had been ruled by that curious mixture of brutality, mild beneficence, and ineptitude ever typical of Spain's colonial ventures. By the 1890's the land was all but unexplored. Riches in minerals, spices, and a hundred natural or potential agricultural products lay at the feet of the conquerors and were ignored. Instead, a few thousand Spaniards tried to get rich quickly through graft, and most revenues were derived through the primitive device of taxing the natives. Under the *encomienda* system, the latter were apportioned among Spaniards and treated as slaves. Sold back and forth, worked like oxen, the Filipinos began to revolt. Within a few dozen years the islands were aflame from the Sulus to Cape Bojeador, and the Spaniards were responding typically by intensifying the harshness of their rule. Thus the years passed and the revolutions continued—large or small, sporadic or chronic, up and down the immense chain that stretched nearly from Formosa to within a dozen miles of Borneo—and the Spaniards could think of no better retort than higher taxes, and new waves of executions and imprisonments.

Whatever Spain gave the Philippines in the form of decent human relations and modern institutions was incidental. Since the system was designed to nurture graft and racism, and to save souls for the Catholic Church, no attempt was made to develop economic factors or the free play of native culture. Occasional reformers who emanated from Madrid were murdered or otherwise rendered impotent. The country was really an enormous mission, rather than a colony operated for commercial ends. Spanish law was paternal but autocratic; despite meaningless decrees, slavery was perpetuated. The people were thrust into a medieval mold, their initiative paralyzed, their education throttled. Taxation kept them poor. Except for a few middle-class pro-Spaniards, the natives were given no chance for advancement. They tilled the fields, worked in the mines, and died without medical care when disease came. Spanish civil rule sat like a millstone around their necks, and Spanish soldiers shot them when they protested, or crammed them into already overflowing jails.

And yet it was not against Spain that the natives periodically revolted. Their motto was *Viva España! Abajo los frailes!* ("Long live Spain! Down with the friars!") The friars had come with the *conquistadores* to convert the heathen. By the nineteenth century practically all Filipinos were Catholics, except for Mohammedans on the southerly islands of Mindanao, Palawan, and the Sulus. (Called Moros, they numbered about one-seventh of the population, and even Spanish zeal had been unable to revise their intractable ways.) Everywhere else the mendicant orders baptized and preached—Dominicans in black wool robes; Augustinians wearing long cassocks covered by a black cloak; Franciscans with coarse brown gowns corded around the waist, and pointed hoods.

By late in the century these three monastic orders owned almost a half-million acres of the best land in the northern islands, including much commercial property in the heart of cities like Manila. Renting out the fields to the natives on a share-cropping basis, they spread through the provinces and took control of the villages. Filipino and Spanish officials alike hesitated to challenge their authority. The natives were impressed into building roads, churches, and convents; but for any Filipino to go to court against a friar meant probable ruin. All but a few tiny parishes in remote districts were administered by Spanish monks, the only representatives of the royal government—inspectors of schools, presidents of the health boards, directors of charities, presidents of the boards of taxation, directors of public works. In general they opposed reforms which endangered their power, and some were distressingly race-conscious. A Dominican newspaper in Manila, referring to a poem about the natives recited at the University of Santo Tomas, remarked: "These verses brilliantly set forth the savage instincts and bestial inclinations of those faithful imitators of apes."

Thousands of miles from the mother country, the Philippines furnished asylum for many such men, as well as others more genuinely devout and respected. Gradually they removed Filipino priests from their parishes and replaced them by Spanish Recollects, a process which was particularly resented. Two secular Filipino priests named Gomez and Burgos campaigned against it in 1871. At the same time another revolt broke out in Cavite Province. By the time it was crushed, forty-three natives had been shot and the two Filipino ecclesiasts (plus another named Zamora) strangled. The garrote was used, an ingenious device of the European Inquisition which caused death by the slow tightening of an iron collar. The date was February 27, 1872. Murdering

Filipino priests was indeed something new. Were the Spaniards beginning to panic?

IV

There are 7,083 islands in the Philippine archipelago, about 4,000 of which have no names, being extremely small and in some cases awash at high tide. Near the end of the century less than 1,000 of them were inhabited, the two largest being Luzon and Mindanao, about the size of Illinois and Indiana respectively. The area of the entire group is slightly smaller than that of the British Isles. From north to south, it extends 1,152 miles. The distance to San Francisco is about 8,000 miles. The climate is tropical but seldom unbearably hot. The record in Manila is 104°. However, the temperature rarely goes below 60° and has been known to reach 112° in Mindanao. The hot season lasts from March to June. Then come the rains. Some places receive over two hundred inches yearly, and the humidity becomes extreme except in the mountains and plateaus of northern Luzon. From October to March the weather turns cooler and fairly dry.

The Filipinos themselves, numbering eight million near the turn of the century, remain something of an ethnological puzzle. Other than about forty thousand aboriginal Negritos, stunted in size and brain power, they are believed to be mainly descended from Malays who streamed into the islands from the South thousands of years ago. There is also some Chinese blood in the Filipino, for China has always been the archipelago's nearest civilized neighbor; and finally there are linguistic hints of a link with India and even Madagascar. Obviously, energetic sailors of many lands settled the islands. As centuries passed, the taller, intelligent Malays shoved the original Negritos deep into the mountainous hinterland. These brown Malay men—not classifiable as Orientals or Caucasians or Negroes—average about five and a half feet tall and

125 pounds in weight. Racially there is no difference between the Mohammedan and Christian groups.

As many as eighty-seven dialects were spoken. However, the confusion was not as great as it may seem, for all the major tongues—Tagalog, Visayan, Bicol, Pampango, and Pangasinan—were of the same Malay origin. Most natives possessed a smattering of Spanish, and every educated Filipino spoke and wrote the language of his conqueror more or less fluently. Tagalogs and other such superior groups had their own written literature long before the Spaniards came. Culturally (except for a few communities that clung to the past) the general level of Philippine Malays was about equal to that of European agricultural peoples, such as those in the south of France. The national budget in the 1890's allocated about a quarter of a million dollars yearly for education, about a third of which was spent in Manila. There was a passion for popular music, and every parish had its own band. Some excellent woodworking, sculpture, and painting were created, but no significant literature was written in any language.

The natives gambled enthusiastically over the national sport of cockfighting, as well as on dice and lotteries; but very little drunkenness and crime existed. Average criminal proceedings in all the islands were under six thousand yearly. No locks or bolts barred the doors of native homes. Family life was extremely devoted. Hospitality ran along Spanish lines; even total strangers were courteously received. On the other hand, Filipinos lied compulsively in their dealings with Spaniards, cheated them, reviled them behind their backs, and harmed them when they could. The residue of resentment and deceit in their souls was directed almost solely against lay and clerical Europeans. The reasons for this are too plain to require comment.

While most Filipinos cultivated the fields, over a million lived in large, fairly modern cities, of which the metropolis of Manila was the cultural and commercial nerve center, dominating the nation to an extent that can scarcely be over-emphasized. In the 1890's Manila's population stood at about a third of a million. The city was divided sharply into two sections. The Old City was completely surrounded by a Vauban-type stone wall, three centuries old, no part of which was less than thirty feet high and forty feet wide. Upon this astonishing structure the Spaniards had mounted three hundred obsolete cannon. The wall was shaped like an oval; to the north lay the River Pasig, about a hundred yards across and not fordable, to the south and southwest shimmered the sea. Moats adjoined the walls. Theoretically they could be flooded by opening sluices which led to the Pasig and the bay, but there was some question whether the mechanism was in working order. The Spaniards had never bothered to find out.

The New, or extramural, City lying across the Pasig was twice the size of the Old. Most neighborhoods had separate names (Binondo, Malate, Tondo, and so on), but they were all really Manila, a sprawling organism featured by dark, narrow streets. Especially in the walled section it possessed a somber, monastic atmosphere. There were few popular cafés and only a handful of theatres. Built not for aesthetic or material pleasures but for defense, it was manned by one Spanish and several native regiments.

But Manila, with its Chinamen and Europeans and sophisticated, citified Filipinos, did not properly typify the Philippines. The true flavor of the islands was encountered in thousands of native villages. Here homes were nipa huts raised on stilts, to avoid small animals and floods. To enter the door, one climbed a ladder. Windows were of braided thatch. To see outside, one removed them. Streets were dusty lanes that resembled their counterparts in the back-country of Arkansas and Mississippi. Over all the rivers flimsy railed bridges swayed. Everywhere the foliage grew incredibly densely—between the houses, lining the roads, and in increasing profusion as the outskirts of the village merged with the jungle, where monkeys chattered and nature held sway. All roads in the Philippines were a disaster. The natives cheerfully characterized them as either *malos caminos* (bad roads) or *muy malos caminos* (very bad roads). In the entire land, there was only one railroad. It led from Manila through Tarlac to the Lingayen Gulf, a total of 120 miles.

In the early 1890's all seemed placid in the islands, or at least normal. Chinese shopkeepers in Binondo, the commercial section of Manila, haggled with customers at their bazaars. Carriages drawn by little ponies clattered throughout the city streets and country roads. The poorest laborers and fishermen of Manila lived, quarreled, gossiped, and died in Tondo's smelly slums. Revolutionary leaders, as usual, plotted their next uprising. Through the towns religious processions passed, and throughout the day church bells pealed. The River Pasig, dividing the Old from the New City (the devout from the profane, one might say), was a chaos of steam launches and fishing boats. Theatres like the *Teatro del Principe* produced entertainment of a ribald sort, accompanied by catcalls and derisive comments from the audience. Throughout the provinces, in a few small arenas, there was bullfighting of an extremely inartistic nature; some toreadors were even known to hang on to the tails of the bulls. The *Hotel del Oriente*, one of the finest in the far east, boasted eighty-three rooms and stabling for twenty-five horses. About a dozen newspapers were published in Manila alone, of which the daily *El Diario de Manila* was most popular. Cockfighting, heavily taxed by the Spanish administration, took place everywhere on Sundays and Thursdays. Row upon row of men, women, and children toiled at the benches of cigar factories.

These places, these people, these activities are a few of the thousand threads that constituted the fabric of the Philippines at the turn of the century.

It was in 1897 that the Mayon Volcano in Albay Province erupted, killing four hundred people who lived in villages around its base. One year earlier the Philippines had also erupted, this time for the last time against Spain. At once the superficially benign aspect of the nation disappeared. Slim little men appeared in the villages and countryside, armed to the teeth with daggers, clubs, bolo knives, and sometimes guns. Again blood flowed in the land and rifles barked after fifteen years of uneasy truce. The 1896 revolt was the most serious yet, and it had been triggered by a gentle, precocious man who had no intention of starting any trouble.

V

Dr. José Rizal was born in 1861, learned to read at the age of three, and soon thereafter learned of the Spanish whips used on his people and of the injustices perpetrated by the friars. He became a poet, philosopher, surgeon, and an artist in charcoal, oils, and clay; and as he traveled through Spain, Germany, England, Italy, and France (speaking the languages of these countries) he perceived the difference between free people and his own oppressed, cringing compatriots. While studying at the University of Heidelberg, he wrote his first protest novel, *Noli Me Tangere*, (*Do Not Touch Me*). It became the *Uncle Tom's Cabin* of the revolutionary movement and marked him to Spanish authorities as a dangerous man.

On the same day that he returned to Manila, the Governor-General executed two documents. One was a safe-conduct paper, the other a statement of charges for "anti-religious and anti-patriot agitation." The doctor was arrested and deported to a little town in southern Mindanao. Yet his was the only program that might have maintained Spanish sovereignty in the Philippines. Warning against armed insurrection, he preached advancement through education and persuasion, and he urged that the economic development of the islands be accelerated. To promote these mild aims he formed the

Liga Filipina. Perhaps there were those in the league more militant, more worrisome to the authorities; at any rate, Rizal, as its head, was in 1896 arrested again. This time he was thrown into solitary confinement and charged with treason.

A dark, muscular, rather handsome man with wavy hair, he sat calmly throughout the mock trial (the evidence required for his conviction was necessarily fabricated) with his arms tied around the back of his chair. One brilliant morning he was driven along Malecon Avenue to the main park of Manila, the famous Luneta, where as a college student he had often walked with his fiancée. (Lying on the beach nine years before, he had said to her, "Do you know that I have a sort of foreboding that some such sunshiny morning as this I shall be out here facing a firing squad?")

It was the social event of the year. Breakfast parties were held on the old walls, and Spaniards of both sexes looked on from their carriages. There was many a *Viva!*, much laughter and applause, all this in contrast to the throngs of silent Filipinos. Troops held them back and artillery was trained upon them. Rizal was not allowed to face his executioners. When the volley hit him he fell and, with a final act of will, twisted his body to face the sky.

Two hundred other Filipino leaders were butchered during the reign of terror, for the revolution had started prematurely four months earlier, when the sister of one of the members of the *Katipunan* ("patriots' league") had betrayed that ferocious society while confessing to a priest. Believing that the *Katipunan* intended to murder them all (which may have seemed true; it contained roughly a quarter of a million members), the monastic and civil officials lost their heads. Other than those natives strangled by the garrote or shot, hundreds were tortured to elicit information by crushing their bones or by hanging them up by their thumbs. Five hundred other Filipinos were imprisoned. Seventy of them died of suffocation in Fort Santiago when a jailer threw a rug over the ventilating shaft. A new governor named Polavieja stated that "for the traitors no punishment seems to me adequate and commensurate with the magnitude of the crime they committed against their king and country." Filipinos arrested in Vigan Province were shipped to Manila tied up like bundles of freight, and then swung out onto the quay by derricks.

By the end of 1896, the revolutionary army in Cavite Province numbered twenty thousand troops, anxious to fight, but discouragingly short of guns and ammunition; nor did they possess uniforms or the slightest training in tactics and drill. Against this horde (mostly Tagalogs) and perhaps half that number elsewhere in Luzon and other islands to the south, the Spanish had arrayed about ten thousand well-equipped Spanish regulars and native collaborators, such as Maccabebes from Pampanga Province.

The outbreak began almost instinctively, and soon most of Luzon was a battleground. First of all, the natives dealt with certain objectionable members of the religious orders. In the village of Imus, for example, thirteen friars fell into their hands. One was killed by being gradually cut to pieces. Another was set afire, after being saturated with petroleum. Still another was pierced through the length of his body by a bamboo split, then doused in oil while alive and turned over a moderate fire. From all parts of Luzon the more apprehensive monks fled frantically to Manila. Most of them got there, but those less fortunate received varying degrees of maltreatment. Some were made household servants of Filipino families. In Olongapo they were hitched to carts and driven like carabaos. Others were simply shot or boloed outright. Meanwhile, having left these rare diversions mainly to noncombatants, the *insurrectos* were fighting Spaniards, and with mixed results. By autumn Polavieja was in the not uncommon colonial predicament of having won most of the pitched battles without being able to end the war. Any Spanish defeat invariably meant that new throngs of rebels entered the field, and Spanish victories were dreadfully arid; for the Spaniards never killed many Filipinos, but merely disorganized them and chased them away. Since the latter were disorganized to begin with, and had all of Luzon to run in, such defeats were borne by them quite cheerfully.

The Governor-General asked for more troops, but since Her Majesty already had two hundred thousand men trying to quiet the Cubans none could be spared at the moment. In any event Polavieja was finished. World opinion had been shocked by the ferocity of his actions, which British and French newspapers in the far east had taken pains to report in harrowing detail. Even the Spanish government at home was embarrassed. When it was perceived in Madrid that he could not even subdue the natives, his health became such as to require his resignation. His successor was General Fernando Primo de Rivera, a somewhat more complex individual who had been instructed to end the insurrection in one way or another; and to assist him in his patriotic labors he was handed twenty-six thousand reinforcements.

Irresistible pressure was now put on the *insurrectos*, who retreated northeast of Manila, trying to reorganize and counterattack while doing so. A headquarters was set up in a mountain cave of Biak-na-bato, a rugged area about sixty miles from the capital. To this romantic spot there wended one day a well-known Manila businessman named Pedro Paterno, escorted by a few revolutionary soldiers. The little procession moved slowly along the forest trails, and upon reaching the cave at Biak-na-bato Señor Paterno dismounted and walked inside. Everyone there knew him. Amid flickering candles he handed over a document. It was from General de Rivera and its contents were surprising. Despite the deterioration of the revolt, it was a bid for peace; and it contained any number of concessions and promises. The insurgent high command conversed in low tones. At length one young man strolled over to Paterno and began to ask questions. This was the twenty-nine-year-old leader of the Philippine Revolutionary Government: Señor Don Emilio Aguinaldo y Famy.

VI

The Filipino revolt was directed by a coterie of remarkable youths who, through contact with books and ideas from the western world that Spain had not been able completely to screen out, had bluntly rejected the dictum that they were serfs or, at best, second-class citizens. José Rizal had been a classic example of a man influenced by this social awakening that mushroomed in the Philippines during the latter half of the century. Aguinaldo was another. But if the former was a catalyst and a symbol, the latter was the Revolution incarnate.

How had he acquired leadership? Certainly he was held in no religious esteem, for he was anti-Church and a Mason. Of all the Filipino leaders he was the poorest orator. He had no advanced formal education, nor had he made much of an informal attempt to develop his mind or sphere of knowledge. Yet this unknown youth had unified, at least in varying degrees, eight million people behind him, and held an unchallenged position on the revolutionary planning staff. It seems inexplicable. Even as a personality he emerges cold, calculating, and unsmiling, a little self-conscious, obsessed not so much by the tragedy of his people as by hatred for Spaniards. Fed up with the "color line," he would prove that the Filipino was not only at the mental level of the European but above him morally and in the thirst for self-improvement. However one may explain his hold on the insurrection movement, this much is certain—he was stubborn, resentful, fanatic, and clever: a bad one, in short, to have for an enemy.

His family was a Chinese-Tagalog mixture, his parents fairly well-to-do landowners in Cavite Province. He had studied law briefly at the College of San Juan in Manila and then returned home upon the death of his father. In 1895 he left again, when a Spanish sergeant who was competing with

Aguinaldo for the affections of a Filipino beauty died under strange circumstances. Next year Aguinaldo returned and married the girl. At the same time he was elected municipal captain of his home town, Kawit. He was already an official of the murderous *Katipunan*. At this time Aguinaldo was not particularly distinguishable from a million other Filipino men near his age—about average height, and deceptively pleasant-looking. Though soft-spoken and dignified beyond his years, he was trying to live down a reputation as an abnormally proficient street fighter. He seemed without much sense of humor. Skilled as a marksman, swimmer, and rider, he had searched out adventure as a teen-age boy by putting to sea on trading vessels working between Manila, Mindora, and other central islands. His past and most of his personal traits were mildly exceptional, but they scarcely seemed to fit him for supreme command. Luck and ability as a military commander catapulted him to fame. After that it may have been his reserve, his dedication to the cause, sense of diplomacy, feeling for the theatrical gesture, shrewdness, and physical courage which did the rest.

His first move was in August 1896, at the start of the revolt. He led an assault on the Spanish garrison in his home town; it was successful and resulted in a goodly capture of rifles and bullets. He then proceeded to the town hall and issued an exhortation for the people to take up arms and join in the fight. At this time the head of the revolution and the *Katipunan* was Andres Bonifacio. A few years older than Aguinaldo, a demagogue and advocate of pure violence, he had studied the French Revolution and knew, or thought he knew, all the right moves. Unfortunately the *insurrectos* in the Manila area under his personal direction lost all their opening battles. At the same time Aguinaldo's troops in Cavite were defeating the Spaniards in one sharp engagement after another. By October, Aguinaldo had become the accepted military commander of the revolution and had issued his first national proclamation, a bombastic affair of the type that has been arousing masses of people for centuries:

> Filipino citizens! We are not a savage people; let us follow the example of European and American nations; now is the occasion for shedding our blood for the last time, that we may achieve our beloved freedom.
>
> . . . the civilization brought to these Islands by Spain during the lapse of three centuries is superficial and, fundamentally, vicious, for she has tried to keep the masses in dense ignorance, to extinguish the fire that burns in the hearts of a group of Filipinos who, for no reason other than that they are educated, are the victims of persecution . . . Spain which, not satisfied with shamelessly exploiting us, to our face calls us carabaos, drones, monkeys, and other vile epithets . . .
>
> Filipinos! . . . The time has come . . . Let us march under the Flag of the Revolution whose watchwords are Liberty, Equality, and Fraternity!

In November he smashed Spanish regulars at Binakayan and forced the veteran Spaniard, General Blanco, to flee with his troops. A costly but spectacular victory, it instantly elevated Aguinaldo to Bonifacio's level, or higher. Within a couple of months he had designed a Central Revolutionary Committee to carry on the war, had organized the villages on an emergency basis to conduct their own legal affairs and contribute to the war effort, and had set up a congress composed of outstanding Filipino patriots to consider the questions of raising men, food, and war taxes. Simultaneously he was running most of the military operations and precariously controlling the excited Filipinos who were in charge of various departments. Seldom has one man done so much so quickly. At a convention during the spring of the following year, 1897, he was elected president and generalissimo. The demotion to secretary of the interior was a cruel shock to Bonifacio, who proceeded to walk out of the convention. Refusing to recognize the new revolutionary government, he tried to form a separate army and government, in which he elected himself president. He called upon the people of the Philippines to follow him; whereupon, for underestimating his taciturn rival, he was arrested, court-martialed, and shot.

Meanwhile, as we have seen, the war had been going badly against the *insurrectos* after the arrival of General Fernando Primo de Rivera late in 1896. From Biak-na-bato Aguinaldo and his cabinet imploringly addressed the outside world . . .

> Contemplate our altars, stained by the religious orders which have converted the most sacred objects into means of enforcing shameless exploitations . . . the friar thinks only of the gold he receives. The poor are treated with contempt and only the rich are blessed.

He sanctioned a tentative constitution along strong democratic principles. A code of civil liberties was created. Universal suffrage was granted. But without military victory all this could be nothing much but words . . .

> Our tyrants rob us of the products of our land . . . Behold the law trampled under foot, converted into a weapon to be used against rather than in defense of Filipinos . . . the native is barred from holding office, arbitrary rule prevails, individual security depending not on natural right, but on the irresponsible will of any of those in authority.

Desperately he and his aides tried to keep the guerilla war alive, and from their mountain fastness they issued a steady stream of orders to a hundred local commanders throughout Luzon. They formed a new cabinet and again elected Aguinaldo president. But no foreign nation paid the slightest attention, and in the meantime the revolution was going on the rocks for lack of rifles. Around Biak-na-bato the *insurrectos*, in strong defensive positions, prepared their last stand. De Rivera sensed trouble—maybe even a disaster—if he attacked the sullen Filipinos at bay there. It was then, as we have seen, that he made his unexpected offer through Señor Paterno.

First he proposed an armistice and a general amnesty. Next he alluded to reforms that the Queen-Regent, in her wisdom and mercy, was desirous of making, and to reparation moneys (not to be construed as bribes) which might be remitted to the Filipino cabinet members, should they change their misguided ways. Protracted negotiations now set in, despite the friars, who wanted the rebels crushed and tried to sabotage the agreement. But the Governor-General had his orders, and Señor Paterno was not standing idly by. Time and again he advised the rebels of Spanish reinforcements pouring in and pointed out with regret how wretchedly armed the insurgents were in comparison. ("This he did not have to tell us," Aguinaldo conceded irritably; for it was common knowledge that only one rebel in ten owned a gun.)

At one time the *Katipunan* had naïvely asked the Mikado of Japan to take over the Philippines. The emperor had neither responded, observed Paterno, nor helped arm the rebels. His arguments were annoyingly accurate and were beginning to take effect; and Aguinaldo and his staff had to admit that if de Rivera's promises were actually instituted further resistance would be meaningless. And while it was peculiar that the Spaniards refused to put anything official in writing, they did agree orally to perform splendid deeds. De Rivera stated that he would expel the religious orders. He would give Filipinos representation in the Spanish Cortes. Filipinos and Spaniards would acquire equal treatment before the law. Filipinos would be hired in high government posts. Freedom of the press would be granted, and the right to form associations. Eight hundred and fifty thousand dollars would be turned over to the leaders of the rebellion, provided that they left the country. The friar lands would be restored to their original Filipino owners.

It all appeared far too good to be true, and one can easily picture the cynical reaction of Aguinaldo and his men. But they needed money desperately. De Rivera promised to pay the $850,000 in three installments, the final amount to arrive when one thousand rifles were handed over to the authorities and the *Te Deum* sung in the cathedral of Manila as thanksgiving for the restoration of peace. February 28, 1898, was the time limit. Two nervous Spanish generals were delivered to Biak-na-bato as hostages. By draft General de Rivera remitted $400,000 to Señor Aguinaldo in the Filipino's own name. De Rivera and other Spanish officials then pocketed the balance.

The agreement having been effected, a peace banquet was held by the *insurrectos*, uproarious with noise, wine, speeches, and rejoicing. The firearms turned in by the insurgents—1,182 of them—were rusty old rifles, deadly only to those who might be so stupid as to fire them, pistols so obsolete nobody knew how they worked, little bronze cannon of the sort used to celebrate marriages, and sundry other guns wrapped in wire and bamboo to keep them from automatically disassembling themselves.

De Rivera harshly denounced the friars, though nothing was done to curtail their powers. Aguinaldo proclaimed the revolution at an end. He and thirty-four other Filipinos emerged warily from Biak-na-bato and proceeded in triumph toward the little harbor town of Sual. Amid much fanfare everybody set sail for Hong Kong. Upon their arrival the $400,000 draft was deposited to Aguinaldo's personal account in a British bank. A junta was formed to work out the mechanics of the next revolt. A few Filipinos who tried to slip back into Manila were apprehended, tossed into jail, tortured, and put to death.

Again an uneasy peace descended upon the Philippines, like that which had followed the abortive revolt of 1871. The *Te Deum* was sung by relieved and exhilarated Spaniards in the enormous cathedral of Manila. De Rivera's amnesty brought several hundred unsophisticated Filipino peasants into his loving net. But the balance of the money due the Hong Kong exiles was not paid, many who had helped lead the revolution were executed, and no Spanish reforms went into effect, nor did de Rivera even bother to make the gesture of publishing them in writing. So, though its leaders were temporarily or permanently gone, the revolution started up all over again. In Luzon new insurrectory councils directed the same familiar guerilla operations. As soon as the people discovered that nothing had changed, fighting started again in Panay and Cebu. Assassinations and street fighting flared in various cities. Guerilla bands raided the provinces of Camarines Norte, Pampanga, Tarlac, Laguna, Nueva Ecija, and Pangasinan, killing and terrorizing the friars and the tiny Spanish garrisons. The Governor-General had been clever up to a point, but he had solved nothing at all, and in a sense he had paid out a fortune in Spanish cash to help the enemy finance a new and better rebellion.

In Hong Kong, during these stirring times, there was much unrest among the exiled revolutionaries. They appreciated the $400,000 gift, of which they intended to make good use at the first possible moment, but it was hard to sit around and talk while their people were fighting the enemy. Also, a vulgar development had come about. A certain member of the Junta, Isabelo Artacho, prompted by a Spanish bribe, was threatening to bring suit for $200,000 in back salaries as secretary of the interior of the Revolutionary Government, having held this office for two months. It was fantastic; yet litigation might tie up the entire $400,000 indefinitely. What to do?

There had been, in fact, a good deal of squabbling almost from the moment when the Filipinos had landed on that lush, green British isle just off the China coast. To his disgust Aguinaldo found that a few men yearned to split up the money—the interest on which was barely keeping them all alive—under the misconception that the funds should have been divided among them to permit the ready pursuit of wine, women, and song. Aguinaldo soon set these individuals straight, in his chilling way, but some grumbling continued behind his back. All of them were men of action, and there was too little to keep them occupied. They took up lodging in dark little rooms (a few with families lived rent-free in a house donated to Aguinaldo), smoked incessantly, plotted day and night, ate and slept erratically, pined for their families and homes, and found themselves vilified by many observers—many Filipinos, too—for selling out the Revolution for personal gain. The $400,000 remained intact, under Aguinaldo's baleful eye.

Since the insurrection was proceeding without them, and since the enemy had broken all his promises, clearly it was time to get back to Luzon. Even in the very vicinity of Manila, under the very noses of the authorities, wild activities were proceeding apace. In February 1898 the United States consul there, Mr. Oscar F. Williams, was reporting to his State Department information already well known to the distraught exiles:

> Conditions here and in Cuba are practically alike. War exists; and battles are of almost daily occurrence. Prisoners are brought here and shot without trial, and Manila is under martial law. The Crown forces have been unable to dislodge a rebel army within ten miles of Manila, and last Saturday, February 19, a battle was there fought. A republic is organized here as in Cuba. Insurgents are being armed and drilled, are rapidly increasing in number and efficiency, and all agree that a general uprising will come as soon as the Governor-General embarks for Spain, which is fixed for March.

Communications between Mr. Williams and Washington had, in fact, become quite lively of late. Previously he had been a forgotten man, an elderly minor official performing insignificant duties in an obscure oriental city. As relations between the United States and Spain deteriorated, his job had acquired much new significance. And still another U.S. consul, a Mr. Rounceville Wildman stationed in Hong Kong, had become alert to dramatic possibilities in the Philippines. Unlike Williams, who mainly contented himself with daily atrocity reports, Wildman was an individual more disposed to bravura. He had already been in touch with Don Felipe Agoncillo, the Junta's agent entrusted with foreign relations, and they had spoken guardedly about possible lines of action to pursue, should America and Spain come to blows. The Filipino flatly proposed an immediate and automatic alliance, on an if-and-when basis. He also offered to buy twenty thousand Springfield rifles; and, Wildman reported, he was "not particular about the price—is willing that United States should make twenty-five or thirty per cent profit." To this communication the State Department replied that he should encourage no advances on the part of Mr. Agoncillo.

Had Secretary Day hastened to brush off these potential allies because we and Spain were not yet at war? Perhaps to support the insurgents would indeed be diplomatically gauche and premature. On the other hand, since we were already doing precisely that in Cuba, Mr. Day's warning was perhaps confusing to our man in Hong Kong. Though rebuffed, he and the gentlemen of the Junta remained obsessed by the idea that the North American republic might soon be in a position to co-operate with the rebel movement.

But while the United States drew steadily closer to her mission of delivering the Cubans from bondage, the Filipinos happened to be in a different category. They were thousands of miles away. Many Americans had never heard of them. Even fewer knew that Spain owned the islands and that a revolution was in progress there, just as in Cuba. For unlike the Cubans the Filipinos had neglected to set up a propaganda bureau in Washington or New York. Not a word had yet been uttered in Congress about Spain's misrule of the Philippines, as against scores of impassioned speeches about matters in Cuba. Although the State Department, too, had warned Spain on numerous occasions about Cuba, nothing had been said about the Philippines. These unhappy islands, one might have concluded, were none of our business. When early in 1898 the *North American Review* carried an article entitled "The Cuba of the Far East," it was the first public reference to the situation there. Aguinaldo and his men were unaware of the cloud of American apathy concerning their cause.

Behind that cloud, however, events were on the move. If the Philippines were an enigma wrapped in a mystery to most people, Mr. Theodore Roosevelt, for one, knew a few things about them and had ideas concerning them. For example, he ascertained that Spain had a decrepit Asiatic Squadron slumbering peacefully in Manila Bay. We too had an Asiatic Squadron, and its commander was about to retire. As assistant navy secretary, Roosevelt was acquainted with the perfect man to take over—an energetic, ambitious sixty-year-old commodore named George Dewey. Gaining him the appointment was complicated by the fact that Mr. John D. Long, who had been prominent in the Peace Society before being named secretary of the navy, mistrusted Dewey's aggressive reputation. Roosevelt called for the commodore and stated, "I want you to go. You are the man who will be equal to the emergency if one arises. Do you know any Senators?"

Dewey confessed acquaintanceship with Senator Redfield Proctor of Vermont, who in turn visited President McKinley that very day. The commodore took command of the Asiatic Station at Nagasaki, Japan, on January 3, 1898. But so incensed was Mr. Long over the wire-pulling that he did not grant him the usual promotion to acting rear-admiral. Rather piqued, Dewey buried himself in the job of studying all the latest charts and data on the Philippines that he could lay hands on. (The current navy information turned out more than twenty years old.) He directed the far-flung warships under his command to assemble at Hong Kong. Thus we find Dewey and his fleet, Aguinaldo and his Junta, and the ebullient Mr. Wildman all there at the same time. The American ships went into dry dock to have their hulls painted and scraped. Having ascertained that they possessed considerably less than their peacetime allotment of ammunition, Dewey took steps to rectify this condition. He wrote home that "our ships are all . . . looking out for a right to protect American interests, of which there are many more than is generally known." Fortunately the helplessness of the Spanish eastern

fleet was notorious. As a fighting unit it was incapable of
crossing the Pacific; it could exert no threat to the American
west coast or to anything else.

Meanwhile another naval move—anything but secret—was
in progress at Port Royal, South Carolina, where the second-
class battleship *U.S.S. Maine* had been ordered to depart for
Key West and thence to Havana, Cuba for a "friendly" visit.
In view of the explosive relations with Spain, Mark Hanna,
for one, compared it to "waving a match in an oil well." Provocative or not, the *Maine*, under Captain Sigsbee, steamed
into Havana harbor the morning of January 25; and there
she lay quietly for three weeks. The sultry evening of February 15 found the captain in his cabin writing a letter to
his wife.

On the other side of the world it was dawn, and it found
Commodore Dewey's fleet knifing southward through the
China Sea. That same morning our clique of Filipino patriots
was arguing irascibly around little tables in the rear of a
Hong Kong café. What was to be done about Señor Artacho,
that dog of a traitor, who was still proposing to sue Aguinaldo
for the preposterous sum of $200,000? Some members of the
Junta would happily have strangled him; instead it was decided to smuggle Aguinaldo out of Hong Kong with the
$400,000. Matters of timing were discussed. First rifles and
cartridges would be purchased—here in Hong Kong if possible, elsewhere if necessary. Then they would charter a merchantman to land them and their goods somewhere near
Manila—perhaps at Cavite—the moment the Spanish-American War began.

A few wanted to attempt an alliance with Japan. Since the
Katipunan had previously been unsuccessful in this respect,
the idea aroused little enthusiasm. The firebrand of the revolution, General Antonio Luna—educated at the University of
Madrid, another student of the French revolution, round-
faced, thick-lipped, swarthy, with dense black hair and a
handle-bar mustache—would have none of it. As the only pro-

fessional military expert of the lot, it was he who would direct
the actual field operations, and this he wished to commence
doing at once.

There was the hunched, paralytic Apolinario Mabini, the
brain of the movement. A thirty-three-year-old attorney,
clean-shaven and balding, he had the piercing eyes of one
feverishly ill and utterly dedicated. General Miguel Malvar,
another trained soldier, was middle-aged, with a satanic little
beard and a Prussian crew cut. Colonel Gregorio del Pilar,
soon to become legendary, was a handsome youth in his early
twenties, member of a distinguished, wealthy *mestizo* family.
The cultured Felipe Agoncillo, Lieutenant Leyba (Aguinaldo's secretary), and a dozen others schemed and seethed
that day, as they had been scheming and seething for weeks.

In New York, Hearst's *Journal,* having headlined on January 25 "OUR FLAG AT HAVANA AT LAST," went on to say with
some prescience: ". . . everything is now ready for the final
scene, and it is to be hoped that it may not be long delayed."
Hearst sent Frederick Remington to Cuba to draw pictures, but (the story goes) the artist telegraphed from there,
"Everything is quiet. There is no trouble here. There will be
no war"; to which Hearst replied, "You furnish the pictures
and I'll furnish the war."

And with equal foresight Henry Cabot Lodge wrote his
friend Henry White at the American embassy in London,
"There may be an explosion any day in Cuba which would
settle a great many things. We have got a battleship in the
harbor of Havana. . . ." On that battleship the evening
passed tranquilly, the silence in Captain Sigsbee's quarters
accented only by the scratching of pen on paper and the faint
hum of dynamo engines. The time was nine-forty.

2

THE
CALL
TO
ARMS

WHAT WITH DEWEY IN THE ORIENT GRIMLY PREPARING for war, and the *Maine* resting at anchor offshore Havana, one might assume that things had gone from bad to worse. Yet they had even improved a little. Some sympathy for the Cuban rebels had evaporated in the States, in view of their annoying policy of burning cane fields owned by Americans; and there was a growing suspicion that these tactics were designed to coax us into extracting Cuban chest-nuts from the Spanish fire. Then, too, a new Liberal gov-ernment in Madrid had already replaced the excessively efficient Governor-General ("Butcher") Weyler. The natives continued to demand total independence and refused to stop fighting; but despite this jarring note it did seem that the crisis was on the wane.

None other than Roosevelt blandly remarked to McKinley in a personal talk that he had not the slightest idea that there would be a war, and then dropped the suggestion that if it *did* come to a fight our Asiatic Squadron ought to block-ade Manila and try to capture that city. The President gave no hint that he heard it. He wanted no part of the war hawks. Before his inauguration he had said to Cleveland, "If I can only go out of office . . . with the knowledge that I have done what lay in my power to avert this terrible catastrophe, I shall be the happiest man in the world." And in his December 6 message to congress he uttered words that were to haunt him and embarrass the expansionists for years. We might possibly have to intervene in Cuba some day, he noted, or we might merely recognize Cuban independence or belligerency; but one thing we would never do:

> I speak not of forcible annexation, for that cannot be thought of. That by our code of morality would be criminal aggression.

Spain wanted peace with the desperation of a field mouse fleeing from a ravenous eagle; and McKinley also wanted peace. Apart from the fact that he had fought in the Civil War and detested bloodshed, he had taken office as the aegis of prosperity (by 1898 the financial panic was over) and he was under pressure from business and other interests to stay out of Cuba. Contrarily, however, he was being prodded by other forces toward intervention. The yellow press, spearheaded by Hearst's *Journal* and Pulitzer's *World*, was hot for war and was exerting an almost hypnotic effect upon public opinion generally and upon congressional attitudes in particular. The affair of Señorita Evangelina Cisneros, a pretty blonde who had been imprisoned and allegedly mistreated by the Spaniards as a spy, was distorted into a famous tearjerker by the *Journal*. A riot in Havana on January 12, 1898, led to fears (ungrounded, as it developed) that the American consulate there was in physical danger. Partially as a result the *Maine* had been rushed to the scene. One of the last straws was the pilfering and publication of a private letter written by Señor Enrique Dupuy de Lôme, Spanish minister at Washington, in which he derided Mr. McKinley as "weak and a bidder for the admiration of the crowd, besides being a common politician who tries to leave a door open behind himself while keeping on good terms with the jingoes of the party." And there was the plain plight of the Cuban people —destitute, war-wracked, and already the object of U.S. charity in the form of food, clothing, and millions of dollars in cash. On top of all else, the *Maine* blew up in Havana harbor the evening of February 15, killing 266 of the 350 men aboard.

Still Mr. McKinley hesitated. To him and to men like Mark Hanna, the epitome of big business and one of the President's closest friends, it seemed insane to inject a dose of war into an organism that was economically healthy for the first time in years. Deploring the war fever, the *Commercial and Financial Chronicle* made this typical statement: "Every influence has been, and even now is, tending strongly towards a term of decided prosperity, and the Cuban disturbance, and it alone, has arrested the movement and checked enterprise." In two months after the *Maine* incident the stock market lost a third of the gains it had acquired so laboriously in recent years. But Mr. Roosevelt shook his fist under Senator Hanna's nose at a Gridiron Dinner and burst out, "We will have this war for the freedom of Cuba in spite of the timidity of the commercial interests."

The dilemma of the president was painful. It arrayed his personal yearnings and closest friends—those, indeed, who had placed him in the White House—against a majority clamoring for war. Hoping for a miracle that would bring both peace and the approval of the electorate, he instructed Minister Woodford in Madrid to work out a cease-fire if possible; and the Spanish government stated its willingness to negotiate. The efforts of the president were viewed by many with contempt. Roosevelt sneered that McKinley had no more backbone than a chocolate éclair. And Secretary of War Alger stated the issue to a senator in basic words: "I want you to advise the President to declare war. He is making a great mistake. He is in danger of ruining himself and the Republican party by standing in the way of the people's wishes. Congress will declare war in spite of him. He'll get run over and the party with him." Almost singlehandedly the yellow press continued its efforts to make a collision inevitable. A *World* cartoon on March 4 showed Uncle Sam rolling up his sleeves, looking toward Cuba, and saying, "Peace, By Jingo, If I Have To Fight For It!" (One reflects, with a sinking feeling, how often throughout history great nations have taken that stand.) On April 2 the *World* ran a banner headline: "GREAT BATTLE MAY BE FOUGHT WITHIN FIVE DAYS." Since we were not yet at war, an explanation grudgingly followed. It was to the effect that there would be "from two to five days more for a polite exchange of formal notes between the United States and Spain—and then war." But it would not be "much of a war."

In the midst of the hubbub, the exhilarated Cuban rebels announced that they would not discuss an armistice—for reasons unstated but all too obvious. And Senator Proctor's speech was almost the last straw, for this respected gentleman had actually visited Cuba and now before a hushed senate described the nightmares he had seen. Of the four hundred thousand natives who had been thrown into reconcentration camps, he asserted, three hundred thousand were dead or dying. At this remarkable estimate, most of the remaining waverers went over to the war camp—even some of the Wall Street crowd—and McKinley stood more alone than ever before. Despite the use of sleeping pills, he neared the breaking point. Roosevelt, upon leaving the White House one evening, met a friend and burst out, "Do you know what that white-livered cur up there has done? He has prepared *two* messages, one for war and one for peace, and doesn't know which one to send in!" On April 4, Secretary of the Navy Long wrote in his diary that McKinley was dangerously sleepless, over-worked, and no longer capable of thinking clearly. It was pathetic how he constantly asked for the latest news. And Charles Dawes (then a young man in the Treasury Department) wrote on March 27 in *his* diary, ". . . the President

proposes to intervene to stop the suffering . . . and his conscience and the world will justify it. He is making a magnificent fight for peace." Again it was that odd theme of going to
war to preserve peace.

The Spaniards, with America demanding that they totally
surrender to the Cubans, on March 31 made further concessions. Woodford sent a warning cable to his chief that the
Spaniards, with their backs to the wall, had retreated about
as far as they could or would. But on April 9 the miracle
McKinley had been praying for arrived. Spain capitulated
both to the rebels and to Uncle Sam, granting (among other
things) an immediate armistice and almost total Cuban independence. It was a remarkable diplomatic feat, certain to
end the insurrection if America accepted it, even if the rebels
momentarily did not; and Mr. Woodford cabled Mr. McKinley: "I hope that nothing will now be done to humiliate Spain,
as I am satisfied that the present Government is going, and is
loyally ready to go, as fast and as far as it can. With your
power of action sufficiently free you will win the fight on your
own lines."

The last sentence is noteworthy in its implications, and if
there was any doubt as to its meaning Woodford spelled it
out: "I believe that this means peace, which the sober judgment of our people will approve long before next November
and which must be approved at the bar of final history. I
believe you will approve this last conscientious effort for
peace."

A note of suspicion, of barely concealed alarm, runs
through Woodford's phrasing. He knew his man, and he knew
the temper of the nation. It is true that McKinley's cabinet
was for peace almost to a man and that leading Republican
senators were still for peace. McKinley, however, on April 6
had already drafted a war message. The Spanish surrender,
as we have seen, arrived April 9. Mr. McKinley made no particular change in his speech, which was loaded with grave
accusations against the Spanish government. Now that Spain

had, in fact, caved in, he merely added a penultimate sentence to that effect. Finally he tacked on the following paragraph and delivered the message on April 11 before a tumultuous joint session of Congress:

> This fact, with every other pertinent consideration, will, I am sure, have your just and careful attention in the solemn deliberations upon which you are about to enter. If this measure attains a successful result, then our aspirations as a Christian, peace-loving people will be realized. If it fails, it will be only another justification for our contemplated action.

The Senate passed a war resolution by the surprisingly narrow margin of 42 to 35, the House concurring 310 to 6. This phrase, clumsy but clear for all practical purposes, was included: "The people of the island of Cuba are, and of right ought to be, free and independent." It also contained an extraordinary amendment, inserted by Senator Henry Teller of Colorado and adopted during the excitement without debate. It read:

> The United States hereby disclaims any disposition or intention to exercise sovereignty, jurisdiction, or control over said islands, except for the pacification thereof, and asserts its determination when that is accomplished to leave the government and control of the island to its people.

Thus the nation finally surrendered to the war god who had pursued her so relentlessly for years. "I think," remarked Senator J. C. Spooner, "possibly the President could have worked out the business without war, but the current was too strong, the demagogues too numerous, the fall elections too near." On April 25 an act of Congress declared that a state of belligerency had existed since April 21, 1898.

II

We recall that Commodore Dewey many weeks before had established his fleet at Hong Kong, only a few hundred miles from the Philippines and an ideal jumping-off point should war come. By February, at which time the Asiatic Squadron was somewhat scattered on training maneuvers, news of the *Maine* disaster reinforced Dewey's opinion that a break was imminent. He purchased the British collier *Nanshan* and the merchantman *Zafiro*, and placed them under private registry as supply ships. Aboard the cruiser *Olympia*, upon which his commodore's flag fluttered in soft tropical airs, he bided his time while the day approached for which he had been born.

Later that month—the twenty-fifth, to be exact—he was not surprised to receive the following telegram:

> DEWEY, HONGKONG:
> Order the squadron, except the *Monocacy*, to Hongkong. Keep full of coal. In the event of declaration of war Spain, your duty will be to see that the Spanish squadron does not leave the Asiatic coast, and then offensive operations in the Philippine Islands. Keep *Olympia* until further orders.
> ROOSEVELT

What doubtless startled Dewey more than the serious (but anticipated) content of the message was that it was signed by the assistant secretary rather than by Mr. Long. Both the latter and Mr. McKinley had long feared the impetuous youngster, and watched him like a hawk, but Mr. Long had made the mistake of temporarily leaving him in charge of his office one afternoon. By evening he had sent the above un-authorized wire to Dewey, had redistributed a number of other ships, had put through heavy new orders for ammunition, and had ordered guns for auxiliary vessels not yet even authorized, much less under construction. Finally he transmitted to congress a message requesting a law to authorize recruiting any number of men to active naval duty. When Mr. Long reached his office next morning he nearly fainted. In his diary he wrote that Roosevelt, in his precipitate way, had caused more of an explosion than had happened to the *Maine*. But the work was done, and wheels within wheels were already turning. Mr. Long, who could have revoked Roosevelt's order to Dewey and his other actions, decided helplessly not to do so.

Commodore Dewey prepared for war with renewed diligence. He asked Consul Williams to come to Hong Kong with information fresh from Manila, and began taking off all needless and inflammable equipment, personal belongings, and woodwork from the ships of the fleet. The *Baltimore* was drydocked, scraped, and painted, all within twenty-four hours, having arrived with stores of ammunition which were transferred rapidly to other units. During these intense activities he had occasion to meet some of the gentlemen of the Filipino Junta, who were, of course, electrified over the implications of the sinking of the *Maine*.

What was said? Dewey denies promising anybody anything. His later testimony before a Senate Committee gives the impression that all they wanted was a free ride with the squadron to Manila:

> They seemed to be all very young earnest boys. I did not attach much importance to what they said or to themselves. Finally, before we left Hongkong for Mirs Bay I received a telegram from Consul-General Pratt at Singapore saying that Aguinaldo was there and anxious to see me. I said to him, "All right; tell him to come on," but I attached so little importance to Aguinaldo that I did not wait for him. He did not arrive, and we sailed from Mirs Bay without any Filipinos.

Other sources close to the scene at the time have a different version. One of them, the writer Mr. A. H. Myers, received the impression that Dewey encouraged the Filipinos to accept American arms and intensify the revolt. He reports that the Filipinos asked, "What will be our reward?" to which Dewey replied, "I have no authority; but there is no doubt if you cooperate with and assist us by fighting the common enemy, that you will be granted your freedom the same as the Cubans will be."

Mr. Myers does not tell the source of his quotation, and

the question—would Dewey help the Filipinos rise without related assurances?—remains unanswered.

Aguinaldo at this time—early April—was on the verge of leaving for Singapore to evade the legal clutches of that traitorous wretch, Señor Isabelo Artacho. While he did not see Dewey personally, he had a few talks with Commander Wood, captain of the *U.S.S. Petrel*. Wood gave him the identical sort of promises. Furthermore, he whispered, as soon as war came the Americans would proceed to Manila to demolish the Spanish fleet. That was no secret, Aguinaldo replied. He wanted to know what the Americans would do *after* their victory.

"The United States, my general," replied the captain, "is a great and rich nation and neither needs nor desires colonies."

When Aguinaldo suggested, "So that we may have the fullest understanding, it will perhaps be in order to put whatever we may agree upon in writing," Mr. Wood hedged; and next day the Filipino perforce left Hong Kong. In contrast to these further revelations Commodore Dewey's testimony continues:

> They were bothering me. I was getting my squadron ready for battle, and these little men were coming on board my ship at Hong Kong and taking a good deal of my time, and I did not attach the slightest importance to anything they could do, and they did nothing . . . finally I would not see them at all, but turned them over to my staff.

Aguinaldo reached Singapore on April 21—a notable date, as we have seen. Scarcely were his bags unpacked at the home of a friend when an Englishman, Mr. Howard W. Bray, called to inquire if he had arrived. Here, indeed, was personified the inscrutable wisdom of the East, for Aguinaldo had traveled secretly and incognito. Mr. Bray was turned away. As he left, he remarked that he was acting for the American consul-general in Singapore, Mr. E. Spencer Pratt. No simple messenger but a wealthy planter who had formerly

lived in the Philippines, Mr. Bray returned that evening, was
put off, came back the following morning, was again spurned,
and tried once more that afternoon. By this time Aguinaldo
was interested, and decided to meet him. He did so briefly,
and a further rendezvous was arranged for nine o'clock that
evening at "The Mansion," a suburban inn on the River
Valley Road. In cloak-and-dagger fashion he, Bray, Pratt, and
Lieutenant Leyba (the general's secretary) congregated and
spoke until midnight, with Bray acting as interpreter.

After Pratt had argued at length that Aguinaldo—who
needed no convincing—should co-operate with Dewey by resuming leadership of the insurrection in Luzon, he divulged
that Spain and America were already at war. Recovering from
his astonishment, Aguinaldo asked, "What can we expect to
gain from helping America?"

"Independence," said Pratt; and in reply to the Filipino's
polite request to put it in writing he continued: "You need
not have any worry about America. The American Congress
and President have just made a solemn declaration disclaim-
ing any desire to possess Cuba and promising to leave the
country to the Cubans after having driven away the Spaniards
and pacified the country. As in Cuba, so in the Philippines.
Even more so, if possible; Cuba is at our door while the Philippines are 10,000 miles away!"

Aguinaldo was impressed by the analogy. He agreed to
place himself and his army at the service of the Americans,
provided that the Philippines were given the same formal assurances as Cuba. As usual, we find him alert, cool, and
faintly suspicious. Could the substance of this present meeting be made a matter of record? he asked. And again there
was that same slight hitch. Only Dewey, it seemed, could
issue a formal statement. Aguinaldo replied that upon hearing from the commodore he would go to work; and on this
note the first meeting broke up.

It has been said ever since that a controversy exists over
its content. If so, it is a needless one. The conservative Singa-

President William McKinley

Emilio Aguinaldo

Insurrecto troops

The U.S.S. *Olympia*

(credit: Official U.S. Navy Photo)

Admiral George Dewey

The Pasig River in Manila

The *Olympia* in action, May 1, 1898

(credit: Official U.S. Navy Photo)

Spanish cruiser *Castilla*, May 1, 1898

General Thomas M. Anderson (front, center) and his staff

Aboard the *Hancock*

A *barrio* in central Luzon

General Wesley Merritt

pore *Free Press* reported the meeting on May 4 as part of a
larger story covering further relations between Pratt, Dewey,
and Aguinaldo. Mr. Pratt sent a clipping to the State Department with the assurance that its description of what happened was substantially correct, and meanwhile telegraphed
Commodore Dewey by way of the U.S. consul at Hong Kong:

> Aguinaldo, insurgent leader, here. Will come Hong Kong ar-
> range with Commodore for general cooperation insurgents
> Manila if desired.

To this Dewey replied that same Sunday: "Tell Aguinaldo
come soon as possible."

When next morning Mr. Bray and General Aguinaldo
joined Mr. Pratt at the Raffles Hotel, the American had wonderful news. The six-word telegram from Commodore Dewey
had grown like Topsy. Without showing it to them, he re-
capitulated its contents, which Aguinaldo jotted down.

> Pratt said Dewey replied that the United States would at
> least recognize the independence of the Philippines under
> the protection of the U. S. Navy. The consul added that there
> was no necessity for entering into a formal written agreement
> because the word of the Commodore and the U. S. Consul
> were in fact equivalent to the most solemn pledge . . .

There is no record of any such a telegram being sent by
Dewey, and the evidence, or lack of it, suggests strongly that
Pratt was deceptive. The *Free Press* reported the American's
assertions without comment. Mr. Bray, when interviewed,
stated his opinion that Aguinaldo had full justification for
expecting Philippine independence under a United States
protectorate. Aguinaldo's handwritten note, too, no longer
exists, if it ever existed. The commodore, at any rate, was involved with more urgent matters, having just received this
communication:

> DEWEY, HONG KONG:
> War has commenced between the United States and Spain.
> Proceed at once to Philippine Islands. Commence operations

at once, particularly against the Spanish fleet. You must capture vessels or destroy. Use utmost endeavors.

LONG

The British, acting under neutrality law, gave him
twenty-four hours to get his ships out of Hong Kong. He
moved to Mirs Bay, about thirty miles away. The Chinese
did not bother to protest, and for two days the crews drilled
with torpedoes and quick-fire guns, and aimed their eight-
inchers at cliffside targets on Kowloon Peninsula. Early afternoon of April 27 the fleet steamed out into the China Sea,
bound for Manila, while the *Olympia*'s band blared "El Capi-
tan" and the men shouted, "Remember the Maine!"

Meanwhile Aguinaldo had been having a final talk with
the ambitious, outward-looking Mr. E. Spencer Pratt. The
American urged him to see that the principles of civilized
warfare were observed by his troops, to which Aguinaldo
readily agreed. Again the subject of Philippine independence
arose; and the Filipino expressed the wish that America
would protect the islands during the transition to self-rule.
"These questions," Mr. Pratt austerely wrote the State Department, "I told him I had no authority to discuss." On the
twenty-fifth, amid a good deal of confusion, he finally put
Aguinaldo, Lieutenant Leyba, and another aide aboard the
British steamer *Malacca*. When they reached Hong Kong, at
2 A.M., May 1, the commodore's anticipated launch was not
there to greet them. At that exact moment Dewey was sipping cold tea on the *Olympia*'s bridge, as his fleet slipped
past Spanish batteries on the island of Corregidor.

Perplexed and disappointed, Aguinaldo went ashore
and was met by Mr. Rounceville Wildman, who explained
Dewey's absence and assured him that the commodore would
soon send a warship back to pick him up. The enforced
delay permitted other business to be transacted. To begin
with, Aguinaldo handed the American consul $50,000. He
then bought a steam launch for $15,000 to be used for trans-

port and communications between the islands, two thousand Mauser rifles at $7 each, and two hundred thousand rounds of ammunition at $33.50 per thousand. These items were to be landed in Cavite as soon as circumstances permitted. Next Aguinaldo ordered a long list of additional armaments and supplies, and to cover them he placed $67,000 more to Wildman's credit.

Aguinaldo stayed at Hong Kong for two weeks, occupied in this interesting way and conferring with Wildman, who dispensed more encouragement and informal promises. Like Pratt, he laid great stress on the Teller Amendment and assured the insurgent leader that the Philippines would receive the same treatment as Cuba. Privately, however, he observed to Washington that the rebel Filipino army might turn out to be "a necessary evil . . . If Aguinaldo were placed in command . . . Admiral Dewey or General Merritt would have some one whom they could hold responsible for any excesses which might otherwise be perpetrated upon the Spaniards . . ." The point of view was, perhaps, callous, but as the days passed the two men had begun to annoy each other. Aguinaldo fretted at the delay in getting to Dewey and at Wildman's evasiveness. The latter wrote his superior that the Filipino was becoming "childish and he is far more interested in the kind of cane he will carry or the breast-plate he will wear than in the figure he will make in history. The demands that he and his junta here have made upon my time are excessive and most tiresome. He is a man of petty moods . . ." Plainly Mr. Wildman possessed an irascible, if perceptive, mind, though he seemed to lack the innocent frankness of Mr. E. Spencer Pratt.

What fun, meanwhile, Mr. Pratt was having in Singapore! He had never known that diplomacy could be so intriguing and that he was so talented at it. He continued to see various Filipino patriots and his correspondence with the State Department became positively voluminous. To enlighten the Washington people, he explained that Aguinaldo aimed at the independence of the Philippines, but that he might temporarily accept American protection along the same lines that might later apply to Cuba. At the same time he forwarded a copy of the proclamation issued to the Philippine people by the insurgent leaders:

> Compatriots! Divine Providence is about to place independence within our reach . . . The Americans, not from mercenary motives, but for the sake of humanity and the lamentations of so many persecuted people, have considered it opportune to extend their protecting mantle to our beloved country . . . At the present moment an American squadron is preparing to sail for the Philippines . . . There where you see the American flag flying, assemble in numbers; they are our redeemers!

Nor could he resist complimenting himself, in another letter to his superiors, for having lined up Aguinaldo's cooperation. As for that dullard, Mr. Wildman:

> Why this cooperation should not have been secured to us during the months General Aguinaldo remained awaiting events in Hongkong, and that he was allowed to leave there without having been approached in the interest of our Government, I cannot understand.

While the State Department absorbed this reprimand and preserved a thoughtful silence, hilarity was reigning at the United States consulate in Singapore one afternoon, where Filipino residents of that city had assembled to honor Mr. Pratt and to thank him for having in effect unilaterally delivered their country from foreign bondage.

It was briskly reported in the *Straits Times*. First a thirty-piece Filipino band played several rousing selections. One Dr. Santos read a speech pledging the eternal gratitude of the Philippines for Pratt's part in bringing Aguinaldo and the Americans together. Mr. Pratt's reply expressed confidence that the Filipinos would govern themselves efficiently, and he reminisced happily concerning his role: "When, six weeks

ago, I learned that General Aguinaldo had arrived incognito
in Singapore, I immediately sought him out. An hour's interview convinced me that he was the man for the occasion; and,
having communicated with Admiral Dewey, I accordingly
arranged for him to join the latter . . ." When he finished,
everyone had begun to feel that the Philippine Islands were
already a sovereign state. Since his listeners were Christians
who drank alcohol—no Moros were present—liquid refresh-
ments were next served.

After a few drinks Pratt became even more congenial.
"Hurrah for General Aguinaldo," he cried; "hurrah for the
Republic of the Philippines!" He walked up and down the
room waving an American flag, then presented it to the Filipinos. More toasts were drunk to America, Dewey, Aguinaldo,
and to Mr. Pratt himself. The band played again. At last the
celebration ended, leaving the consul in a state of euphoria.
He wrote his superiors in Washington all about it. Finally he
was making his mark on history! But several days later the
sphinxlike silence of the Department of State was broken, and
the coded words that emanated therefrom were an icy chill
displacing the heat of the consul's Raffles Hotel suite: "Two
hundred twelve received and answered. Avoid unauthorized
negotiations with Philippine insurgents. DAY." It was the entire message.

Pratt responded apprehensively: "I neither have nor
had any intention of negotiating with the Philippine insurgents . . ."

There was nothing wrong in getting Aguinaldo's assistance
"if in so doing he was not induced to form hopes which it
might not be practicable to gratify."

Too late Mr. Pratt perceived the tomahawk en route to
his scalp and tried to fend it off. "I declined even to discuss
with General Aguinaldo the question of the future policy of
the United States with regard to the Philippines. I held out
no hopes to him of any kind, committed the Government in
no way whatever. . . ."

Inexorably the State Department turned to Mr. Pratt's clippings from the *Straits Times*, which he had suggested making public in America, and commented in these terrifying terms: "The extract . . . has occasioned a feeling of disquietude and a doubt as to whether some of your acts may not have borne a significance which this government would feel compelled to regret."

"Feel compelled to regret"! But this was almost gutter language! For while Pratt was outward-looking, he was looking in the wrong direction. The Philippines were not about to acquire independence, nor was he about to receive a promotion. Instead he was shortly dismissed from the consular service.

III

During Aguinaldo's laborious journeys on slow steamers from Luzon to Hong Kong to Singapore and back to Hong Kong, and while Dewey proceeded from Washington to San Francisco to Nagasaki to Hong Kong to Mirs Bay and finally to Manila, the commander of the Spanish Asiatic Fleet preserved a grave lassitude verging on coma. Surely this was not due to overconfidence. The Spanish problem—and it will recur in this narrative—was not how to win, for this was patently impossible, but how to appear gallant and resourceful in defeat. Admiral Patricio Montojo's best ship was the 3,500-ton *Reina Christina*, an unarmored cruiser. He possessed six others, three made of wood, one of which was a hulk which had to be towed. This feeble collection of ancient tubs, euphemistically termed men-of-war, totalled about 12,000 tons. In opposition, Commodore Dewey had 19,000 tons in the form of four armored cruisers, one unprotected cruiser, one gunboat, and the Coast Guard revenue cutter *McCulloch*. American firepower almost doubled that of the Spanish. Yet the British who cheered and waved off the American fleet, as

it left Hong Kong Harbor, thought the Yanks were doomed.
At the Hong Kong Club there had been no betting on the
Americans, even at heavy odds. A British regiment had entertained Dewey's officers at dinner one evening before their
sailing, and the commodore recalled that the prevalent remark ran to this effect: "A fine set of fellows, but unhappily
we shall never see them again."

There were tangible reasons why the Americans had been
written off. One was Spanish mines. In Dewey's memoirs,
and in a hundred other records and accounts of the day, the
fear of mines is incessantly reiterated. The entrance to Manila Bay, ten miles wide, is broken up into small channels by
the islands of El Fraile, Caballo, and Corregidor. The Spaniards had had months in which to lay a deathtrap here. Another fear was of the land-based shore batteries on the
Manila waterfront. With his back against them, it was estimated, Montojo's firepower afloat would be tripled.

Both apprehensions were groundless. Not one Spanish
mine had ever been laid in the harbor approaches until
April 19, when Montojo was instructed to do so by the Ministry of Marine. His fourteen mines had neither fuses nor
cables; in a pitiful attempt somehow to comply with orders,
a few torpedoes were strung up in the channel near Caballo
Island. Even this was done badly, for they were positioned
in such a manner that they could not be contacted.

The shore batteries were simply abandoned. Spanish merchants would not allow the admiral to place his fleet under
the protection of the city's guns, for doing so would invite
American fire that might damage commercial property near
the waterfront. The admiral bowed to superior logic. He
moved his fleet units to Cavite, and here they anchored in
the shallowest possible water off Sangley Point, so that after
they had been sunk their superstructures would be above
water and their crewmen could cling to the masts until rescued. The concept was brilliant, though 224 of these sailors

had no fear of drowning, for they had deserted their ships the moment war was declared.

With calamity impending, the new Governor-General, Basilio Augustin y Davila, turned to prayer and issued a booming manifesto:

> The North American people, composed of all the social excrescences, have exhausted our patience and provoked war . . . The struggle will be short and decisive. The God of Victories will give us one as brilliant and complete as the righteousness and justice of our cause demand . . .

> A squadron manned by foreigners, possessing neither instruction nor discipline, is preparing to come to this Archipelago with the blackguard intention of robbing us of all that means life, honour, and liberty. Pretending to be inspired by a courage of which they are incapable, the North American seamen undertake as an enterprise capable of realization the substitution of Protestantism for the Catholic religion . . .

> Vain designs! Ridiculous boastings!

> . . . The aggressors shall not . . . gratify their lustful passions at the cost of your wives' and daughters' honour, or appropriate the property that your industry has accumulated . . .

> Filipinos, prepare for the struggle . . . let us resist with Christian decision and the patriotic cry of "Viva España!"

Little imagination is needed to picture the apathy with which the Spaniards greeted this announcement, and the derision of the Filipinos. Archbishop Nozaleda assured his "beloved sons" that the gentiles, if victorious, would make them all slaves; and he begged the Filipinos to fight on Spain's side. Augustin had made his gesture merely for the record. Admiral Montojo, a sad-eyed little old man, decided to make one too. He took a few of his ships (those that were able to move) to Subig Bay, north of Corregidor, to give the impression that he was aggressively steaming out into the China Sea to meet the U.S. fleet. Upon arrival, he heard that Dewey

was nearing Lingayen Gulf. He hurried back to Sangley
Point and prepared helplessly to receive his visitors. The
stage was now set for the tragi-comedy well known to most
Americans.

We have seen that in the early morning hours of May 1
Dewey reached Corregidor, some three miles from the mainland of Bataan to the north and some twenty miles from the
shoreline at Cavite, where the Spanish fleet wanly sat. At this
point the Americans were detected by a battery on El Fraile.
A few shots were exchanged. The tension was great, for
mines were anticipated here. The commodore kept sipping
cold tea as his ships slid through the opening. Nothing
happened. By 4 A.M. the entire fleet had entered the broad
waters of Manila Bay and speed was reduced to four knots.
Men off duty were told to sleep or relax. Coffee and hardtack
were served. The combination of hot coffee and cold tea disturbed the commodore, who lost his breakfast over a lee rail
as dawn broke. He was wearing a little golfer's cap atop his
white uniform, having mislaid his uniform cap the previous
day.

The Spanish fleet was not sighted offshore Manila, and the
Americans turned westward toward Cavite. The enemy
opened fire. When the *Olympia* closed to a range of five thousand yards, Dewey turned his column to starboard so that it
paralleled the Spanish line.

"Take her close along the 5-fathom line, Mr. Calkins,"
he said to the navigator, "but be careful not to get her
aground." The gunners, stripped down to shoes and trousers,
stood silently by their guns. One shell burst just beyond the
Olympia. Dewey made no sign until 5:41, when he called
down to the conning tower, "You may fire when you are
ready, Gridley." The day was brutally hot and windless. Below decks Chief Engineer Randall of the *McCulloch*, a
portly man, collapsed and died of heat prostration. The first
American shell was thrown from an eight-inch rifle in the
Olympia's forward battery. For two hours an enormous mass

of projectiles was exchanged, and upon the placid waters of
the bay a pall of smoke settled, so dense that accurate aiming
became extremely difficult. The American fleet made five
slow passes before the Spaniards, closing the range slightly
each time.

By seven-thirty the commodore had begun to grumble
and fret. No damage to Spanish ships was at all apparent. It
is true that the Spaniards were proving extraordinarily inef-
fective. Their seven ships moved around aimlessly, often getting in each other's way, making senseless rushes and sorties,
firing with bewildering volume but seldom making a hit. Yet
not one seemed to have been sunk or disabled. To punctuate
Dewey's gloom, he was told that his five-inch ammunition
was running low. In dismay he directed the fleet to stand
out to the middle of the bay, purportedly for breakfast.

One gunner shouted, "For God's sake, Captain, don't let
us stop now. To hell with breakfast." The ammunition rumor
turned out to be incorrect, and firing was resumed. During
the interim, the smoke had cleared. It was seen then that the
enemy was fearfully hurt. By noon, after the *coup de grâce*,
all seven Spanish ships were sunk and several other auxilliary
vessels scuttled or captured. Three hundred and eighty-one
of their men were dead or wounded. In contrast, Dewey's
force had suffered only minor damage, eight men had been
slightly wounded, and only Mr. Randall had died. It was the
most one-sided victory in the annals of naval warfare; and
while Montojo had no chance from the beginning it is also
true that the inaccuracy of Spanish fire was epochal. After
six furious hours Dewey's vessels had been hit only twenty
or thirty times and the worst damage was a broken deck beam
on the *Baltimore*.

Meanwhile, Manila shore batteries having been firing at
him sporadically, Dewey sent the Spanish governor a curt
note threatening to bombard the city unless he stopped it.
He did. Dewey then demanded the use of the cable to Hong
Kong. This was refused, whereupon the *Zafiro* dragged the

harbor and cut the cable which was Manila's only modern communication with the outside world.

Thus in one day the commodore had performed a number of legendary deeds. He had told Gridley to fire when ready, he had hauled off for breakfast in the middle of a great battle, he had demolished the enemy, and finally he had pawkily withdrawn from the United States of America. He had cut the cable to spite the Spaniards, of course, but the by-product was curious; for the following wire had already been sent to Madrid by Señor Augustin:

> Our fleet engaged the enemy in brilliant combat, protected by the Cavite and Manila forts. They obliged the enemy, with heavy loss, to manoeuvre repeatedly. At 9 o'clock the American squadron took refuge behind the foreign merchant shipping.

This depressing information was published in American newspapers Monday, May 2. On the following day, and for a few days thereafter, somewhat sadder and wiser telegrams from Admiral Montojo were reported in Spain. A ray of hope was sighted in Washington, despite Dewey's unaccountable silence.

The commodore's problem was bizarre. He had just won a great naval victory, and some flunky in the Hong Kong telegraph office was refusing to accept messages not originating in Manila. The Americans were far from being in Manila. It would take an armed invasion, in fact, eventually to put them there. Dewey therefore sent the *McCulloch* to Hong Kong with the news. She arrived May 5. After two days of wrangling and red tape there, her skipper cabled the following message to Washington:

> MANILA, May 1, 1898
> The squadron arrived at Manila at daybreak this morning; immediately engaged enemy and destroyed the following Spanish vessels: *Reina Christina, Castilla, Antonio de Ulloa, Don Juan de Austria, Isla de Luzon, Isla de Cuba, General*

Lezo, and *Marques del Duero, El Correo, Velasco,* one transport, *Isla de Mindanao* . . .

DEWEY

And then this:

MANILA, May 4, 1898

I have taken possession of the naval station at Cavite, Philippine Islands, and destroyed its fortifications . . . I control bay completely and can take city at any time, but I have not sufficient men to hold . . .

DEWEY

Crowds gathered along the waterfront and stared at the foreign squadron, some people even climbing on the walls of the batteries that had been so recently firing at it. For their benefit the *Olympia's* band played "La Paloma" and other Spanish tunes, wafted gently ashore by the cool sea breeze. It was a strange interlude, one that surely could not last, and yet the days passed and the American fleet brooded there silently and inexplicably.

Back in Washington, Mr. McKinley confessed that before the battle he "could not have told where those darned islands were within two thousand miles!" We shall see that this statement was probably apocryphal. Officially the war was being fought for Cuba alone, and the Spanish fleet had been attacked to eliminate it as a possible menace to our west coast. The Spanish garrison in the Philippines, however, was remote and less than negligible as a war factor. To blockade and invade Spain herself, if possible, would have been comprehensible policy. As applied to the Philippines, such tactics hinted at broader objectives. While the United States had no naval station in the far east and international law forbade the use of neutral ports to a belligerent, Dewey had no need to stay at Manila. Sailing back to San Francisco would have been simple and natural. His job was presumably done. But the last clause of his wire dated May 4 hints that it had only begun. It is true that Dewey was under orders to con-

tinue offensive actions in the Philippines, and that it might
have seemed not only ignoble but technically improper for
him to slink away. Probably he could have disregarded those
nine-week-old instructions, for there was no Spanish navy
left to fight in Philippine waters. The administration, however, made no move to recall him and his fleet. To do so would
have been a political blunder of the first magnitude; also,
Secretary of War Russell A. Alger records that the decision
to send an army of occupation to the Philippines had been
reached before Dewey's triumph at Manila. This is verified
by Mr. McKinley's directive to the commanding general of
the army, dated May 4, that he assemble troops in compli-
ance with "verbal instructions heretofore given." That same
month Mr. Lodge wrote "Teddy" that a substantial army was
about to be sent there. Events were proceeding with haste,
nor was there much secrecy about them. "Unless I am utterly and profoundly mistaken," exclaimed the Senator, "the
Administration is now fully committed to the large policy
that we both desire." Had he been advised of these prior
"verbal instructions?"

One more set of facts indicates that serious land fighting
against some foe was contemplated in the Philippines. Late
in April, Major General Nelson A. Miles, the army's ranking
officer, was instructed to furnish recommendations for a
Philippine invasion force. On May 3, before Dewey's victory
was known here, he asked for approximately three infantry
regiments and three artillery battalions—some five thousand
troops in all. To the War Department that figure seemed sufficient at the time. Major General Wesley Merritt, the army's
number-two man, was given command. At the moment he
was at Governor's Island, New York, in charge of the Department of the East. A week later he left for San Francisco to
organize the expedition, and there he received concise instructions from the President himself. He was to go to the
Philippines and, with the help of the navy, defeat the Spaniards there. Next he was to establish order and then United

States sovereignty. In so doing he was to assure the Filipinos that his country wished only to protect, not fight them. Finally and incidentally, he was to take over public property and start collecting taxes. Three days after this interview, the general found that he still failed to understand just what to do. Was he to seize the entire country, he inquired, or just the capital city? After three additional days McKinley replied that all the islands must be given order and security "while in the possession of the United States." It was a serious tangent from traditional policy. Technically, since we were at war with Spain, it was our duty to harm and harass the enemy as much as we could, anywhere we could. The Teller Amendment barred us only from Cuba. As to rebel soldiers, naturally we would not fight them. Why should we? It was taken for granted that the semi-savages of the islands would not challenge our motives; and the State Department added a pious memorandum of its own, one befitting this most pious of all Washington agencies: "The United States in entering upon the occupation of the islands . . . will expect from the inhabitants . . . that obedience which will be lawfully due from them."

IV

In Hong Kong, Apolinario Mabini, noting among other things the strange inaction of Rear-Admiral Dewey (who had been promoted), penned a searching memorandum to his chief. Essentially, he said, the war was nothing but an effort by the United States to preserve valuable interests in Cuba. The United States would win it. Having done so, she would ask for at least part of the Philippines as indemnity. This would be tragic (he wrote reflectively), especially since the Philippines had little recourse other than ingenuity with which to ward off their new possessor. "Let us be sensible: the Americans, like the Spaniards as well as all European nations, covet this very beautiful pearl of the oriental sea . . ." Mabini's analysis, while prophetic, was not especially new to Aguinaldo, who had been doing some hard thinking of his own in recent weeks.

And while the American people, as Mr. Dooley's saying went, had not previously known whether the Philippines were islands or canned goods, they too were learning fast. Already there was speculation about what to do with the "captured islands." Senator Beveridge stunned a large audience before the Middlesex Club in Boston with a speech that brought imperialism out into the open and forecast not only the significance but the future course of the war—and this four days before Dewey's victory:

. . . we are a conquering race . . . we must obey our blood and occupy new markets, and, if necessary, new lands.

American factories are making more than the American people can use; American soil is producing more than they can consume. Fate has written our policy for us; the trade of the world must and shall be ours . . . American law, American order, American civilization, and the American flag will plant themselves on shores hitherto bloody and benighted, but by those agencies of God henceforth to be made beautiful and bright.

. . . In the Pacific is the true field of our earliest operations. There Spain has an island empire, the Philippine Archipelago. It is poorly defended. Spain's best ships are on the Atlantic side. In the Pacific the United States has a powerful squadron. The Philippines are logically our first target.

At Bangkok, Siam, our minister there, John Barrett, put the idea in different words when interviewed by a newspaperman: "It is of the greatest importance that the United States should take the Philippine Islands. Their value is not realized at home. They are richer and far larger than Cuba, and in the hands of a strong power would he the key to the Far East."

The New York *Times* had changed its editorial mind with celerity. On May 3 it stated that we could not dream of retaining the Philippines but must turn them over to Great Britain. On May 4 it reiterated that "not in any event" could we take the islands. One paragraph later it confessed that if Britain turned them down, we might have to take them after all. After five days it had become plain "that paramount necessity will compel us to assume for a time" the job of ownership and administration. Coming from America's greatest newspaper, and a pro-administration one to boot, this six-day turnabout was most significant.

These and several other widely published statements had come to the recent attention of General Aguinaldo. His always dormant suspicions awakened. Now it was more desirable than ever to talk frankly to Admiral Dewey, more vital than before to assume firm insurrectionary control of the islands as soon as possible. Imperialism, which abhors a vacuum, might be checked by a *fait accompli* in the form of a victorious Filipino army and an established Filipino government. The *McCulloch* arrived at Hong Kong in order to deliver Dewey's momentous cables, as we have seen, and to pick up Aguinaldo. On the evening of May 16 the Filipino leader (with seventeen of his staff) finally boarded her for the last leg of his historic odyssey.

Aguinaldo has recorded his feelings during the quiet voyage that ensued. They picture a man deeply perplexed. Was he to be a cat's-paw in this new war to be waged under the direction of the United States Navy? Would his own people support him? Surely his return would placate those who thought he had abandoned his country for gold. Had Spain been true to the promise not to harm his family? Now that he was returning, what was to stop the Spaniards from seizing them as hostages? And always there was the key question: What assurances would he receive from Admiral Dewey, and how valid would those assurances be? For two and a half days, as the little cutter drove southeast through the China

Sea, Aguinaldo and his staff pondered and discussed what lay before them.

The *McCulloch* dropped anchor in Manila Bay the afternoon of May 19. Without delay a launch came alongside and took off Aguinaldo, Colonel del Pilar, and Lieutenant Leyba. After being piped aboard the *Olympia,* they were descended upon by a gray-haired, fatherly figure resplendent in white full dress uniform. It was Rear-Admiral George Dewey, and he was holding out his hand and smiling broadly. Like Mr. Pratt and Commander Wood and Mr. Wildman before him, he too had interesting tidings for Emilio Aguinaldo.

3

DEWEY
AND
AGUINALDO

O F ALL THE FUTILE CONTROVERSIES IN UNITED STATES
history, there are few to match that concerning Dewey's alleged commitments to Aguinaldo. "It is the word
of a Malay adventurer," observed the Hartford *Courant*,
"against the word of an American admiral and gentleman
. . . We believe George Dewey." The admiral never bothered to put anything in writing; the Filipino swears he
itemized everything; and while the former implication may
hardly be regarded as suspicious, the other proves nothing.
Dewey says he never suggested that Philippine independence would arise out of the insurgents' co-operation with
him, and even claims that he never considered Aguinaldo as
an ally, although he "did make use of him and the natives
to assist me in the operations against the Spaniards."

If this appears something of a contradiction, Aguinaldo's
version is equally dubious. The admiral could not guarantee
Philippine independence. He was only a military commander;
as such he was not an independent agent, and Aguinaldo

knew it. Though Messrs. Pratt, Wildman, and Williams at times came perilously close to promising the Filipinos self-government, it is hard to imagine the more circumspect Dewey doing so, nor does a single scrap of paper exist to prove that he did. From Hong Kong, it is true, Rounceville Wildman wrote Aguinaldo at about this time to rest assured that the Spanish-American War was being fought to free the Cubans "not for the love of conquests or the hope of gain," and that his countrymen were "actuated by precisely the same feelings for the Filipinos." There had been other such assurances and Dewey was to supply (or imply) many more. While Mabini and Aguinaldo entertained something less than full confidence in these quasi-official pronouncements, they pinned their ultimate hopes on the Teller Amendment, even though, strictly speaking, it pertained only to Cuba. At heart they assumed that when Dewey called on Aguinaldo to take action as a co-belligerent it meant the automatic recognition of their government. America's actions—then and later—spoke to the Filipinos louder than Dewey's words, whatever those words may have been.

Affairs at the outset were muddied by misunderstandings. While the issue was crucial, and both sides vaguely recognized it as such, at the moment neither was concerned about technicalities. Their immediate problem was Spain. Only Mabini looked a trifle further than that. It was one of those moments when history moved too fast for its participants. The assumed attitude of the Americans was that they intended to whip the Spaniards and set the natives free, and the latter were excitedly taking it for granted. It was not until several months later that the controversy exploded, among other explosions more literal and devastating. By then it had become a moral issue almost unparalleled in American policy and politics. Yet it would be superficial to dismiss the squabble as an exercise in semantics; for from this breakdown in communications (or diplomacy) evolved a disaster in the an-

nals of colonialism which compares with the Sepoy Mutiny
or France's 1830 Algerian intrusion.

Dewey and Aguinaldo needed each other's aid. From this
seed war blossomed. Largely due to non-meeting of the
minds, the two nations blundered into each other much like
the United States and China a half-century later in Korea. It
must also be noted that Filipino naïveté played its part. After
three centuries of servitude the natives were filled with sudden hopes. The men of the Junta remembered McKinley's
recent phrase linking forcible annexation with criminal aggression. They noted Mr. Lodge's even more recent Senate
speech: "We have grasped no man's territory, we have taken
no man's property, we have invaded no man's rights. We do
not ask their lands." It was hard not to believe this sort of
thing; and to compound confusion there were marked differences of opinion among the natives themselves. Some, like
Luna and Mabini, demanded total independence. Aguinaldo
vacillated between this and a temporary U.S. protectorate arrangement. At the moment he was even willing to fight the
Spaniards under American military direction. But the amount
and kind of American protection varied widely among those
who desired it. At one extreme it was little more than sym-
bolic, at the other something close to outright ownership.
With the Filipino leaders themselves so divided, and the
American position contradictory in the extreme, the possibility of a *modus vivendi* was not good from the start.

It is against this confused backdrop that events now developed. Simple compromises which might have solved everything were never explored. Washington was surprised by
Dewey's sudden, fantastic victory and had no policy for in-
heriting an insurrection. The rebels jumped to certain conclusions. Dewey was given no instructions to speak of. He
and Aguinaldo proceeded together against the Spaniards, but
their initial dealings ignited a new train of powder.

II

Upon boarding the *Olympia* (with the honors due a general officer, says Aguinaldo; not true, replies Dewey), Aguinaldo plunged into immediate conference with the admiral. His first question was whether the American had really sent Pratt the telegram recognizing Philippine independence under the temporary shelter of the U. S. Navy. He had indeed, said the admiral, and assured his guest that America was uninterested in colonies. Next (so it is said), Dewey asked Aguinaldo if he could induce his people to rise quickly and decisively against the Spaniards. The general replied that events would speak for themselves. "Well, now," exclaimed the admiral, "go ashore there; we have got our forces at the arsenal at Cavite, go ashore and start your army." He gave him sixty-two Mausers, some captured Spanish arms, and a supply of ammunition. That night Aguinaldo slept aboard the flagship. The following day, before going ashore, he conferred again with Dewey. With some embarrassment, he spoke of prevalent suspicions that the American government might not recognize insurgent authority over the islands, and that the two sides would soon be fighting each other. Dewey scoffed at the rumors and reiterated that Philippine independence was assured. He advised Aguinaldo to compose a Philippine national flag, but not to unfurl it until Spain was defeated.

(When subsequently questioned by Senator Carmack: "You did want a man there who could organize and arouse the people?" the admiral, irritable under long interviewing, replied, "I didn't want anybody. I would like to say now that Aguinaldo and his people were forced upon me by Consul Pratt and Consul Wildman.")

Thus ended the first two meetings. They have become somewhat legendary. The honor of both the Philippines and the United States rests upon them. Patriots of both nations have therefore interpreted them as might be expected; but we shall never know precisely what George Dewey told Emilio Aguinaldo, nor shall we speculate further. Aguinaldo closes the matter by stating flatly: "In the archives of the government in Washington and in almost all the history books on the Philippine-American War, it is of record that both [sic] Dewey, Pratt, and Wildman completely denied having made every promise that they had made to me."

The general went ashore at Cavite on May 20. In its gossipy way, the Singapore *Free Press* reported: "Admiral Dewey was very much pleased with him, and has turned over to him two modern field pieces and 300 rifles, with plenty of ammunition. General Aguinaldo is now organizing an attack on the Spanish land forces, and a decisive battle may be expected soon." The two men saw each other daily for a time, and the Filipino followed Dewey's instructions to the letter on military and administrative matters. But he had little to do with him after the army came, the admiral later recalled.

News of Aguinaldo's return spread like wildfire through the provinces, throwing the population into a new uproar. A flood of volunteers engulfed the ex-Spanish arsenal, which with all its weapons and stores had been turned over to the *insurrectos*. Almost to a man, Filipino militiamen formerly attached to the Spanish army went over to their compatriots with twelve thousand precious rifles. The insurgents, admits Dewey, "could have had any number of men; it was just a question of arming them. They could have had the whole population." At headquarters, for several days, the problems of food, money, uniforms, and the allocation of weapons were overwhelming. With his wife and infant son, Aguinaldo moved into the home of the former Spanish naval commandant and tried to co-ordinate this final and most hectic phase of the revolution.

At first few Americans on shore or aboard the squadron

paid much attention. Then it was seen that thousands of natives were arriving, and endless crates of rifles and ammunition were being unloaded along the slender pier that pointed eastward, like a finger, at the mainland across the bay. With a flicker of interest the American sailors learned that this barefoot native mob was supposed to help them lick the Spaniards. After a few days the mob seemed to have acquired some simple coherence. The men drilled in little groups on the parade ground, feebly stirring the dust, as seen from a distance. They cleaned and disassembled and reassembled their new weapons. Plainly they were disciplined, and what impressed the Americans who came into contact with them was their confidence and desire to kill Spaniards. Lieutenant Leyba, Aguinaldo's secretary, dined aboard ship with several of Dewey's officers one evening and stated evenly that an offensive would take place within a week. It would proceed up the neck of land that attaches Cavite to the main island, and then northeast along the beach toward Manila. At this point, he thought, the first serious battle would take place. Having won it, his people would then capture Manila. The Americans listened ironically and agreed among themselves that the modest, immaculately uniformed youngster was talking nonsense. And yet the Filipino army multiplied before their very eyes; there was no secret about its lethal intentions as that sunny week flickered by. Was it possible that these untutored peasants could actually win America's war?

The admiral had his doubts. "I was waiting for troops to arrive, and I felt sure the Filipinos could not take Manila, and thought that the closer they invested the city the easier it would be when our troops arrived to march in. The Filipinos were our friends, assisting us; they were doing our work." Indeed they were; and yet, when told that a general attack was scheduled for May 31, Dewey urged caution. Would it not be better, he queried Aguinaldo, to wait until his men were better armed and trained? But on May 28 some three hundred Spaniards raided a Filipino ammunition train, and in the skirmish which followed the Europeans were all killed or captured. The incident made the insurgents even harder to restrain.

They had even collected a comical little navy—eight Spanish steam launches and five larger ships big enough to carry a few captured three-inch guns—and these vessels now commenced darting about the bay under their new Filipino flag, quite insolently getting in everyone's way. Matters were moving quickly. Aguinaldo's earlier deference had given place to a disquieting assurance. In conferences with Dewey and other officers his cool reserve seemed to have deepened into something resembling hauteur. Very erect, a little vain, his jet-black hair pompadoured back, he spoke little and often merely smiled instead of answering questions. He fingered his sword and joked mildly about the $25,000 price laid on his head by the Spaniards. He was really becoming a bit difficult. Sourly the admiral wrote Washington that his protégé was getting a "big head." On May 24 he had proclaimed a temporary dictatorial war government (naming himself president) to exist until a constitutional convention met.

His official statement contains many a pointed phrase. The United States, he said, was "undoubtedly disinterested," and the Filipinos were quite "capable of governing for ourselves our unfortunate country." He sent a copy in Spanish to Dewey on the *Olympia*, and the latter endorsed it to the Navy Department without bothering to have it translated. The admiral was weary of all the proclamations. This was the fifth or sixth that had reached his desk and (as we shall see) he had other pressing problems on his hands. But they kept coming thick and fast, all exceedingly long and overwrought in tone and written in Spanish or Tagalog, and Dewey kept passing them along without comment.

A great day was June 18, 1898, when Aguinaldo issued the Philippine Declaration of Independence. It was ordained a national holiday in perpetuity, and natives of all provinces celebrated as never before. Invited to attend the ceremony at Filipino headquarters, Dewey declined. It was mail day, he explained politely; and the somewhat startled Malays were left to draw their own conclusions. Five days later the dictatorial government was abolished. In its place, as promised, a revolutionary regime was established, providing for a congress, a cabinet, a supreme court, and so on; and its obvious intention was to set up a *de facto* government carrying the warning tag: "Hands off."

Dewey forwarded a copy of the document to Washington by ordinary steamer mail instead of by cable, with an accompanying letter which stated in part: "In my opinion these people are superior in intelligence and more capable of self-government than the natives of Cuba, and I am familiar with both races." And later he added, "Further intercourse with them has confirmed me in this opinion." One perceives where the admiral's rather cursory sympathies lay. But how much weight would they carry among the hardheaded, outward-looking politicos back home? Could he, for example, influence a man such as Henry Cabot Lodge who, with an excitement rare for him, had just written Henry White in London that the Philippines "must be ours . . . We hold the other side of the Pacific, and the value to this country is almost beyond imagination"?

The Filipinos wondered if they were about to be handed over from one master to another. Hastily they pressed their new government into being, although its congress would not convene for some weeks. There was little to distinguish it from the American system. The president was granted somewhat greater power than his U.S. counterpart. The legislative branch was unicameral. Departmental secretaries—Foreign Relations, Marine and Commerce, War, Public Works, Police, Justice, Instruction, Hygiene, and Treasury—were all appointed by the executive and corresponded closely to U.S. cabinet posts. The body of jurisprudence was taken almost intact from the code of English-speaking peoples. Congress itself was to be composed of representatives elected by popular vote in each province. All this was largely the brain child of Apolinario Mabini. Paralyzed from the waist down since 1895, he lived in a wheel chair and had been spared the more severe Spanish reprisals. Now he was known as Aguinaldo's "Dark Chamber"—his right-hand man, the writer of his most important papers, the intellect, the planner without whose instructions Aguinaldo seldom spoke or acted on any matter of state.

Several days after its proclamation, the document was signed by ninety-eight Filipino officials and one Artillery Colonel L. M. Johnson of the United States Army. Since Admiral Dewey failed to report the event to Washington, it is not known when it came to the attention of the State Department. There is no record of any comment thereupon—adverse, complimentary, or noncommittal—by that body. It was, in fact, Washington's glacial silence which perturbed the revolutionaries more than any overt act. Dewey patted Aguinaldo on the back and told him to start up his army, but after their first two meetings he said nothing about the beauties of the infant government, which seemingly could have died in childbirth for all that America cared. Proclamation after proclamation, government after government, came into being. The foundling lisped and prattled and stretched out its dimpled hand, but Uncle Sam had eyes only for little Cuba.

III

The London *Times* predicted that America would annex the islands or sell them to someone else perhaps Great Britain. Upon learning of this, Aguinaldo flared up and addressed a message (the poor fellow did not even know his ally's name) to "The President of the Republic of the Great North American Nation":

DEAR AND HONORED SIR:

I come to greet you with the most tender effusion of my soul . . . to shake off the yoke of the cruel and corrupt Spanish domination, as you are doing to equally unfortunate Cuba . . .

At the same time, as I am always frank and open, I must express to you the great sorrow which all of us Filipinos felt upon reading in the *Times* . . . that you, sir, will retain these islands . . . But we found a palliative to our sorrow in the improbability and suddenness of that statement, as common sense refuses to believe that so sensible a public man as you would venture to make an assertion so contrary to common sense . . .

Oh, sir, you are greatly injured by this statement, which ought to be regarded merely as a diplomatic trick invented by the friends of Spain . . .

I close by protesting once and a thousand times, in the name of this people, which knows how to fight for its honor . . . a people which trusts blindly in you . . .

It was plaintive, and devoid of that sonorous formality with which heads of state ought to communicate; and perhaps Mr. McKinley found it beneath his dignity to respond, for he did not respond. Only in his private notes do we find a memorandum, handwritten around this time, which may possibly be linked to Aguinaldo's message. It reads: "While we are conducting war and until its conclusion we must keep all we get; when the war is over we must keep what we want." And as for Dewey he continued to blink at the march of events. He never dreamed, he later confessed, that they wanted independence, and if the statement seems dubious it is at least partially verified by his inaction at the time. He wrote Washington scarcely a word about the Philippine independence movement. He was an admiral, a fighting man; these other affairs were not his concern. When an officer called his attention to the flags on Filipino boats he shrugged his thick shoulders. No government would recognize a "little bit of bunting that anyone could hoist." They could call it a Filipino flag, if they wished, but he assuredly would not. The admiral could be cool to political realities at times, and surely this phase does not find him at his best. Yet we must note his dilemma. If he knew nothing about Filipino aspirations he might appear obtuse, whereas if he knew all about them he would seem to be encouraging Aguinaldo under false pretenses. What to do?

He waited for Washington to deliver an army, hoping meanwhile that native troops would keep the Spaniards off balance. With only 1,743 naval officers and men, he could not capture Manila, nor did his orders allow him to depart. He had won a naval victory and occupied a sliver of beach on an Asian bay eight thousand miles from home. In classic naval tradition he was blockading the city behind that bay. Now what?

Whatever Dewey did or did not do, the Filipinos saw their own opportunity and were seizing it without hesitation. In a flash 2,800 Spanish troops in Cavite Province were cut off, surrounded, and shortly captured. The entire Spanish garrison at Caloocan, just outside Manila, fled into the walled city. When Malabon was seized by the insurgents, Spanish resistance in Bulakan collapsed; whereupon some seven thousand troops fell back, as though magnetized, toward a final defense line running through the northern suburbs of the capital. It is needless to recite further instances of convergence upon Manila by Spanish troops in nearby provinces such as Bataan, Cavite, and Bulakan. By the middle of May the rebels firmly gripped all of southern Luzon except for Manila. Admiral Dewey's bulletin of June 6 to the Navy Department is an understatement occasioned by the fact that he was not in daily touch with rebel military progress: "Insurgents have been engaged actively within the province of Cavite during the last week; they have had several small victories, taking prisoners about 1,800 men, 50 officers; Spanish troops, not native."

By then the Filipino avalanche had, in fact, swept over

not merely Cavite but most of Luzon. A few fortified outposts held out, but for all practical purposes that enormous island was already lost to Spain. The rebel army moved its several field guns here and there (sometimes by boat) with telling effect. A few hundred Spaniards holed up inside the large church at Cavite Viejo could not be dislodged by assault, whereupon the *insurrectos* shelled them from the arsenal all across Bacoor Bay. With the Americans watching in astonishment, fairly accurate Malay artillery demolished the structure and sent the enemy hurrying northward toward the Old City.

By this time Aguinaldo's army under Luna's command was an instrument of considerable merit and almost excessive enthusiasm. Never again would it be better organized, more adequately equipped with weapons, ammunition, and supplies. It numbered about thirty thousand, exclusive of small hit-and-run groups (some of which were hard to distinguish from brigands) that operated as far south as the Moro islands. Led by generals who would soon glorify the history books of little brown children—Ricarte, Pio del Pilar, his brother Gregorio, Noriel, Montenegro, Garcia—the insurgents slowly squeezed the Spaniards out of the suburbs into the heart of Manila. Soon the swollen, overcrowded metropolis was surrounded by fourteen miles of trenches, and the upper Pasig River was sealed off, should any Spaniards foolishly consider escaping into the interior. On June 27 the rebels delivered their most devastating blow when Montenegro's regiment captured the only pumping station which supplied Manila. Spanish pleas to let the water flow for the sake of humanity were triumphantly rejected.

Dewey was now keeping Washington informed somewhat more alertly and had cabled: "Insurgents continue hostilities and have practically surrounded Manila. They have taken 2,500 Spanish prisoners, whom they treat most humanely. They do not intend to attack the city proper until the arrival of United States troops . . ." And late in June: "I have given him [Aguinaldo] to understand that I consider insurgents as friends, being opposed to a common enemy . . . he has kept me advised of his progress, which has been wonderful . . . Have advised frequently to conduct the war humanely, which he has invariably done."

His progress had been such that as July dawned the Spanish-American War in the Philippines was, in effect, over. There only remained the matter of storming besieged, blockaded Manila. The success of that operation was a foregone certainty. Was this to be the sole function of General Merritt's invasion force? The State Department had spoken of "entering upon the occupation of the islands." Had Señor Aguinaldo rendered such occupation anomalous?

The American public was intent on the progress of the war in Cuba, so much closer to home geographically and psychologically. Nothing much seemed to be taking place in the Philippines. Few American reporters were yet on the scene. Frank Millet of *Harper's Weekly* had not arrived, nor John Bass of the same publication, nor had even the New York *Times* begun covering events at first hand. One of the few United States journalists who reached Manila Bay that June was John T. McCutcheon of the Chicago *Record*. While his dispatches were more or less drowned in the Cuban flood, some who read them may have discerned a flaw in the general assumption that the Philippine archipelago was already American property. On the twenty-fourth he cabled:

> Imus, Bacoor, Las Pinas and Paranaque were captured in less than a week . . . Over in Cavite the calm passionless statements of great victories that Aguinaldo gave us were being substantiated every day . . . Closely following the remarkable insurgent successes in Cavite Province, where the whole district had been captured in eight days, came stories of other successful operations in Pampanga Province; Maccabebe and San Fernando were captured and the great Spanish General Molet fled in terror to Manila . . . Our respect for the insurgent prowess has grown a great deal . . .

Anyone even superficially in touch with Philippine events could perceive that the thirteen thousand Spanish troops in Manila under commander-in-chief General Fermin Jaudenes had come to the end of a long road.

IV

In America something of a national prayer-meeting was in progress. So total had been Dewey's victory that it seemed hard to explain on mechanistic grounds. Had providence willed the slaughter of Spaniards against the loss of not one American in battle, the destruction of an entire enemy fleet against negligible damage to U.S. vessels? Was Spanish marksmanship really that atrocious? "If I were a religious man," reflected Dewey, "and I hope I am, I should say that the hand of God was in it"; and Senator Beveridge insisted, "Blind is he who does not see the hand of God in events so vast, so harmonious, so benign"—events including, incidentally, the annexation of Hawaii a few weeks later. The mouthpiece of William Randolph Hearst crowed, "How Do You Like the *Journal's* War?" Commodore Dewey was made a rear admiral on the permanent list; but this was not enough, and Congress hurriedly appointed him to the new and exalted rank of Admiral of the Navy. A Dewey craze swept the nation:

> They're making Dewey buttons,
>   They're making Dewey hats,
> And "Dewey's" imprinted
>   On collars and cravats.
> They're making Dewey tobies,
>   And thus they make cigars;
> They're making Dewey cocktails
>   To push across the bars.

For once even Theodore Roosevelt's statement that the admiral had won a victory greater than any since Trafalgar, except for Farragut's, seemed sober in the context of the times. A Dewey-for-President boom started, and an unmelodious ditty swept the land like a pestilence:

> Oh, dewy was the morning
> Upon the first of May,
> And Dewey was the Admiral,
> Down in Manila Bay.
> And dewy were the Regent's eyes
> Them orbs of royal blue,
> And dew we feel discouraged?
> I dew not think we dew!

It was now that big business moved into the prevailing, irresistible current of the times. Speaking of the ownership of the Philippines by a progressive, commercial power, Assistant Treasury Secretary Frank Vanderlip alluded to the project as "alluring." He envisioned the formation of great companies to create railroads there, to exploit the forests, and develop sugar, tobacco, and mineral industries. The Secretary of State, too, had requested a report on Philippine industrial and financial matters; in the main it stressed Manila hemp. There were, it seemed, vast tracts of uncultivated land where it flourished with vigor, and all that was needed was capital to open it up. It was all alluring, very much so, and as the guidon of American commerce Mr. McKinley himself evinced a growing curiosity. Of Dewey he inquired concerning "the desirability of the several islands, the character of their population, coal and other mineral deposits, their harbor and commercial advantages . . ."

All this is not surprising, for we have already noted expansive inclinations on the part of the administration. But as to those commercial interests who had previously deplored the thrust toward war, the line reversed itself. In the phraseology of the day, it broadened its outlook. The stock market soared and even conservative rail issues advanced an average of $2.79 per share the week after Dewey's exploit. On May 5 the *Wall Street Journal* reported that "some broad-minded men" now felt that a coaling station and naval base in the Philippines would not really be asking too much; and the *American Banker* six days later referred to our new tactical position "as respects the inevitable partition of the Chinese Empire." A reporter from the Seattle *Post-Intelligence* interviewed James J. Hill on June 1 and learned that the Great Northern railroad baron, who until Dewey's victory had denounced imperialism, was now in favor of retaining the Philippines. "If you go back in the commercial history of the world," he announced spaciously, "you will find that the people who controlled the trade of the Orient have been the people who held the purse strings of nations." Chambers of commerce in San Francisco and Seattle petitioned McKinley to keep not only the Philippines but Guam and the Carolines, and any other real estate which might be liberated from Spain. In sum, it may be said that American business had swerved generally toward an imperial position after initially resisting it.

In doing so it reflected the spirit of the people, which was in turn reflected (or conditioned) by the periodicals of the day. Under the impression that we already owned the Philippines, the Providence *News* admitted that "we do not know much about our new possessions in the far Pacific, but what little we do know indicates that they are of great value . . . They are certainly well worth keeping." The Philadelphia *Record* concurred: ". . . willy nilly we have entered upon our career as a great power." And while the Boston *Herald*, for one, warned of tampering with the two-edged Monroe Doctrine blade, most other people and periodicals had few qualms. The most unabashed attitude, perhaps, was expressed by the Chicago *Times-Herald*:

> We find that we want the Philippines . . . We also want Porto Rico . . . We want Hawaii now . . . We may want the Carolines, the Ladrones, the Pelew, and the Mariana groups. If we do we will take them . . .

With the triumph of a lawyer who finds a loophole in a tax clause, the Milwaukee *Sentinel* observed that we had no "formal or implied" duty to refuse the Philippines. When *Public Opinion* polled 65 newspapers it found that 28 favored permanently keeping the islands, 16 were against it, and 21 were undecided but apparently moving toward annexation. Wonderingly the Washington *Post* discovered that ours was, indeed, "a strange destiny . . . an imperial policy," one that we would have to learn to live with. "A new consciousness seems to have come upon us," this publication continued; "—the consciousness of strength. It might be compared with the effect upon the animal creation of the taste for blood." And it all seemed to be happening without our volition. We "find" that we want this or that. The desire arrives "willy nilly." New appetites "seem to come upon us." We are not actors; we are acted upon; but sweltering with his regiment in San Antonio that May Roosevelt expressed matters less polemically in a letter to Henry Cabot Lodge: "Give my best love to Nannie, and do not make peace until we get Porto Rico, while Cuba is made independent and the Philippines at any rate taken from the Spaniards." And early the next month, aboard the *Yucatan* in Tampa, he gave vent to new fears and frustrations: "The navy has had all the fun so far, and I can only hope that peace has not been declared without giving the army a chance at . . . the Philippines." A cartoon in the *Rocky Mountain News* shows Uncle Sam sticking American flags into various Spanish islands and remarking, "By gum, I rather like your looks." For a brief moment the nation thought very little, and surrendered to an orgy of patriotic dreams.

In those stirring days it was still possible to state the case in the manner of former Senator James Eustis, speaking before an exhilarated audience at the Manhattan Club: "Dewey has settled the question . . . he has conquered foreign territory, and I am afraid that he has given Uncle Sam a damn big appetite for that particular brand of food." But to justify the abandonment of traditional foreign policy required a more basic rationale. It was at hand, and its name was destiny. Had not the New York *Sun* written: "The policy of annexation is the policy of destiny; and destiny always arrives"? Whatever that meant, it set a theme which others improvised upon. Expansion, said the great Mahan, arose through "no premeditated contrivance of our own"; our wishes made no difference at all; it was "natural, necessary, irrepressible." We were therefore helpless. Said Secretary Hay, "No man, no party, can fight with any chance of success against a cosmic tendency." To crave colonial possessions, intoned Chauncey Depew, was in the blood and no power could stop it.

(Whether or not it was a cosmic tendency or a blood disease, General Merritt in San Francisco was taking no chances. On May 15 we find him writing Mr. McKinley that "the expedition must be fitted out very carefully . . . It seems more than probable that we will have the so-called insurgents to fight as well as the Spaniards." Two days later he complains that his allotted force of two regiments is insufficient "when the work to be done consists of conquering a territory 7,000 miles from our base, defended by a regularly trained and acclimated army of from 10,000 to 25,000 men and inhabited by 14 millions of people, the majority of whom will regard us with the intense hatred both born of race and religion." Meanwhile, he had to make do with what he had—the 14th and 23rd Infantry, a few batteries of light artillery, some five thousand assorted Krag-Jorgenson and Springfield bayonet-equipped rifles, and a few hundred shotguns and revolvers of mixed calibers—not much, but perhaps enough to assist destiny until more of everything arrived.)

And allied to determinism was the obligation, honestly felt, to uplift those waste places which the war might throw across our path. "Duty determines destiny," said Mr. McKinley, combining both themes (Who determines duty? the *Nation* wondered)—and he elaborated: "The war has brought us new duties and responsibilities which we must meet and discharge as becomes a great nation . . ."—implying that America entered upon the task with the reluctance of a bachelor adopting a squalling orphan. It would be barbarous, said the New York *Tribune* on May 5, to give the Philippines back to Spain or to relinquish them to their own folly. The key turned. Those who favored annexing the islands brushed aside the idea that the Filipinos could govern themselves. In the words of one writer:

> Cannibals govern themselves. The half-ape creatures of the Australian bush govern themselves. The Eskimo governs himself and so do the wildest tribes of Darkest Africa. But what kind of a government is it?

One shudders at the thought. And as for his own land:

> . . . this launch of State . . . sails out in her search for American freedom, American prosperity, American ways, a Christian religion, the little red schoolhouse, and the American home.

Formerly anti-war and generally anti-imperialist, the organized Protestant church now descried another outlet for missionary activity. Was it not the duty of the world's strongest Christian nation to lead the heathen to Jesus? Dewey's victory crystallized a latent conviction that the hour was ripe for a new moral offensive. Mr. McKinley and his wife, both ardent Methodists, did much to help the cause. "Do we need their consent," he asked, "to perform a great act for humanity?" And the Philippines were an even more worthy target than Cuba, for they were substantial in size and population and paved the way for God's work in China.

Only Catholics opposed the program, fearing a calamity to their faith in the Castilian colonies. The Pope's Spanish sympathies were well known. A crisis was averted when on May 18 American archbishops circulated a statement to the effect that U.S. Catholics would follow the flag and that Catholic priests would pray for an American victory on all fronts. Then followed a swing toward expansion by many of the Roman faith, although at no time in the years to come did the number reach a majority, nor did their fervor approach that of Protestant and Jew.

Speaking on "The Christian Conquest of Asia" at Union Theological Seminary, the influential Reverend J. H. Barrows suggested that "wherever on pagan shores the voice of the American missionary and teacher is heard, there is fulfilled the manifest destiny of the Christian Republic . . ." A Methodist paper went further: "Every Methodist preacher will be a recruiting officer." We would be selfish to decline ownership of the Philippines, the *Religious Telescope* thought; to do so would be an actual crime in the eyes of God. Religion had joined the great crusade, hand-in-hand with duty and destiny.

V

The *Olympia* swung gently at anchor beneath a burning sun. From a wicker chair on her forward deck Admiral Dewey surveyed the bay, the city, the arsenal. His shirt open at the neck, he fanned his face with a palm-leaf fan and perspired under a white awning. He was worried. On May 20 he had been informed by Washington that three Spanish battle cruisers—*Carlos V, Pelayo,* and *Alfonso XII*—plus some transports might have left for the Philippines with an undetermined number of troops. A month later the rumor was confirmed, and with interest. From Gibraltar the U.S. consul reported a Spanish fleet under Admiral Manuel de la Camara off Ceuta and sailing eastward. Composed of two armored cruisers, six converted cruisers, and four destroyers, it was in theory more powerful than Dewey's squadron. Should it defeat the Americans it could then waylay U.S. troop transports en route to Manila. Agitated cables began to flow between Manila Bay and the Navy Department.

The latter advised Dewey that the big-gun U.S. ironclads *Monterey* and *Monadnock* were being rushed to the scene (at their distressing top speed of six knots) but could not arrive until late in July. Dewey assured Washington somewhat doubtfully that in the event of an attack his squadron would try to give a good account of itself. On June 17 Camara stood out from Cadiz at high speed. It developed that he was convoying three transports carrying two infantry regiments and a battalion of marines. The Spanish fleet reached Port Said on June 26. Following urgent arguments by U.S. Consul Ethelbert Watts, it was refused coal there by the British and Egyptian governments. Elated, Watts expected the Spaniards to double back to Cadiz. Instead they continued toward Suez.

Informed of these developments, Dewey wired next day: "No change in the situation since my telegram of June 17. Five German, three British, one French, one Japanese men-of-war in port. Insurgents constantly closing in on the city . . . Shall the *Monadnock* and the *Monterey* arrive in time? In my judgment, if the coast of Spain was threatened, the squadron of the enemy would have to return."

The same idea had occurred to the Navy Department, which cabled the admiral on June 29: "Squadron under Watson, the *Iowa*, and *Oregon*, the *Yankee* and the *Dixie*, the *Newark* and the *Yosemite*, and four colliers preparing with all possible despatch to start for Spanish coast. The Spaniards know this."

And on July 5: "Camara reported to have passed Suez Canal . . . after having coaled in Mediterranean Sea. Intends to coal again in Red Sea and thence direct to the Philippine Islands."

Allowing Camara ten knots, the ironclads six, and the transports twelve, they would all arrive about August 1. Dewey personally thought Camara would appear first. Without battleships, he further assumed, he would be at the mercy of the *Pelayo* and *Carlos*. He decided that if Camara did not turn back he would cruise east, pick up the two ironclads, return, and then smash the new Spanish fleet. General Anderson having already arrived with the first troop expedition, Dewey asked him what he would do. The army man replied that he would take thirty days' rations and march into the hills east of Cavite to await Dewey's return.

At this point Camara turned back. Unfortunately for the drama, his coaling situation was hopeless, his converted cruisers weak, and he had already been told to avoid any encounter which had no prospect of success, and to beware of the useless sacrifice of his squadron. His gesture had not been seriously planned; and whatever reality it may have possessed was dispelled by the American threat to bomb Spanish coastal cities and by his fuel problem. There would be no second naval engagement in Manila Bay.

With the suspense over, montony set in. Over and over the sailors soapstoned the decks, washed their laundry, went through listless dry-run gun drills, and waited for the war to end. Meanwhile, they watched the progress of the insurgents, and visited them and their prisoners at the arsenal, the jail, and the adjacent hospital. Filipinos passed back and forth in their little boats calling out, "*Americanos amigos!*" Gifts and conversation were exchanged. One officer of the *Petrel* writes:

> But the more we knew the Filipino the more we got to know what hatred is . . . Their hatred of the Spaniard was the accumulation of the hatred of their forefathers for generations, added to their own. And while each man's hatred seemed to be directed against the Spaniards in general, it was principally directed against the soldiers and the priests, and was based on some wrong to his own personal family, and to the families of his friends and relatives. His hatred of the priests concentrated in his hatred of the Archbishop; and it seemed that in all the world there could not be another man so hated as the Archbishop of Manila.

The days passed in somnolence and peace, for it was understood that if shore batteries did not bombard the fleet Dewey would also hold his fire. Usually a dead calm lay over the sheet of water between the ships and the city. It was hot and humid, and the men watched longingly for ripples that signalled a breeze. Almost imperceptibly the great ships rocked at anchor. As the last streaks of daylight disappeared, a launch from the *Olympia* scurried about and gave the evening countersign.

All evening, every evening, sleepy men stayed on watch and at the secondary batteries. No lights burned, except for searchlights which swept the surface of the silent bay, fairy wands that touched the hulls and spars of full-rigged merchant ships and men-of-war, and silhouetted them against the brooding darkness. During some nights heavy clouds piled up and a storm burst. With searchlights useless, the men peered tensely through the rain for possible enemy torpedo boats. These midsummer-night torrents soon ended, muttering their way into silence. Once more searchlights probed the greenish-gray waters. When they picked up a strange object, the officers of the day spoke into voice tubes and guns swung around to bear upon it.

By morning the sea had again turned placid and blue, and a faint breeze tiptoed in from the shore. The men changed watches, yawning and joking in low tones. A new day had dawned in the Philippines. Would it be a tempestuous one?

4

THE
SIEGE
OF
MANILA

FAR FROM THESE PLACID SCENES, IN ANOTHER MILIEU where Congress and the citizenry were clamoring for immediate invasions and victories, former Civil War General Russell A. Alger, now secretary of war, was attempting to place almost nonexistent American armies upon the soil of Cuba and the Philippines. Elderly and benign, he was blamed from the start for the delays and confusion which reigned. Yet it was not his fault that the army was unprepared to fight a major war. Since the Civil War the main preoccupation of the impoverished War Department had been to administer patronage and dole out companies for endless Indian skirmishes which involved hardly the slightest problems in staff work or communications. That spring the regular establishment consisted of 28,183 men. In Cuba Spain had about 100,000 effectives, in Manila nearly 13,000. McKinley called for 200,000 volunteers. In short order he got them, and more—the majority lifted intact from the National Guard, the balance untrained; and after three decades of somnolence Mr. Alger's department now faced the appalling overnight prospect of feeding, clothing, arming, and equipping a quarter of a million men.

Nor were the Guard formations an unalloyed boon. Primarily social and political clubs, they had little equipment, an easygoing type of discipline that bordered on negligence, and scarcely any cavalry or artillery; and except for years of close-order drill they knew little more about war than the other volunteers. They elected (and demoted) their own officers and took orders not from the War Department but from the governors of their respective states. When congress ordained that each state militia body be mustered intact into the federal army, all did so—with varying degrees of misgivings and protest except for one New York regiment, which flatly refused to fight under strangers and which never did enter the war. Efficient new Danish Krag-Jorgensen rifles were available only for the regular army. Volunteers received old Springfields which fired black powder and were considered fairly useless in combat. There was not an ounce of smokeless powder in the arsenals and no prospect of getting any in the immediate future. Other articles were desperately short—canteens, blankets, summer khaki, haversacks —and the cupboards of the Commissary Department were also close to bare. Complaints about "embalmed beef" began to be heard as soon as the men reached their mobilization points. In the heat of that spring and summer they were outfitted, insofar as possible, in heavy blue uniforms designed for winter duty. The first camps to be set up were most unsanitary. Medical services were meager. Due to an insufficient number of latrines, and certain practises which followed, typhoid fever began to spread. Some regiments brought measles with them; and swarms of prostitutes spread venereal disease. Conditions were so bad at Camp Merritt, a damp, sandy blight near San Francisco's Golden Gate Park (where pneumonia and bronchitis also became epidemic), that a board of medical advisers recommended abandoning it altogether and moving it to another site.

Matters were not commencing well, and it made no difference that the troops were enthusiastic and anxious to fight.
They had little to fight with, and inadequate means of getting to the scenes of action. Daily besieged by scores of people wanting special favors, Mr. Alger had to conduct the war
(he grumbled) "during the greater part of the night and
Sundays," while telegrams piled up on his desk:

"Not one Iowa regiment mentioned in any expedition
against Spaniards."

"Will it not be possible to have Seventh California Regiment ordered West Indies or Manila? . . . Very anxious to
go to the Front."

"Twentieth Kansas disappointed at not being sent to Manila. Say California and Iowa assigned ahead of them. They
are as well drilled and efficient as other regiments."

"Great disappointment if Fifty-first Iowa doesn't sail on
Arizona. Is such an order possible? Meeting being held.
Please answer."

Meanwhile Major General Wesley Merritt was, in effect,
advising Adjutant General H. C. Corbin that his men could
not swim from San Francisco to Manila. Where were the
transports? "I am not complaining, but report the facts, as
they do not seem to be understood in Washington." The wire
crossed one from Corbin, who had lugubrious tidings of his
own. Batteries B and G, for example, would arrive without
horses and could not be supplied with ammunition for "several weeks." Three days later, via an irascible note in which
one senses the frustrations and mounting ire of the department, the general was sharply informed that there would be
no trained cooks aboard ship: "For a hundred years the soldiers of the Army have cooked for themselves, and it is not
understood why at this late day changes should be made."

Yet it was all more or less inevitable during the first weeks
of this or any other war in this or any other democracy; and
behind the confusion a good deal of effective improvisation
was taking place. In this respect America's unpreparedness

was a kind of asset, for with few known formalities to restrict them local commanders got things done by common sense in unconventional ways. Horses were purchased on the spot, company commissions were appointed informally, food and other items were ordered from local merchants, corporals and sergeants supervised training and construction duties normally allotted to field-grade officers; and slowly the chaos of late-April subsided. By the middle of May several thousand Guards, regulars, and volunteers from western states— California, Nebraska, Oregon, Wyoming, Colorado, Idaho, Minnesota, Utah, Kansas, Montana, South Dakota—had trickled into Camp Merritt, and the first expedition, incredibly enough, was scheduled to depart for Manila Bay in precisely one week.

II

The Philippine expeditionary force, designated as VIII Corps, was commanded by a sixty-two-year-old West Pointer, one of the Civil War "boy generals." As a cavalryman in that conflict, Merritt had been brevetted six times for gallantry. Under Custer, he later earned a reputation as an outstanding Indian fighter. A cool, contemplative officer tending toward fat, with hard gray eyes and wavy white hair, he had asked for the Philippine assignment. Now he regretted having done so. He was not friendly with General Miles, and his request for 14,400 troops, 6,000 of them regulars, had been denied somewhat too brusquely. Outranking everyone in the army except Miles, he also had become obsessed by a conviction that the Philippine operation was a side show unworthy of his status. There is evidence that he requested a transfer (which was refused) to the Cuban expedition shortly after reaching San Francisco.

The camp which bore the general's name was not calculated to improve his disposition, resembling as it did a vast

picnic ground rather than a military establishment. It was
not fenced in, and hordes of mothers, sisters, wives, and
sweethearts roamed the area. Some of them infiltrated the
kitchens and proceeded to overfeed and sicken the men with
cakes, cookies, and puddings. San Francisco was much too
close, and the men kept wandering off and getting into
mischief. "There were plenty of girls to go around of all nationalities," one private wrote, "including the cuddly Japanese . . ." At saloons like the Poodle Dog, the men sang,
drank, and celebrated in the immemorial ways of soldiers on
the eve of battle. It was a problem for their officers to keep
track of them. They kept pouring into the receiving offices,
and milling around, and at first there was nothing much for
them to do. Hundreds had arrived in summery "ice cream"
trousers, linen dusters, and seersucker jackets. On foggy and
windswept dunes they were drilled in these odd costumes
for days on end, and the San Francisco *Call* was impelled
to remark sourly on May 18, "If marching up a hill and
marching down again is all that is necessary to constitute a
soldier, then most of the volunteer troops . . . have nothing
more to learn."

Hardly a man among the volunteers knew his commanding
officer. (One colonel dressed in civilian clothes was refused
entrance to his own headquarters area. When he identified
himself, the tall guard grinned, bent down, and whispered
into his ear, "Try the next sentry. He's easy.") Through an
error in Washington, some essential matériel had been
shipped east for the Cuban expedition. Few lieutenants or
noncoms knew how to make out a supply requisition or a
morning-report. So untutored were the Kansas officers that
Merritt complained about them directly to the War Department. Only the 23rd Infantry, some artillery, and fragments
of the 14th Regiment—all regulars—contrasted with the chaos
of their surroundings. Baffled and resentful, Merritt cabled
Mr. Alger that he was "at a loss to understand that it is the
intention of the authorities that I . . . proceed to the Philip-

pines and occupy such part of the islands as I may be able."

But his problems were no worse than General Shafter's in Tampa. They were merely somewhat different. San Francisco was a government depot for army supplies, a superb harbor with plenty of rail facilities. Since the War and Navy Departments did not own a single transport or troopship at the outbreak of war, it was up to Merritt to get them. Ship captains were reluctant. Financially the offers were attractive, but they feared what the army might do to their property; and it was only after threats and haggling that the general was finally able to charter the *City of Peking*, the *Australia*, and the *City of Sydney*. The apprehensions of their skippers were well grounded, for immediately these vessels were ripped apart to accommodate sleeping quarters and army messes. Hodgepodges of unsorted supplies and makeshift carpentry, they were ready to sail with a day or two to spare.

It had been hoped that the first contingent would embark on May 21, but its assigned commander did not arrive until the evening of the twenty-third. Brigadier General Thomas Anderson, an imperious Civil War veteran, had one day in which to inspect his command, for it was to sail without fail on the twenty-fifth. Numbering about 2,500 men, it included all the artillery and regular infantry, plus the California and Oregon volunteers.

When that dawn arrived the men broke camp, laughing and chattering like magpies, and under forty pounds of equipment marched through the city toward the Pacific Mail dock. Throngs of civilians lining the streets began to infiltrate the ranks of the 1st Californians as they wheeled up Van Ness Avenue. Soldiers and onlookers burst into tears; women flung themselves upon their men; fathers joined the march and carried their sons' blankets and haversacks. "The march of the regiment was not a glorious spectacle," reported the *Bulletin*. "It was piteous." For the first time the meaning of imminent war seemed to strike home. When one sobbing boy dropped his rifle at the corner of Market and

Third, a white-haired lady darted in among the men, picked it up, placed it on her shoulder, and marched alongside him. Amid cheers, frantic waving of flags, and screeches of steam whistles, the city police force at its head, the wild parade surged on.

By late morning, every man having crossed his gangplank, the three ships moved out into the bay and dropped anchor. Here further supplies were taken aboard. Ferries and other small craft surrounded the troopships. Women threw roses and Red Cross badges at the soldiers. One flung a rolled-up flag like a spear toward the men at the *Australia*'s rail. It caught one under the eye; blood spurted. There was a horrified pause until someone shouted, "Oh, he's all right! He's a soldier. He isn't hurt." Bands afloat began to play and a mournful song drifted across the waters:

> Brave boys are they
> Gone at their country's call,
> And yet, oh yet, we cannot forget
> That many brave boys must fall.

This would have been an apt moment for the departure of the conquerors; but for two anti-climactic days the ships sat in the bay, and it was not until Wednesday afternoon, May 25, 1898, that the blue "proceed" signal was broken out on the forepeak of the flagship *Australia*. Again a pandemonium of whistles, saluting guns, and fluttering handkerchiefs erupted, and again launches, tugs, yachts, and tenders clustered around the transports. Passengers aboard the huge ferryboat *Ukiah* sang "The Star Spangled Banner," "Hail Columbia," and "Yankee Doodle." The *Peking* backed a little, then shoved her bow into the swell and headed for the Golden Gate at a bold twenty-knot clip. Anxiously watched by thousands of eyes ashore, the three hulls, partially obscured by their own clouds of smoke, grew faint in the twilight. Far at sea lookouts hailed, "Six o'clock and all's well. Port light is burning bright." A forlorn cluster of three specks on an endless sea, the first armed expedition ever dispatched by the United States to conquer and annex a foreign land was under way.

III

"It's the rolling that affects one, not the pitching," an ashen-faced chaplain observed. Seasickness affected many of the men, and in the close quarters their nausea was transmitted to others. Aboard the *City of Peking* a thousand troops had been jammed into a sleeping area measuring about sixty by four hundred feet. Ventilation was poor, and the stench caused hundreds to flee to the upper decks. With mess facilities limited, meals were served only twice a day—generally "beans that had seen better days and pork strong enough to stand off a Spanish battalion". Most beef had spoiled due to a failure of the *Australia*'s cold storage rooms. Straw mattresses were infested by "graybacks." Underwear deloused in steam, it was learned in dismay, at once disintegrated; and those men without a second pair wore none for days thereafter. The 2nd Oregon Regiment had not been issued army shoes. Fresh water was at a premium, since each ship was able to distill only about eight hundred gallons daily. To cap it all, measles broke out on the *Australia*.

The men bore it all good-naturedly enough, and by Friday most of the seasick cases had begun to recover. Some feeble wigwagging passed back and forth. The *Sydney* sent those aboard the *Peking* a sarcastic invitation to dinner. Any number of whales were spotted; always they turned out to be porpoises. A rumor spread that all Filipinos were cannibals, and the men appraised each other as potential steaks on a savage menu. A tarpaulin swimming tub filled with sea water was erected on the *Australia*. The soldiers piled in, a dozen at a time, while others scolded and waited impatiently.

As the expedition plugged southwest at nine knots the

heat increased, and more men stayed above decks day and night. Constantly they wrote letters, argued, perpetrated small practical jokes, and grumbled. "It's all worn out," said one private of his rifle. "The rifling is almost gone and there's no telling where it will shoot. I don't know but it's more dangerous to be behind it than in front of it." A sergeant remarked, "I got a new pair of shoes today, but they didn't have eights and I had to take tens. I guess I can make paper insoles for them . . ." And another: "They tell me Manila is three degrees hotter than hell. What do you suppose my underclothes are made of? Cotton flannel!"

Speculation that they were bound for Hawaii was confirmed on June 1, when the top of Diamond Head showed dead ahead. All troops were given two days of leave in Honolulu—a continuous ovation with everything free ("Couldn't spend a dime," ran the phrase)—carriage rides, drinks, cigars, meals, curios, native dances, the beach at Waikiki. Then the ships again stood out to the open sea, escorted now by the cruiser *U.S.S. Charleston*.

In his cabin aboard that warship, Captain Henry Glass opened sealed orders and learned that the convoy's next stop (like Magellan's) was to be not Manila but Guam, in the Spanish Marianas. Upon arriving there on June 20, the *Charleston* fired thirteen shells at its antiquated little fort. After a shocked silence, a launch put out from the shore and approached the cruiser. It contained the Spanish port captain, who stated, "You will pardon our not immediately replying to your salute, Captain, but we are unaccustomed to receiving salutes here, and are not supplied with proper guns for returning them."

"What salute?" asked Glass, perhaps ironically. He informed them that their two countries were at war and asked for the surrender of the island and its Spaniards, including the Governor. When this message reached the latter, he replied in a quaint note: "The military regulations of Spain forbid me to set foot upon a foreign ship of war . . . However, I shall be happy to see you in my office in the morning."

The Captain's rebuttal was to send a boatload of marines ashore. Despite the protests of the Governor at this so-called act of violence, the American flag was raised over the government building, to the glee of the natives, whereupon the expedition put to sea once more, with sixty Spanish prisoners. (When news of the incident reached the United States, Henry Lodge remarked, "Why the President should have taken those islands, unless he expects to hold on to the Philippines, I cannot conceive.") And nine days later the expedition crept slowly into Manila Bay and anchored near Dewey's flagship off Cavite.

IV

Nobody at home knew anything about it. The Manila cable was still cut, and only the Gilbert-and-Sullivan episode at Guam had yet been reported to our puzzled but approving populace. And the innocence here was matched by that prevailing in Manila Bay. Not an American on the scene, with the exception of Dewey and a few newspapermen, was acquainted with the Philippine Islands or understood exactly what was to be done there. The name Aguinaldo was even less familiar to them. And what it all had to do with Cuba was another mystery which few even tried to comprehend. Until very recently General Anderson had been a colonel in Alaska, and his ignorance of politics and problems in the land he was to invade was probably more monumental than that of any commander in history under similar circumstances. On July 1, nonetheless, he started landing his men to fight another war in his long and stolidly martial career.

The first contacts between American and Filipino troops were wary and disquieting. In the dirty, narrow streets of Cavite menacing bands of insurgents held sway, and the outnumbered Americans felt like intruders in a quarrel that

was none of their business. All the larger Spanish homes and
mansions were occupied by Aguinaldo and his aides. A few
antiquated barracks had been condescendingly turned over
to Anderson's force, close to the shoreline, where the tropical
odor of Spanish corpses bubbled to the surface, a memento
of Dewey's smashing victory. The wrecks of Montojo's ships
protruded starkly from the shallow waters. One government
building had been converted into a prison containing two
thousand gloomy and disheveled Spanish prisoners. The general atmosphere, all in all, tended to dispel the illusions held
by many volunteers concerning the glories of war. Meanwhile the *insurrectos*, busy at their beloved paper work,
cleaning and reloading cartridge shells, loading and unload-
ing supplies on carts, conferring, and distributing arms, paid
little attention to the *americanos*. They yearned and plotted
to get at the Spaniards in Manila, and they intended to do so
shortly with or without their new allies. By now they had
pushed the enemy out of Malabon, San Francisco, Cavite
Viejo, Imus, Bacoor, Los Pinas, Paranaque, and Malabai; and
only Malate and a honeycomb of Spanish trenches still stood
between them and the moss-covered walls of the capital.

Their forward "First Zone" was commanded by a pure
Malay general, Mariano Noriel, heavily built, bulletheaded,
flat-nosed, and copper-colored. A pleasant young man despite his pugilistic appearance, he wore the dark-blue gingham uniform common to both Spanish and insurgent officers.
Second in command was Lieutenant Colonel Juan Cailles,
part French, part Hindustani, the type of man who always
gravitates toward adventure and war. For a time he had
served with the Spaniards; now (a Hollywood star born decades too soon) he was to be the mainspring of the impending
Manila attack. About thirty years old, slim, classic-featured,
with piercing black eyes and a silky mustache, he inclined
a good deal toward the melodramatic. Except for a red-
and-blue ribbon on his hat, and riding boots, he wore no sign

of rank; and this was typical of all Filipino commissioned personnel.

And while the insurgents prepared to attack, the Americans under Anderson could do nothing momentarily but occupy their one small base. The rainy season had begun, with intermittent downpours throughout July; and during this interlude the little body of men unhappily hung on and awaited reinforcements. They were coming. On June 15 a contingent of 3,500 men commanded by Brigadier General Francis V. Greene had left San Francisco. Twelve days later Merritt and his staff set sail. And the fourth and final expedition of the summer put to sea June 29 with five thousand men under Brigadier General Arthur MacArthur, father of little Douglas MacArthur. By late July some twelve thousand American land troops were in the Philippines; and already it had become clear that U.S.-Filipino relations lacked that camaraderie usually present between military associates. One reason for the strain is described by an American major in an official report:

> Almost without exception, soldiers and also many officers refer to the natives in their presence as "niggers" and natives are beginning to understand what the word "nigger" means.

A more deep-seated factor grew out of conversations between Aguinaldo, Dewey, and various U.S. generals which invariably mirrored a painful discrepancy in interests. Dewey summarized matters for Anderson the day the latter arrived: "If the United States intends to hold the Philippine Islands, it will make things awkward, because just a week ago Aguinaldo proclaimed the independence of the Philippine Islands from Spain and seems intent on establishing his own government." They decided to see him the following morning. Upon leaving the *Olympia,* the admiral said to the general, "We'll make this call just as unofficial as possible, no sidearms, no ceremony, give no indication to Aguinaldo that we take his government seriously."

At insurgent headquarters they found the Filipino surly and withdrawn. "The insurgent chief," Anderson reported, "did not seem pleased with the incoming of our land forces . . ." He bluntly asked Anderson whether the United States would recognize his government. Taken by surprise, the general replied lamely that as a mere soldier he was not empowered to recognize any government. Aguinaldo declined to attend an American Fourth of July celebration to be held in Cavite, because the written invitation addressed him as "general" rather than "president." It was not an auspicious beginning.

After a few days Aguinaldo returned the visit. Pointedly to indicate his status, he brought along his entire cabinet, military staff, and the inevitable military band. After a minimum of small talk, he asked. "Does the United States intend to hold the Philippines as dependencies?"

Caught in the middle, still trying to reconcile Aguinaldo's avowed intentions with his own orders, Anderson tried a new and slightly more plausible tack: "I cannot answer that, but in 122 years we have established no colonies . . . I leave you to draw your own inference."

Reflectively Aguinaldo said, "I have studied attentively the Constitution of the United States and in it I find no authority for colonies, and I have no fear."

That very day the insurgents arrested two American officers for encroaching upon their lines. Upon hearing of this, Anderson dispatched a note to Aguinaldo recommending that the Filipinos keep their hands off American personnel. But the problem of separating the two armies was becoming difficult, for Anderson had already commenced expanding his holdings. During the middle of the month he ferried most of his men across the bay and landed them near Tambo, a village on the east shore three miles below Manila. Here they dug in, their left flank on the shore, their trenches facing the rice paddies and swamps which lay between them and the walls of the Old City. So now, with the insurgents holding the entire perimeter of the bay above and below the capital, and with Anderson's command clinging precariously to two beachheads, the insurgents on land surrounded not only Spaniards but Americans; thus, to attack Manila, the latter would have to penetrate, bypass, or co-operate with the Filipino army, which in that sector under Noriel numbered ten thousand men.

Anderson needed *lebensraum*, transport, and other supplies, and it was all too plain that Filipino civilians had received orders to relinquish nothing. The General's missives (now addressed obliquely to "your excellency") took on a more acrid flavor: "General Anderson wishes you to inform your people that we are here for their good and that they must supply us with labor and material at the current market prices." When Aguinaldo replied evasively, Consul Wildman got into the argument. Americans had gone to war solely to relieve the Cubans (he scolded Aguinaldo) and had to be trusted whatever the final disposition of the conquered territory might be. For this he was slapped down by the State Department—"your action disapproved and you are forbidden to make pledges or discuss policy." Yet the arrival of more and more U.S. troops seemed to speak for itself. The Filipinos knew they could capture Manila alone, possibly assisted by Dewey's naval guns. Why were the Americans coming in such large numbers? Aguinaldo could not help wondering "whom the Americans expected to fight." He reminded Dewey and Anderson that his army and government controlled the islands.

With heavy sarcasm Anderson advised Aguinaldo on July 22 that "your fine intellect must perceive . . . that I cannot recognize your civil authority." The Filipino replied that the Philippine Republic existed, whether America liked it or not, and that henceforth no more troops were to be landed without his written permission. To this serious pronouncement there was no answer at all, while Americans continued disembarking almost daily for two more weeks. Aguinaldo seethed. The honeymoon was quite obviously over; and Dewey warned Washington: "Situation is most critical at Manila. The Spanish may surrender at any moment. Merritt's most difficult problem will be how to deal with insurgents under Aguinaldo, who has become aggressive and even threatening towards our Army."

Throughout all these dealings General Anderson had become increasingly uncomfortable. A forthright, grizzled old war horse, he disliked the game of words which he found himself playing; and while he bore down hard on Aguinaldo, his cables to the War Department were phrased almost imploringly. As early as July 18 he had warned: "I think I should state to you that the establishment of a provisional government on our part will probably bring us into conflict with insurgents." Three days later: "I submit, with all deference, that we have heretofore underrated the natives. They are not ignorant savage tribes, but have a civilization of their own . . ." And next day: "Aguinaldo declares dictatorship and martial law over all islands. The people expect independence." But the general, under the impression that he had made an important discovery, could not curtail the march of events. With the arrival of Greene's contingent it was clear that somebody would have to give.

The only American whom Aguinaldo really respected—that protective father image, Admiral Dewey—now exerted personal pressure on him to shift Noriel's forces eastward to make room for U.S. regiments; and reluctantly the Filipinos evacuated the beaches of Pasay, Tambo, Baclaran, and Paranaque with all their laboriously constructed new entrenchments. When Noriel protested, Aguinaldo smiled and said, "You are being tragic. They're our allies, always remember that!" As American flags went up all along the line, Noriel and Cailles relinquished their advanced headquarters at Fort Antonio Abad and side-stepped sullenly a full four miles to Makati. But could even Aguinaldo enforce more such withdrawals? Already he was being sharply criticized by Luna and Mabini for this concession, which, they predicted, would only lead to further humiliations.

V

Separated by a third of the circumference of the globe from their source of supply, half encircled by semi-hostile Filipino troops, the Americans were now entrenched at Camp Dewey, a former peanut farm near Tambo. The heat was oppressive and rain kept falling. At times the trenches were filled with two feet of water, and soon the men's shoes were ruined. Their heavy khaki uniforms were a nuisance; they perspired constantly; the loss of body salts induced chronic fatigue. Prickly heat broke out, inflamed by scratching and rubbing. Within a week the first cases of dysentery, malaria, cholera, and dengue fever showed up at sick call. The Americans tried to improve their trenches, a task which resembled that of Sisyphus, for in the rain the saturated black loam washed down as fast as it was thrown up.

The men fretted. They had volunteered to fight Spaniards gloriously in Cuba, and a dreary siege operation thousands of miles from home was not to their liking. On and off, for twenty-four straight days in July alone, it rained. From reveille at 0445 until taps at 0900 the troops ate, slept, drilled, and worked in drizzle and downpour. They went to bed wet, woke up and donned clothes that were still damp, only to be soaked all over again. In July and August the incredible total of twenty-eight inches of water fell, and heroic countermeasures were called for—frameworks built two feet above the ground, laced with bamboo strips, and then covered by a pup tent, a blanket, and soggy masses of banana leaves. The contraptions resembled a Rube Goldberg cartoon, but they worked.

Nauseous "goldfish" rations (Alaska canned salmon) had been furnished in overgenerous quantity by the War Department, under the impression that it would be ideal for the tropics. So oily that it burned like a torch when dry, it was traded whenever possible (the natives actually liked it) for fruit, rice, and eggs. Loving womenfolk back home mailed more of the same. It was hard to render thanks, but one Oregon genius wrote: "Tears came at the sight of your present. How it made me want to be home again!" And moodily, across that one-time peanut field now referred to as a drill ground, the men marched and countermarched in water half a foot deep. On July 28 Oscar Davis, war correspondent for the New York *Sun,* cabled:

> We're saturated now. It beats all creation how it can rain out here . . . You don't mind an occasional soaking. It gives excuse for taking a drink. But one has something to do down here besides change his clothes and drink whiskey.

In Cavite the Americans seemed like giants to the natives. Fierce-looking, unshaven, wearing wild West hats, they loafed and smoked, visited the shops, strolled the streets, flirted with Filipino girls, and played with the "pickaninnies." Further north, newcomers kept coming ashore in driblets that continued for weeks, two hundred at a time, on *cascos* that resembled Chinese junks. "It was a dispiriting thing," wrote one navy man from the little *Petrel,* "to see one of those brown-colored cascos filled with men clothed in dark brown trousers, blue shirts and brown hats, the brims of the hats pulled down, being towed very slowly toward the beach under a dark grey sky and over a miserable choppy sea, the rain pouring down on them incessantly. We could see the cascos start towards the beach, and then we lost sight of them in the gloom."

By early August communications, once so spirited and almost courtly, between Aguinaldo and the American commanders had dwindled to a bare minimum. No longer did the rival commanders visit each other, nor did Aguinaldo offer his services, nor did the Americans make further overtures.

Aguinaldo had moved his headquarters to Bacoor, ten miles away, from where he continued to obstruct American efforts to acquire labor and supplies. Quartermaster Major Jones visited him and was told that the general was indisposed. When he returned in two hours, Aguinaldo was reportedly asleep. The American now scribbled out an angry note: "We are here to befriend the Filipinos . . . the return we are asking is comparatively slight . . . We are prepared to purchase five hundred horses at a fair price, but we cannot undertake to bargain for horses with each individual owner." The Philippine president passed it on to General Anderson, who backed up his major and remarked cuttingly that when a U.S. commander was asleep he knew enough to empower someone else to act for him. Aguinaldo responded that, much as he would like to help, he had no transport to spare. He then asked irrelevantly if there had been any word from Washington concerning the recognition of his government. At this point Anderson was probably wishing that he had never left Alaska. In the end, Aguinaldo allowed a few horses, carts, and wagons to be doled out—just enough to keep the Americans in chronic but not crucial difficulties.

Armed with instructions from McKinley to establish supreme political control over the natives of the islands, Merritt arrived July 25 just in time to catch the full force of a southwest monsoon. For eight endless days, unable to debark, his expedition sat offshore the Tambo beach. There was no breakwater, the sea hit the shore with eight-foot breakers, and it was not until August 2 that the *cascos* were loaded and set drifting ashore. A few were swamped in the surf, and the harassed navy men were sometimes unable to help. When one officer called upon the *Rapido* for assistance, its skipper replied, "Who in the devil are you, anyhow?"

"I'm Colonel Pope, chief quartermaster."

"To hell with the Pope! I take my orders from Commodore Dewey. Get out of my way or I'll swamp you!"

In disgust Merritt abandoned Tambo as a landing area,

and men and supplies were taken off more smoothly during high tide near the mouth of the Paranaque River, a mile from Camp Dewey. Frigid and bored, the general remained on the *Newport* with his staff. Neither he nor Aguinaldo bothered to call on each other. His relations with Dewey were also meager and formal; from the start they disliked each other. He visited Cavite and Camp Dewey only once. No longer the dashing cavalry commander of old, he confided to his aides that he was tired of the army and wanted to retire or enter the diplomatic service.

He ordered all correspondence between his command and Aguinaldo stopped, until he could "enforce my authority in the event that his pretensions should clash with my designs." On July 28 he called for General Greene and told him somehow to juggle the rebels out of their lines. An intelligent, sensitive officer in his early fifties who, after graduating from West Point, had spent a year as military observer in the Russo-Turkish war, Greene turned out to be a most adroit negotiator. Soothingly he persuaded young Noriel to slide his command eastward one more time. Greene then moved in one battalion each from the 18th Regulars and the 1st Colorado Volunteers. The Americans now controlled the vital Pasay-Manila road and had worked up to within eight hundred yards of the Spanish powder-magazine fort and outer trench zone. Next Greene threw forward strong outposts and constructed a new trench line, directly behind which he placed all the Utah light guns. On July 31, for the first time in this war, U.S. land troops came under enemy rifle fire. Along a fairly broad front Merritt was now ready for an independent assault upon the Philippine capital.

VI

Surrounded and blockaded for ten weeks, that city was nearing the end of its endurance. Its only meat was horseflesh and a little buffalo beef. Bananas were twenty-four cents each; flour, rice, and mangos were practically gone; and only the rich dined adequately, although at enormous cost. The poorest ate dogs, cats, and rats. Thousands of *évacués* had been quartered in churches and college buildings. Nobody knew when the Filipinos and Americans were coming, and nerves were taut. All the foreign consuls had appealed to Dewey to allow their nationals out of the city, and with his permission an exodus of British, French, and other expatriates had been taking place since early May. Many Spaniards, nonetheless, clung to their dreams. Surely, they thought, there would be no annexation. *Mañana* the *norte americanos* would go away; *señor* and *señora* would promenade on the Luneta at dusk, just as they had always done, and the Filipinos would step aside to make way for them. But the natives refused to step aside, and many ugly incidents occurred. It was racism and discrimination turned upside down.

Three times Aguinaldo presented surrender terms to Governor Augustin. Hoping for reinforcements from the mother country, he refused them. The British consul, Mr. Walker, died of a minor illness aggravated by malnutrition. Spanish officers, by and large, had given up hope and spent most of their time lounging in cafés, while their off-duty troops roamed the city and suburbs. Ragged and emaciated, they tried to browbeat or steal food from those merchants who still had anything to sell; but mostly they lived on scraps and dried fish and tried to figure out ways of surrendering or otherwise saving their skins. They included about four hundred sailors from the ex-fleet, formed into a useless and demoralized brigade.

In July Augustin cabled Madrid by roundabout means that his situation was doomed. In reply he was instructed to turn over his command to General Fermin Jaudenes, who assumed the governorship (an unusually empty honor) on August 5.

During the day all was quiet. At night the city became

sparklingly alight, almost normally so, and around ten o'clock
sputtering rifle fire started up between the Spanish and insurgent lines in the suburbs. After about an hour it stopped.
Except for these exchanges, during which nobody advanced,
there were no more battles. The insurgents served sporadically. Between periods in the line they went home for a week
or two, handing over their positions and rifles to other soldiers when they left. Sometimes when their ammunition gave
out they walked away in a body to get it replaced. It was all
quite casual, and everyone knew that the Americans would
soon call the tune.

If nothing else, the Spaniards had prodigious amounts of
small-arms ammunition, which they expended in volleys
whenever insurgent and American skirmishers revealed themselves. The Filipinos enjoyed drawing it, hidden as they were
in trenches and thickets, but they hesitated to advance against
it. Only those who had formerly served in the Spanish army
knew much about the weapons they were using. Mausers had
a hinged front sight which could be turned flat, and often
the rebels fired away without raising it. Behind their trenches
they indifferently strolled about, explaining to the Americans
that the enemy was afraid to stand up and take horizontal
aim.

One evening the Spaniards opened up with heavier volleys
and a few 3.2-inch guns. A volunteer U.S. battalion panicked,
believing it was under attack, and sent a courier to headquarters. "General," he cried, "send reinforcements, send
every man, send every company, we're whipped, we're
whipped." Dubiously Greene ordered some dismounted cavalry and part of a regular regiment into the lines. En route
ten men were killed and forty-three wounded by Spanish bullets soaring high (as usual) over the front. Although the
Spaniards had never left their trenches, this false alarm resulted in the first U.S. casualties and the useless expenditure
of sixty thousand rounds of rifle ammunition. The Americans
were instructed not to return enemy fire unless Spaniards

could be seen advancing from their trenches; and one newspaperman quoted a sergeant thus: "Now you fellows, look
a-here! You're not to load your guns unless I order you to,
and if we begin to fire I don't want to see you sittin' down on
your hunkers in the mud . . . I want you to prance right up
on top of the breastwork and give them dagos hell!"

The Americans grumbled, but endured three more such "attacks" and ten more casualties without firing back. (Fortunately the Spanish Mausers, despite their great penetrative
power, were high-velocity, small-bore weapons of poor killing
power. By comparison, the cumbersome .45-caliber American
Springfields sounded like small cannon, emitted a cloud of
black smoke, and caused fearful injuries.) After August 3 the
firing died down to nearly nothing. Americans, Filipinos, and
Spaniards rested, watched, and passively awaited the de-
nouement.

VII

Why the United States seemed so intent on a key role in the
capture of Manila was not clear at the time. Aguinaldo co-
operated in hopes of avoiding antagonisms that would preju-
dice the recognition of his government. Dewey and Merritt
were simply under orders to take the city and establish American sovereignty. They did not know whether such sovereignty was to be temporary or permanent, nor was it their
business to know. As for relations with the insurgents, Dewey
surmised where he stood. Secretary of the Navy Long had
already cabled him, "Report fully any conferences, or co-
operations, military or otherwise, which you have had with
Aguinaldo . . ."

In reply, the admiral reported that several conferences had
been held, but that he had refrained from helping him in any
way. Doubtless the Navy Department did not take this plain
inaccuracy too seriously, in view of the admiral's previous

admissions that he had given the Filipinos arms, turned the
Cavite arsenal over to them, and so on. In any event, Long
did not quibble but merely cabled back that it was desirable
"not to have political alliances with the insurgents or any
faction in the islands that would incur liability to maintain
their cause in the future." And Dewey assured his chief that
he had "entered into no alliances with the insurgents . . ."

Yet even the apolitical admiral had not been born yesterday, and he understood as well as anyone that the Philippine
Islands faced a historical crisis. Perhaps Washington did intend to acquire part or all of the islands, or did intend to make
treaty arrangements with them. It was not his to reason why;
but in any event by August it was no secret that some degree
of association or assimilation was inevitable. Henry Lodge
summed it up in a July letter to Roosevelt: "I had a long talk
with the President . . . He is not giving much consideration
to the Philippines but the question in his mind is how much
he will take there. I think his imagination is touched by the
situation, and I think he grasps it fully." If, however, the
United States should ultimately decide to step aside, other
nations were ready to move in. The previous month Germany's foreign minister (von Bülow) had written his ambassador at Washington, "His Majesty, the Emperor, deems it a
principal object of German policy to leave unused no opportunity which may arise from the Spanish-American War to
obtain naval *fulcra* in East Asia." Great Britain was known to
have offered to buy the islands if America decided not to keep
them. Both Britain and Germany were determined that the
Philippines should not drift into each other's orbit, and the
latter was intent on at least a naval station there. Germany's open acquisitiveness explains why Number 10 Downing Street was anxious to settle for American possession of
the archipelago.

Thus the Spanish-American imbroglio found Germany on
Spain's side, in a manner of speaking, for the Kaiser preferred
feeble competitors rather than young, vigorous ones like the

United States. And while the British and French were ostensibly neutral, at heart they hoped Spain would be allowed to hold the Philippines, and for much the same motives as Germany. Spain's weakening grip spelled opportunity for everyone else.

As for Russia, fearing England's growing power in the far east and the prospect of a strong Anglo-American alliance there, she too hoped the Philippines would stay with Spain. And finally there was Japan, militarily second-class but already showing disconcerting signs of ambition and greed. Her government approached the State Department at about this time, suggesting that if we were unwilling to administer the archipelago alone, they would be willing to help out. The offer was politely declined.

The scene that summer, all in all, was reminiscent of wolves surrounding a wounded stag. They all wanted a morsel, and they all feared to challenge the growing might of the United States—a nation already at war and in a position to take on, if necessary, more comers than Spain. Yet there was no denying that the Philippines were "up for grabs," and many a man proffered advice and warnings. Consul Wildman in Hong Kong, for example, wrote the State Department:

> I wish to put myself on record as stating that the insurgent government of the Philippine Islands cannot be dealt with as though they were North American Indians, willing to be removed from one reservation to another at the whim of their masters . . . the attempt of any foreign nation to obtain territory or coaling stations will be resisted with the same spirit with which they fought the Spaniards.

Aboard the *Baltimore* in Manila Bay, Consul (ex-Consul, to be precise) Oscar Williams penned a more roseate note to Mr. Day in Washington:

> I hope for an influx this year of 10,000 ambitious Americans, and all can live well, become enriched, and patriotically as-

sist your representatives in the establishment and maintenance of republican government . . .

But the views of Mr. Bray, in the Singapore *Free Press*, were in stark contrast:

. . . it is simply ridiculous to imagine that eight to ten millions of such people can be bought and sold as an article of commerce without first obtaining their consent. Let all those who are greedy for a slice of the archipelago ponder well over this before burning their fingers.

He meant American fingers, but his words also applied to Germans. For in Manila Bay a queer wrangle was taking place between Admiral George Dewey and Vice-Admiral Otto von Diederichs.

5

THE
SPANISH
COLLAPSE

WITH TEUTONIC THOROUGHNESS VICE-ADMIRAL VON Diederichs and seven of the eight warships which comprised his Asiatic Squadron had arrived to safeguard German interests—a grand total of one import firm. English, French, and Japanese naval detachments were also at the scene, but the German concentration was stronger than Dewey's and its actions were, to say the least, disconcerting. As early as May the *Raleigh* had been forced to fire a shot across the bows of a German ship which ignored an identification pennant. When von Diederichs called personally to demand an apology, Dewey pointed out that a war was going on and that his blockade regulations governed the shipping in Manila Bay. He also observed that the German naval force seemed disproportionate to that nation's responsibilities there. Von Diederichs responded stiffly and not quite relevantly, "I am here by order of the Kaiser, sir." He could not confess that those orders were to negotiate with the Spaniards for an invitation to mediate between them and the Americans.

So he crudely intruded, while Dewey sat in his wicker chair under the *Olympia*'s forward guns, and watched, and smouldered. When German vessels persisted in knifing through his flotilla without saluting, he dispatched this curt message: "Don't pass the American flag again without seeing it." But von Diederichs' men-of-war continued to behave as though they controlled the bay, anchored wherever they pleased, saluted only the Spanish flag flying from the shore, and landed sacks of flour for their beleaguered friends. German officers entertained Spanish officials and ladies in their wardrooms, and were in turn invited to parties within the city. Rumors flew among the European colonies in Manila that von Diederichs would soon intervene with more than social pleasantries.

The Germans took interminable soundings off the mouth of the Pasig River and occupied Mariveles Harbor for several days, under the pretense of conducting drills on shore. Dewey inquired gravely of von Diederichs if Germany or the United States were the blockading power. When the German cruiser *Irene* went so far as to prevent insurgent troops from capturing the Spanish naval post on Grande Island, Aguinaldo complained to Dewey, who sent the *Raleigh* and *Concord* to chase the *Irene* away. The consequences were twofold and unexpected. For it was the Americans—not the insurgents—who proceeded to occupy Grande Island. And again it was von Diederichs who protested. Dewey listened passively to the German emissary and then exploded, "Do you want war with us?"

"Certainly not."

"Well, it looks like it, and you are very near it." And he added that "as we are in for it now, it matters little to us whether we fight Spain, or Germany, or the world; and if you desire war, you can have it right here. You need not cable to Berlin, nor need I to Washington; you can just have war here and now." Back home the affair was splashed across front pages; and America showed that her martial spirit was still in full bloom. "We take no crowding," warned the Philadelphia *Press*. That the Kaiser had instructed von Diederichs to snatch up any possible stray bits of Pacific real estate seemed clear (and was later proved); still, at the moment, the United States had little more right to the Philippines than any other foreign power. In the words of the Detroit *Tribune*, the Monroe Doctrine did not apply to the universe. And while the New York *Times* editorially admitted that "we may not particularly care about taking the Philippines" it continued, "expansion is a new idea with us. The defense of our rights is an old habit."

Even more inspired was the Atlanta *Constitution*, which welcomed war with Germany as another step toward delivering the peoples of Europe from oppressive, outmoded monarchies. In addition:

> Americans resent any kind of arrogance, but when it is displayed by a despot whose lunatic reign has excited the contempt and indignation of all who believe in human liberty, the feeling goes deeper . . .

It might have been the year 1917. The violence of the reaction startled the German chancellory, plus the fact that Captain Chichester, commanding the strong British squadron at Manila, had gone out of his way to show support for Dewey. As spring and early summer waned, the leaden mind of Vice-Admiral von Diederichs slowly came to realize that Dewey and Merritt were not there to free the Philippines and then set them adrift, nor solely to whip the Spaniards, nor to round out the Cuban crusade. And when the extent of American interests in the islands was suggested by Mr. Hay to the German ambassador in London, the interfering tactics of von Diederichs ceased, much to the regret of our yellow press.

No longer distracted, Admiral Dewey was now able to assist General Merritt in creating another and even more unusual tableau—the capture of Manila by a battle which was not to be a battle.

II

Seated gloomily beneath a large mango tree in Camp Dewey, General Anderson asked Father McKinnon, "Why in the name of common sense don't some of you Catholics enter Manila and tell that arehbishop of yours to call this thing off?" The Californians' chaplain remarked, "I believe I could walk right down the beach and into Manila without any trouble at all." On the spur of the moment he started off. A torrent of rifle fire sent him scurrying back. He tried again. Halfway across the eight hundred yards of sand between the American and Spanish trenches, a bullet went through his hat. He kept walking. Upon entering the enemy lines, he was taken to Archbishop Nozaleda. The conference came to nothing; Governor-General Jaudenes declined to end hostilities just yet. For some time he had been negotiating desultorily with the American commanders, while both sides waited for U.S. troops to arrive. By early August the first three expeditions had landed and the fourth was preparing to do so. Still, Jaudenes' problems involved something more than merely putting out a white flag.

One was to let the Americans in while keeping the Filipinos out. The other was to salvage both Jaudenes' neck and Spain's honor. In solving these simultaneous equations, the Americans and Spaniards drifted into an alliance against the insurgents. Some weeks before the British consul had outlined surrender terms that might be acceptable to both sides, but Augustin had turned them down because the Americans were then too weak to hold off the insurgents. Dewey had refused to consider them for the identical reason—"because I had no force with which to occupy the city and I would not for a moment consider the possibility of turning it over to the undisciplined insurgents." Since these were the natives who waged war "most humanely," whom he had termed more capable of self-government than the Cubans, the admiral had evidently revised his views. When the British consul died, intermediation was taken over by the Belgian consul, M. Edouard André; and, as U.S. troops poured in, everything began to fall into place. Jaudenes promised that he would not use his artillery if the Americans refrained from shelling Manila. He reiterated that, if the insurgents were excluded, Spanish resistance would be noisy but innocuous. In turn, Dewey and Merritt intimated that the mildness of their terms would depend upon the superficiality of such resistance. These preliminary exchanges took place in secret the first week of August. Then came a flurry of open communications largely designed for the ultimate salvation of Señor Jaudenes:

On August 7 Dewey and Merritt advised him that their bombardment might begin within forty-eight hours. "This notice is given in order to afford you an opportunity to remove all noncombatants from the city."

The Governor replied bleakly that he was "without place of refuge for the increased numbers of wounded, sick, women and children who are now lodged within the walls. Very Respectfully and Kissing the Hands of Your Excellencies . . ."

It would be regrettable, the Americans pointed out, if the helpless city had to suffer a bombardment that could be avoided. They asked for its outright surrender, including the Spanish troops therein.

In response Jaudenes alluded to his dire straits—"which unfortunately I have to admit"—and asked for time to consult Madrid.

On August 10: "In reply we respectfully inform your excellency that we decline to grant the time requested."

Fixed (so to speak) or not, the fight could not be long delayed. The Governor talked matters over with the British vice-consul, Mr. Ramsden, and the German consul, Herr Kruger. Ramsden complimented Jaudenes upon his skillful handling of a deplorable situation and congratulated the Spanish army on its courageous showing thus far. Spanish honor was more than satisfied, he assured Jaudenes; he could surrender with an easy conscience.

We learn without surprise that Herr Kruger differed. The Spaniards, he stated, had not yet done all they could. As a Prussian army officer, he did not feel that the dictates of military honor were fully met. Jaudenes agreed with Kruger until the door closed behind his visitors. He then changed his mind. Ramsden was absolutely right. The case was hopeless; he had done all that was humanly possible without reinforcements; there were the noncombatants to consider. Then, too, Dewey and Merritt had just delivered another forty-eight-hour ultimatum, and this time they meant it. Above all, there were the insurgents—*los diablos negros*—who would surely loot Manila and massacre his countrymen if given the chance. It was fortunate indeed, he reflected, that Washington entertained the same humanitarian sentiments as he did. He sent for the Belgian consul.

That afternoon the mock battle was arranged. The navy would assume positions opposite Fort San Antonio Abad at nine the following morning, August 13, and would shell only that structure and the impregnable walls of the Old City. Simultaneously the Spaniards would withdraw, the *insurrectos* would be checked, and the Americans would advance. After having fired a proper number of shots, the *Olympia* would steam forward, flying the international surrender signal "DWHB," whereupon the Spaniards would hoist a white flag and officers of both armies and fleets would meet on the shore to formalize the surrender terms. "It is intended that these results shall be accomplished without the loss of life," Merritt wrote his brigadiers. And to deal with the Filipinos, who had waited three hundred years to enter Manila in triumph, General MacArthur's brigade,

in the event that it can pass the enemy line on the road leading to Singalon, will leave a force in the Spanish trenches at this point of crossing with instructions to permit no armed

bodies other than American troops to cross the trenches in the
direction of Manila.

Such token forces could not in themselves restrain Luna's
thirty-thousand-man army; but once again the pen would
prove itself mightier than the sword.

III

Some little harmony had existed between Aguinaldo and the
Americans until the arrival of General Merritt. At this point,
it virtually disappeared. Merritt claimed that he had been ordered not to deal with the insurgents. No such instruction
appears in any existing document. Indeed he had been told,
"No rupture with insurgents; this is imperative." His mode of
complying, however, was unique; he simply ignored them for
two weeks, vaguely hoping, perhaps, that they would go
away. Aware that arrangements of some sort were being
consummated without him, Aguinaldo reacted as may be
imagined. Mr. Williams thought it advisable to cable Washington of "the exceedingly embarrassing situation which
confronts General Merritt through the officiousness of the insurgent chieftain, Aguinaldo. According to all accounts this
young man's success has completely gone to his head." The
young man in question, more uneasy than Mr. Williams
guessed, sent a staff officer to ascertain the details of the impending attack. No answer having been elicited, he telegraphed American headquarters several times. None of these
queries was acknowledged. He proclaimed (for the third or
fourth time) the independence of his nation and called upon
the world to recognize its sovereignty. As in the case of former
such pronouncements, this one was greeted by a dead silence,
although with a twinge of nervousness Merritt cabled Adjutant General H. C. Corbin on August 1: "Situation difficult.
Insurgents have announced independent government; some

are unfriendly . . . It may be important have my whole force before attacking if necessary to hold insurgents while we fight Spaniards." But a large log-jam was developing on the west coast at the time, and Corbin could only reply, "Six thousand troops at San Francisco. Can charter no more transports."

Former consul Oscar Williams was neither an important nor a brilliant diplomat, but he knew his Filipinos from years of experience, and in his glum, practical way he could see that the situation was taking an alarming turn. He advised Aguinaldo to cool down and accept a "union" (the term was left vague) between the Philippines and the United States. The reply—ironical and unquestionably composed by Mabini—is worth quoting at some length:

> I congratulate you with all sincerity on the acuteness and ingenuity which you have displayed in painting in an admirable manner the benefits which . . . would be secured by the union of these islands with the United States of America. Ah! that picture, so happy and so finished, is capable of fascinating not only the dreamy imagination of the impressionable Oriental, but also the cold and calculating thoughts of the sons of the North.

He personally conceded that many benefits might flow from such an association. But:

> Will my people believe it? I . . . do not dare assure you of it . . . I have done what they desire . . . because acting in any other manner they would fail to recognize me as the interpreter of their aspirations and would punish me as a traitor, replacing me by another more careful of his honor and dignity.

If the United States intends to annex the islands, why not recognize its legal government first and then "join with it?" Why not co-operate with the Filipino armed forces? Already his compatriots complain that the "labor, fatigue, blood, and treasure" of the Filipinos have been used cynically by the American commanders to further their own aims.

> But I do not believe these unworthy suspicions. I have full confidence in the generosity and philanthropy which shine in characters of gold in the history of the privileged people of the United States.

Tell the American government to recognize the Filipino government, he continued, to understand:

> that in the midst of their past misfortunes they have learned to love liberty, order, justice and civil life, and that they are not able to lay aside their own wishes when their future lot and history are under discussion. Say, also, that I and my leaders know what we owe to our unfortunate country, that we know how to admire and are ready to imitate the disinterestedness, the abnegation, and the patriotism of the grand men of America, among whom stands pre-eminent the immortal George Washington.

Mr. Williams failed to report these sentiments to his government, nor their plain implication that the natives would fight rather than be annexed.

Up to this time there had been no direct threats; but now Dewey showed his hand. Fearing that if the insurgents took Manila gross injuries to the city and its Spanish inhabitants would follow, he ordered the Filipinos not to cross the Manolele River between their front and the city. If they did, he warned, he would send the *Petrel* into the stream to bombard their lines. Scarcely had this been swallowed by the native high command when General Greene requested that American field guns and their personnel be permitted to occupy certain forward Filipino entrenchments. With some restraint, Aguinaldo asked for a written memorandum. It would follow, Greene replied; but to save time it would be best to emplace the guns first and write the note later. The transfer occurred so quickly that American artillerymen were in and the Filipinos were out before the volatile Luna got wind of it.

So far so good; and with curious negativism the New York *Times* reported:

DEWEY IS NOT IN DREAD

He Has Not Cabled Washington
That the Philippine Insurgents
Have Grown Defiant

Notwithstanding . . . the Administration has come into possession of information which leads it to believe that the rebels in the Philippines are going to prove a far more troublesome problem to deal with than the Spaniards.

But the following day:

MERRITT SEES TROUBLE AHEAD

The Situation at Manila is
Unsatisfactory and Dangerous

THE INSURGENTS SULKING

And on that same date the *Times* continued to make discoveries:

INSURGENTS NOT OUR ALLIES

Aguinaldo, the Rebel Leader of the
Philippines, Has Grown Arrogant, and
Is a Hindrance

Next morning, August 3, the possible consequences of their defiance, sulking, and arrogance were made plain:

MANILA REBELS ARE MAD

They Would Turn Like Savages
Upon the Priests and Nuns
and Slaughter Them

Alarmist copy of this kind, however, did not emanate from correspondents at the focal point. Oscar Davis cabled *Harper's Weekly* from Cavite that Aguinaldo had saved our troops much hard campaigning; and on August 6, writing for

the same publication, John F. Bass reported: "We forget that
they drove the Spaniards from Cavite to their present in-
trenched position, thus saving us a long-continued fight
through the jungle." A most unprogressive gentleman, he simply concluded, "Give them their liberty and guarantee it to
them."

Those were dangerous days, smelling of crisis and death;
and even George Dewey, as he negotiated with the pliant
Spaniards, was in an edgy mood. His orders to subordinates
early in August have a brief and peremptory flavor. The
Filipino flag on every little launch and *casco* hustling cheerily
about the bay struck him as an affront to the dignity of the
American fleet. One day he swept up all the Filipino skippers
and, on the *Olympia's* deck, lectured them to the effect that
their national emblem was worthless and their "mosquito
fleet" an annoyance. When one Tagalog muttered something
under his breath, Dewey asked for a translation. The interpreter said, "He says, sir, he will get even with you."

"Throw that man overboard," responded the admiral. The
deed was done, and Aguinaldo had a new outrage to protest.
But who, after all, was Aguinaldo? A Tagalog nonentity,
leading a mob of savages who would take to their heels at the
sound of American rifle fire, suggested the Buffalo *Commercial;* furthermore, "Whose dog is he—to-day? He is an in-
triguer who accepts bribes. Whose retainer does he hold now?
Possibly Germany's." And that first week in August, before
the war with Spain was over, before Manila had been attacked, before any negotiations, conciliatory or otherwise,
had been opened with the native government, the journal
Public Opinion reached the end of its patience:

> There has been enough trifling with Aguinaldo . . . He has
> been tolerated and meanwhile has been undergoing a sort of
> civil service examination to decide whether he and his fol-
> lowers are capable of administering the government of the
> islands wisely and well . . . He must be made to submit at

once to the authority of the United States . . . The first test
of ability to command is a willingness to obey.

The acid test of Aguinaldo's willingness to obey occurred
some twelve hours before the scheduled attack. From his office aboard the *Newport,* General Merritt sent a signal officer
ashore in a pounding surf to deliver a message to General
Anderson. The latter was to instruct Aguinaldo to stay out of
the city. On the spot he composed and telegraphed the following message to *insurrecto* headquarters at Bacoor:

Do not let your troops enter Manila without the permission
of the American commander. On this side of the Pasig River
you will be under our fire.

One pictures the consternation which attended the arrival
of this bombshell, confirming the significance of Dewey's
earlier warning not to cross the Manolele; and one regrets
that there is no written record of the undoubtedly picturesque
dialogue between the Filipino gentlemen in Aguinaldo's office
late that balmy evening. We only know that the Philippine
president at length decided to comply, but without telling
Anderson so. Thus the Americans were left wondering if, after
all, they would have to take Manila by actual force—and from
their so-called allies.

IV

The American army in the Philippines had been organized
into a single division of 8,500 assault troops under General
Anderson, split into two brigades commanded by Generals
Greene and MacArthur. General Merritt himself had never
visited the U.S. front lines, and suspicions mounted that he
would not be there during the attack. On August 11 he attended a conference at Camp Dewey which lasted for several
hours, and then returned to the *Newport*. There was no hint
of what had been said, no indication that the general would

take the field, and the war correspondent Frank Millet writes: "This confirmed the impression which was rapidly gaining ground, that the enemy was expected to make no resistance, but would yield at once on the proper display of force on our side." The statement needs qualifying. Dewey and various generals were the only Americans who knew officially that the fight had been prearranged. A few others (including the newspapermen) may have had their suspicions; but unquestionably the enlisted men and most junior officers anticipated a costly battle. Spanish blockhouses and entrenchments outside the capital comprised an excellent defense system, and the last obstacle—the huge walls of the Old City—was certainly nothing to joke about. When the Utah and Astor batteries, the California, Oregon, Colorado, and Nebraska volunteers, and the regulars moved into position the evening of the twelfth, the air was tense with excitement, some apprehension, and relief that the long, rainy weeks of waiting were at an end.

As bugles rasped out reveille at four o'clock next morning a fine drizzle was descending. In the haze, signal communications between ships and shore broke down. Shortly after dawn heavy thunderstorms struck, pelting the thousands of khaki-clad, slouch-hatted troops and converting the roads into porridge. With heavy booms, insurgent cannon on the Pasay road opened up. The Spaniards did not reply, and it was seen that the muzzles of their field guns within Fort San Antonio had disappeared. "This was significant, and did not look like business," commented Mr. Millet. Out in the bay, the British battleship *Immortalité* struck up Dewey's favorite march, "Under the Double Eagle," and Captain Chichester quietly moved his ships between the German and American squadrons. The gesture was much appreciated. By ninethirty Dewey's fleet had steamed into its assigned battle positions and the *Olympia* opened fire on the fort with her five- and eight-inch guns. The others followed suit.

After about ten minutes one officer said to the captain of

the *Petrel*, "Captain, I shouldn't be surprised if this whole performance was a sham. Don't you notice how slowly the Olympia is firing? And I don't think she is firing her eight-inch at all. Besides I just saw a signal from Manila, and I have not seen the Monterey fire at all, and no one has fired at us."

Commander Wood smiled and replied, "Yes, I shouldn't be surprised if it were all a sham."

The naval shelling soon ceased. Now the land batteries went into action, the infantrymen hauled themselves out of their muddy entrenchments, and in dense, straggling ranks proceeded through the suburbs of Malate and Ermite toward the walled city.

The Colorado Volunteers (three hundred of them still without shoes) on the extreme left of Greene's brigade had been assigned the capture of Fort San Antonio. Their route led along the beach, crossed a ford, and traversed patches of marshland. They splashed along, shouting happily, followed by their regimental band. Led by a fat bandmaster with a cornet, it was playing "There'll Be a Hot Time in the Old Town Tonight." There was scarcely any Spanish resistance, and the men found war wonderfully simple and amusing. The fort being empty—which seemed quite natural that dreamlike day—it was captured without much difficulty. When the full brigade reached the Luneta, a deserted and wet and gloomy expanse, they found a white flag flying from the walls and some seven thousand armed Spaniards standing on them. It was plain that these men and those in the nearby blockhouses were not firing at the Americans—"a mystery," writes Aguinaldo sardonically.

During these innocuous events, MacArthur's men on the right were engaged in something resembling actual fighting. Several dozen casualties were suffered in passing through Singalon, after which the brigade entered Manila by way of the Paco district.

Certain elements of confusion had attended these operations. The Spanish surrender flag, hoisted since eleven o'clock, had little effect upon the attackers for two hours. Few of the enthusiastic Americans, jostled and elbowed by throngs of *insurrectos* also determined to get into the city, could see that signal hanging limply in the murky air. The battle, they thought, had scarcely begun. On they surged, and the alarmed Spaniards began firing back. Near Santa Ana insurgents collided with Spanish troops, whereupon a savage little skirmish took place. On MacArthur's right flank, Americans and Filipinos began exchanging shots, for both U.S. brigades had been instructed to drop off detachments at various road junctures to keep the natives back.

It was at about one o'clock—with Spaniards retreating from the trench zone, Americans advancing, Spaniards surrendering, insurgents hurrying along the roads in company with U.S. troops, Americans trying to restrain the Filipinos, the two allies in a state of swirling excitement, firing and swearing at each other, the Spaniards' huge, dirty, white sheet fluttering listlessly atop a corner of the hoary old wall, rifles crackling from all directions—that General Greene finally cantered up to the Puerta Real gate. His raincoat splashed with mud, he galloped through to take the Spanish surrender in the Governor-General's office—too late. Flag-Lieutenant Brumby and Colonel Whittier, representing Admiral Dewey and General Merritt respectively, were already in conference with the authorities. Feeling somewhat unnecessary, Greene departed. The capitulation seemed well in hand anyway, and all that remained to be done was to stop the war. A good deal of scattered shooting was still going on. Two thousand insurgents had somehow worked their way southeast between the Nebraska regiment and the Pasig River bridge. Others were coming up, some of whom were surreptitiously firing at the Americans from cover. The crack of Spanish Mausers could still be heard from a few houses in the southern suburbs. Insurgents on the Paco road pressed against the Californians; sporadic shots were fired, and some Americans went down.

In a blind fury, others began firing back. As the afternoon passed, these and other such irregularities were ironed out.

All this time the naval guns had been silent. The sailors watched the fight as it unfolded dimly through smoke and rain. They had lunch; meanwhile they kept their guns trained on the enemy batteries. The Spanish flag still waved unaccountably over the city. Two hours passed. At 2:23, Lieutenant Brumby's launch returned. He climbed the sea ladder at the *Olympia's* quarterdeck and shouted to the admiral, "Well, they've surrendered all right."

"Why don't they haul down that flag?"

"They'll do that as soon as Merritt gets 600 or 700 men in there to protect them."

Dewey said, "Well, you go over and tell General Merritt that I agree to anything."

Except for fifty American casualties, the engagement had been consummated according to plan. The Americans were in the city and the insurgents were not. Diligent Lieutenant Brumby personally lowered the Spanish flag over Fort Santiago and ran up the Stars and Stripes while dark-eyed señoritas sobbed convulsively and melodramatic Spanish cavaliers muttered curses. Through some miracle, U.S. troops and Filipinos had not drifted into a full-fledged showdown. The Spaniards demanded and received a surrender contract awarding them the honors of war, in line with the theory that they had voluntarily handed over the city and had not lost it through force. Sixty years after the battle, one wonders what difference it made. The United States took title to all public funds and property pending the final Spanish-American peace settlement; and except for the second word the last article of the capitulation was verbatim with that enunciated by General Scott when he captured Mexico City:

> This city, its inhabitants, its churches and religious worship, its educational establishments, and its private property of all descriptions are placed under the special safeguard of the faith and honor of the American army.

A sham battle which saves hundreds of lives is preferable to a real battle. On the other hand, six Americans and forty-nine Spaniards had died to salvage Señor Jaudenes' reputation. Since Dewey and Merritt could have received the surrender of the city unconditionally and without even a demonstration, had they insisted, they became the object of some muted criticism at the time, and some not-so-muted criticism afterward. Obviously an American ultimatum, coupled with a threat to release the insurgents, would have forced Jaudenes' hand. Dewey and Merritt probably cooperated with the enemy because they were inexperienced in diplomacy, and because psychologically they were on Spain's side as opposed to a common adversary—the Filipino *insurrectos*. The incident aroused much astonishment among neutrals in the capital city. In the words of one Englishman:

> The Archbishop of Manila told me, and it was generally admitted by the British and foreign inhabitants, that the capture of the city was one of the most disgraceful farces in the history of modern warfare. The relatives of the . . . men who were literally butchered in this prearranged opera bouffe performance should demand, through their congressmen, an investigation.

But this was written (perhaps overwritten) some months after the facts became known. Two days following the capitulation, the Los Angeles *Times* reported it not too accurately but rather more conventionally:

MANILA GIVES UP TO DEWEY

The American Admiral Batters
The Forts of the Spanish
With His Big Guns

Places This Country in a Position
To Demand Cession of Needed Territory

And Mr. John Goodnow, American consul-general in Shanghai, also felt that we needed the Philippines. That same Tuesday, August 16, the Associated Press quoted him thus: "We should hold the Philippine Islands, the Caroline Islands and the Ladrone Islands, also Cuba and Porto Rico. It does not matter whether we call them war indemnity or what. We need them in our business." But the New York *Times* rose above such sordid considerations: "It has been a just and worthy war . . . the world is better for it . . . we are better for it."

Governor Jaudenes, however, was no better for it. The elaborate plan cooked up between him and the Americans had tragically miscarried. In Madrid the public prosecutor, after an investigation, brought the unlucky little general to public trial and demanded his life imprisonment for state treason. And this was not the least of the curiosities involved in the capture of Manila. It need not have been captured at all, for the Spanish-American War had already ended.

V

It had appeared for a time that the conflict off America's east coast might amount to something. There was the matter of Admiral Cervera's fleet, its whereabouts unknown. Would it bombard or invade Boston or New York? Though a friend of Senator Lodge had predicted to him that if the Spaniards landed at New York they would be selling oranges before they got beyond Fourteenth Street, other individuals were more apprehensive. The enemy fleet was, fortunately, en route to Cuba. Upon reaching Santiago Harbor it was bottled up and destroyed. Meanwhile land operations in Cuba had ended with the capitulation of the Spaniards there on July 16. About a week later Puerto Rico was occupied almost bloodlessly by forces under General Nelson Miles, and Spain hurriedly sued for peace while she still held Manila.

This was July 26, and it found the president in a quandary neatly summarized by the headlines: "WHAT TO TAKE. Queer

Question Arises as to the Islands." Washington was insuffera-
bly hot that weekend, and McKinley invited his cabinet to
evaluate matters while cruising down the Potomac on a light-
house tender. The islands in question were, of course, the
Philippines. It was obvious that we would divest Spain of
Cuba, Puerto Rico, and Guam. The protest of the French
ambassador (acting for Spain)—that taking Puerto Rico
evinced "a spirit of conquest inconsistent with the declaration of disinterestedness with which the United States had
commenced the war"—being unanswerable, it was not answered. As to the Philippines, opinions differed. McKinley
could not make up his mind. The Secretary of State suggested annexing merely a naval base, presumably Manila.
The president joked that Judge Day only wanted a hitching
post. Treasury Secretary Gage and Navy Secretary Long
agreed with Day. Contrarily, Attorney General Griggs desired the entire archipelago, and so did the Secretaries of
Agriculture and the Interior.

It was the kind of impasse McKinley detested; but on the
thirtieth came a helpful dispatch from Admiral Dewey that
Manila might capitulate momentarily. If that were really the
case, it was plain that the march of events impelled us to retain the islands temporarily until we could decide what to
do with them. Why capture Manila for nothing at all, and
then abandon it? It made no sense; and reluctantly those
cabinet members opposed to annexation went along with a
clause in the peace protocol which stated that: "The United
States will occupy and hold the city, bay and harbor of Manila pending the conclusion of a treaty of peace which shall
determine the control, disposition and government of the
Philippines."

In Madrid, when the French ambassador relayed the protocol he had tried to soften, consternation reigned. "This demand," protested the Spanish government, "strips us of the
very last memory of a glorious past and expels us . . . from
the Western Hemisphere, which became peopled and civi-

lized through the proud deeds of our ancestors." But they had no good alternative, and furthermore a protocol was only an armistice, a temporary cease-fire. Surely the eventual treaty would be more lenient. On the afternoon of August 13 Spain signed. But it was not until several hours later—early morning, Manila time—that the capture of that city took place. The cable which Dewey had cut on May 1 was still cut; in fact, he did not hear of the August 13 armistice until August 16.

Madrid also learned of the Manila episode after the signing of the protocol. With some relief, the Spanish foreign minister plausibly pointed out that all military operations occurring thereafter were without legal value; the seizure of Manila was null and void. But law was one thing and possession another. The United States *had* captured that city, and was still holding it, and many signs indicated that she would continue to hold it. The sword was mightier than the pen. And as to the insurgents, those nearly forgotten little brown men, the Associated Press reported tonelessly from Washington on August 17:

> It had been thought in some quarters here that the showing heretofore made by the insurgents would lead to their receiving a certain amount of recognition in the way of joint action between the United States forces and those of the insurgents when the city was occupied, but the instructions sent tonight were based on occupation by the United States alone.

On the day Manila was captured Dewey had cabled his superiors a question which put everything in a nutshell: "Since occupation of the town and suburbs the insurgents on outside are pressing demand for joint occupation of the city . . . Is government willing to use all means to make the natives submit to the authority of the United States?" Due to the zigzag means of transmission, it arrived six days later, at which time Acting Navy Secretary Allen replied that there was to be no joint occupation with the insurgents; Dewey was to use any means in his judgment necessary to that end. Ten thousand miles away, the gentlemen in Washington could not possibly understand that the insurgents were wild with disappointment and ready to fight. Mabini exclaimed that they had a perfect right to enter Manila without permission. Around noon of the day of the capture, the civil governor of Cavite wired Aguinaldo: "At this moment the bombardment of Manila is taking place, and we are not able to see even the shadow of an American general." Generals Pio del Pilar, Noriel, and Ricarte were in an especially ugly mood. That evening four thousand Filipino troops pressed against the American line at Malate, causing General Anderson to wire Aguinaldo at Bacoor a message implying that the Filipino army would soon be permitted entry:

> Serious trouble threatening between our forces. Try and prevent it. Your forces should not try to force themselves into the city until we have received the full surrender. Then we will negotiate with you.

The rank and file of the native army and its officers could not understand why they had been barred from their own capital city. Around the outskirts, it is true, matters were different. On August 13 del Pilar had captured the suburbs of Pretio, Tondo, Divisoria, and Paseo de Azcarraga. Noriel's command had occupied Singalon and Paco. They continued to hold the waterworks and had made additional gains to the north of the city. Pouring into Malate, they assumed a contemptuous, chip-on-the-shoulder attitude which infuriated American detachments supposedly in control of that town.

At ten-thirty on the fourteenth, General Pio del Pilar telegraphed Aguinaldo: "Most urgent. Ask send general to arrange avoid conflict which is probable." In Santa Ana and Pandakan, insurgents under General Ricarte routed five Spanish companies, and a few squads in civilian disguise even infiltrated the Old City through various gates on the south and east. It was under these chaotic conditions that Aguinaldo finally replied to Anderson, and the tone of his message speaks for itself:

> I received a telegram. My interpreter is in Cavite. In consequence of this I have not answered until now. My troops are forced by yours by means of threats of violence to retire from positions taken . . . To avoid a conflict . . . your soldiers should correspond to the conduct imposed upon mine.

The pressures on Emilio Aguinaldo (who had just achieved the ripe age of thirty), the temptation to fight America then and there, must have been enormous. Although conservative elements of his cabinet under Paris-educated Pardo de Tavera favored a wait-and-see policy, they were outnumbered by a radical faction which controlled the army. Under Mabini and Luna, this group was bitterly opposed to any line of action other than immediately driving out the American volunteers before the regulars arrived in force. Yet as this day and the next passed, Mabini began to perceive that they had been outflanked; and wearily he said, "We have not yet finished the war with Spain, and we must not provoke another with America. We are not in a position to conduct two wars."

There were some grounds for optimism. After all, the United States only held Manila and Cavite. The surrender terms suggested that America was barred from extending her grip on the islands. Furthermore, American occupation of Manila enabled the insurgents to diversify their forces and take firmer command of the rest of the archipelago. Hoping to come to a reasonable settlement with the hated *norte americanos* in time, Aguinaldo decided to tread lightly.

On the evening of the fourteenth, two conferences were held between Filipino and American generals. Merritt said that he feared conflicts between Spaniards and natives unless the United States alone controlled Manila and its suburbs. Since the natives could see nothing improper about fighting Spaniards, with whom they were still at war, they refused to leave the suburbs. The meetings settled nothing. Next day the same Filipino commission presented a long series of demands concerning joint occupancy of Manila, other matters of civil control, the implied recognition of Philippine sovereignty, and so on. Anderson ignored them. There was nothing to talk about until they withdrew from the city limits, he asserted. But what were the city limits? Had the Spaniards left any blueprints? Nobody knew. How far back would the native army have to retreat, even assuming they agreed to do so? The Filipinos also suggested that the terms "insurgent" and *insurrecto* be abandoned by the Americans. They had been insurgents against Spain, but they were now independent and the United States did not own them. The Americans continued to call them insurgents.

VI

Almost overnight Manila seemed to return to normal. Native shops opened for business. So did the banks and custom houses. Little tramcars clattered along as though nothing had happened. Newspapers resumed publication. The sun, actually and coincidentally, came out. The cable between Manila and Hong Kong was finally restored, and the first message was from President McKinley. With unconscious irony he congratulated Merritt's army for its gallantry in the assault on Manila. American soldiers, big and rough-looking in their dirty brown uniforms, were everywhere. There was no looting, no disorder.

Merritt proclaimed military law and asked for the co-operation of the people of the islands, concluding with a passage bluntly and primarily aimed at the native army: ". . . so long as they preserve the peace and perform their duties toward the representatives of the United States they will not be disturbed in their persons and property, except insofar as may be found necessary for the good of the service of the United

States and the benefit of the people of the Philippines." He appointed General MacArthur provost-marshal of the city, General Greene in charge of finances and customs, Captain Glass naval officer of the port. Other officers took over the courts, sanitation, public works, and education. Everything was now functioning with American precision and good will. Only Aguinaldo, his Philippine government, and his thirty-thousand-man army obstinately refused to enter into the spirit of the hour. What to do about them? Dewey suggested to Washington that if it were up to him he would stamp them out once and for all. The advice he received in return was less violent but not particularly helpful. He was, "while maintaining a position of rightful supremacy as to the insurgents, to pursue, as far as possible, a conciliatory course to all."

It was easier said than done. If things were quiet in Manila, relations with the insurgents were still most unsatisfactory. The surrounding troops were actually increasing in number rather than dwindling. Since they declined to give up the waterworks, the metropolis was still being forced to subsist on rainwater. To get the pumps operating, Merritt made a few concessions. The insurgents were given access to the city, provided they carried no arms. Filipino products were to be admitted free of duty. Insurgents and their sympathizers were promised preference in municipal jobs not held by Americans. If and when the Americans left the Philippines, Aguinaldo, in an odd phrase, would be left "in as good condition as he was found by the forces of the government." On the other hand, that young man had to withdraw his troops from the suburbs.

He agreed, but by the end of August those troops had not yet stirred. Then came a sharp reminder from Merritt, but still (except for a few token withdrawals) the Filipino army stood pat. It began to look very much as though the stalemate would hold until a final treaty with Spain was negotiated, for better or worse. In the interim, American soldiers settled down to the strange job of running an oriental city.

138   LITTLE BROWN BROTHER

The situation, though improved, was still far from stable. One reason why Aguinaldo did not intend to relinquish more territory was that America might conceivably leave the Philippines upon concluding a peace settlement with Spain. In that event, he wanted to be in the best tactical position to crush the remnants of Spanish power in Manila. Therefore his armies leaned against the tiny perimeter which enclosed the uneasy foreigners. Merritt held the city, Aguinaldo the rest of Luzon. It was humiliating to the American commander that his authority extended not one foot outside the Old City limits. And as the two armies brushed against each other incidents began to crop up. In Cavite on August 24, for example, the native governor, Riego de Dios, wired his president that two allegedly "drunken Americans" had been killed by his soldiers. General Anderson wrote Riego that he and his troops must leave the city. "One of my men has been killed and three wounded by your people. This is positive and does not admit of explanation or delay." But to his man Aguinaldo wired tersely, "Give up your life before abandoning that place."

Large supplies of arms were still reaching the insurgents from Hong Kong and Shanghai. Received at Dagupan, they were taken by rail down to Aguinaldo's new headquarters, the strategic town of Malolos, twenty miles north of Manila. The one and only Philippine railway had been repaired by the natives and was now being operated solely by the Philippine war government. Aguinaldo requested the free use of the Pasig River for his boats. Merritt brushed him off on Admiral Dewey. Aguinaldo demanded occupancy of part of the Paco district. Merritt did not answer. Bored and obdurate, he was about to leave the Philippines he hated so thoroughly, and he knew it. His successor would arrive within a week. Meanwhile he went through the motions of performing a job of diplomacy. Between him and his equally untalented co-negotiator, Admiral George Dewey, they managed to convert the potential friendship and co-operation of the population into suspicion and resentment. The president and governing cabinet of that people, generally treated like corporals under the command of the ranking Americans, were already considering ways and means of ousting the foreign authority. In the words of the deputy consul-general at Hong Kong, written the following year:

> It is perhaps futile to speculate upon what might have been accomplished at this period had the American government been represented by diplomats instead of soldiers in the Philippines . . . war might have been averted . . . The crisis was at hand and our diplomacy was not equal to the occasion. It was of an order below that exercised by the Filipinos themselves. Thrown upon their own resources, ignored by the American authorities, they became obstreperous and sullen, unreasonable and assertive.

From Batangas came a telegram to Aguinaldo: "Arms have landed, materials leaving tomorrow, expect us overland"; and this inventory followed:

> Havanas [rapid-fire guns] 2; cigarettes [ammunition] of same kind, 3502; cigars [rifles] 492; cigarettes of same kind, 500,000; chopped [Remington] and straight cut [Mauser] . . .

The tree was bearing bitter fruit. Late in August Wesley Merritt left for Paris to participate in the Spanish-American peace conference. For a long time to come events would be largely shaped by his successor.

6

BETWEEN
WAR
AND
PEACE

TALL AND HULKING, WITH OLD-FASHIONED SIDEBURNS THAT
sprouted in various directions, a Harvard Law School
graduate of 1861, Ewell S. Otis had served with distinction in the Union Army, rising from captain to brevet brigadier general. When the Civil War ended he joined the regular army. Awarded the temporary rank of major general of volunteers in 1898, he left hurriedly for the Philippines that July. His unfamiliarity with the islands, the Filipinos, and the revolution was normal for those archaic times, in which generals were not briefed in the modern sense of the word but were merely furnished troops, maps, and the enemy's name. In this case the war was over when he reached the islands; Otis had nobody to fight. From the start he therefore reduced the complexities of the unexpected situation which he had been bequeathed to their simplest common denominator. There was no problem; his instructions were clear. The tedious old lawyer in khaki bent over his mountain of papers and repeated in an incongruously thin, treble voice that there was only one government in Manila

—the United States of America—and that the Filipinos had to submit and be "good Indians."

Having been shot in the head during the Civil War, he suffered from insomnia and solaced himself with work. All papers, however trivial, had to be channeled through his office in the imposing white palace of the former Spanish Governor-General in Malacanana Park. His day began there at seven-thirty, continued until five o'clock, resumed at eight, and ended at midnight. He never held a review, was never seen in dress uniform. Too busy to visit the American field positions, on one occasion he composed a long reprimand to an officer who had incorrectly filled out a six-dollar supply requisition. On another, he left headquarters to verify personally the valuation of a dead army mule. He delegated no meaningful authority to anyone, regardless of rank.

Immediately upon taking command of VIII Corps he became enmeshed by documents. As compulsively as he dealt with them, they began to pile up. He stuffed the later ones in drawers. Soon his desk was jammed inside and out. Next he had tables shoved up against both sides to hold the overflow. It was incredible, almost ludicrous; and General MacArthur privately referred to him as a locomotive bottom-side up, its wheels revolving at full speed. Dewey called him a pincushion of an old woman. Otis said Dewey's victory was not much of an affair and that the admiral acted as though he were God Almighty.

He was not unintelligent and possessed a remarkable memory for facts and figures, but since he had no concept of past and present Philippine history his rule was marred by a series of initial blunders, the first being his appointment of Father William McKinnon as superintendent of Manila schools. McKinnon (whom we met earlier) was likeable and competent, and being a Catholic he saw nothing amiss in staffing the faculties with Spanish friars and nuns. The Filipinos were disturbed, and in the United States a typical comment was voiced by the San Francisco *Monitor:* "While the

Evangelical churches have been talking and planning, a
Catholic priest steps in . . . the missionary boards of all sects
should hurry up and send their agents to the front before all
the offices are given away." Otis refused to relieve McKinnon.
Much encouraged, the friar orders tried to stage a general
comeback and implored the American commander to restore
their real estate and civil control functions. When Otis proceeded judiciously to consider these demands, knowing nothing of one of the basic issues which had touched off the
revolution, the uproar swelled. Unmoved, he requested that
Aguinaldo release all Spanish friars and nuns held as prisoners of war. The Filipino denied that he was holding any nuns;
as for the friars:

> . . . apart from the abuses committed by the priests . . . they
> have taken up arms against the revolution . . . In Manila,
> during the siege of the town by your forces, all the eccle-
> siastics, organized and uniformed, formed a part of the
> municipal armed guard . . . The convents have been the
> most impregnable defenses where the Spanish combatants,
> together with the priests, shielded themselves in order to at-
> tack the revolutionists, and this government preserves quite
> a number of muskets taken from the ecclesiastics.

Despite pressures on him from Washington, Otis was
forced to drop the subject. Meanwhile, other frictions had
lately developed within the capital. U.S. patrols took pleasure
in stopping Filipino officers in the Old City and searching
them before the eyes of their fellow natives. An American
guard shot a boy for stealing a banana from a Chinese. As
under Spanish rule, houses were searched without warrant.
Angry crowds gathered in Binondo when an American killed
a boy and a woman during an argument about closing up a
gambling den. One officer wrote: "One morning while I was
officer of the day a Filipino soldier strolled over to one of the
sentries on the outpost of the First South Dakota and asked
the man for a cigarette. As the Filipino was unarmed, the
American was somewhat off his guard, and, as he started to

search his pockets for the desired smoke, was terribly cut across the face by a bolo which the ruffian suddenly drew from under his clothing. Though blinded by his own blood, the plucky soldier managed to settle the score then and there, fairly blowing the man's head off with a short-range shot with his big Springfield."

Soldiers overseas have seldom been averse to liquor, and some Americans shocked the temperate natives by their behavior. Many a Filipino civilian was punched, or slugged with a beer bottle, many a fruit vendor jostled and robbed of his wares. On the other hand, General Pio del Pilar, a brutal man with a most unsavory reputation, provided provocations of his own. His men were a constant menace to Spaniards within the walled city, collected so-called "taxes" from apprehensive natives there, and even succeeded in kidnapping some American troops for a few unpleasant hours. In retaliation, guards began permanently confiscating as souvenirs not only the sidearms but the bolos of Filipinos who entered the city. The insurgents repeatedly tried to draw the fire of the American troops. Often they entered far within the U.S. lines and taunted their rivals to retaliate. General Anderson himself was prevented by Pio del Pilar's troops from proceeding up the Pasig River in a steam launch. In a rage, he wrote Otis asking how long he would have to submit to such interference.

All autumn the strain grew. Otis had arrived with more infantry, cavalry, and artillery, raising total U.S. strength in the islands to 15,559 officers and men. These reinforcements were inexplicable to the insurgents except on the most obvious grounds, and the later capture of their records proves that they now considered war with America practically inevitable. They strengthened their lines around the encircled capital. At Malolos the revolutionary government issued a bewildering stream of manifestoes, all subtly or flatly tending to arouse the countryside to the probability of impending conflict. As they threw up more trenches and barricades, they mounted field guns with their muzzles pointed at U.S. troop positions. On September 9 six hundred Americans tried to shove back the insurgent lines at St. Lazaro, were forced back, finally penetrated them, and made an exhaustive reconnaissance. Aguinaldo sent written orders to his field commanders to shoot if necessary, should any further such incidents arise. From Pineda, however, Colonel Cailles wired Aguinaldo on September 13 tidings that undoubtedly sobered him:

> I inform your excellency that we have no Mauser cartridges; I hear there are many in Batangas . . . I ask your excellency to order General Noriel to send us shells . . . I am sorry for our soldiers. I see that the more they work and the more they expose their lives the less they receive. Since your excellency has charged me with these operations no one has given me a cent to meet the expenses of the headquarters at Pineda. More than *ten* superior and other officers eat there at my wife's expense. She has no more. We do not smoke. I am perplexed. Patience. I suffer everything for my most beloved and unforgettable president.

Next day his mood had improved, for in a cemetery he had discovered two boxes containing ten thousand Mauser cartridges. A Spanish soldier had told him where to look. "I gave him a present," he reported modestly. Also, "three rich men of Manila promise to supply all of our forces with rice and provisions . . . I am now most happy."

From Pangasinan the native general wired Aguinaldo that four Americans had arrived with Protestant propaganda printed in Tagalog. The president responded that this was "only a pretext to study our territory; so make them understand that the people don't want any other religion."

And the commander at Angono wired that six Americans had come in a *banca* to take photographs and to climb the mountain, and according to the boatman twelve others would also arrive soon. Today these innocent soldiers are clearly distinguishable as the predecessors of millions of sightseeing GIs of future wars, but at Filipino headquarters there was

General Gregorio del Pilar

The *China* leaving San Francisco, June 15, 1898

3rd Artillery and Astor Battery disembarking, July 26, 1898

ring line near Santa Mesa the morning after the outbreak

American killed by shrapnel

Street fighting in the outskirts of Manila, February 5, 1899

General Merritt and staff aboard the *Newport*

Apolinario Mabini

Filipino Officers

Antonio Luna

Generals Merritt and Otis with staff officers, posing before the governor's mansion ("The Palace") in Malacanana Park

Native district (possibly Tondo) at midnight, February 4, 1899

General Elwell S. Otis

much alarm and Aguinaldo advised his man to keep the Americans away, or at least to confiscate their cameras.

In November came this message from proud, handsome, part-Spanish General Mascardo in San Fernando: "Most urgent. Have received telegraphic order from War Department which says: 'Prevent American troops from disembarking.' In case they insist what am I to do? May I begin firing?" Aguinaldo telegraphed, "Answered affirmatively."

And Cailles again: ". . . there are 3,000 Americans in front of our position at Singalong. I do not know what they wish; if they enter Pineda I open fire."

These incidents and threats were stabs of lightning in a murky sky; but at Malolos, a rambling market town with an enormous monastery and church, ninety-five Filipinos were engrossed with the more prosaic problems of creating a viable government. The congress which convened there on September 15 included the most gifted intellectuals in the Philippines —lawyers, doctors, engineers, painters, teachers, and top businessmen—for at last the well-to-do, educated natives had flocked to the revolutionary movement started by the poverty-stricken radicals of 1896. That sunny day the new Philippine national emblem floated from every nipa hut; the Pasig band played as never before; parade after parade of civilians in holiday attire and soldiers with tri-color cockades on their hats filled the main street. The open-air meeting was formally convened by Emilio Aguinaldo himself, looking uncomfortable in swallowtails. In low tones he read a short address. It had a good deal to do with the Monroe Doctrine; America for the Americans, the Philippines for the Filipinos was its gist. And after lunch—which Consul Williams and several American newspapermen attended as guests, in an old convent converted into his palatial home—he received more friends and delegates with the serene, masked expression which had become his trademark.

Next day the congress ratified the declaration of independence as its first order of business. Approval of Mabini's constitution, however, was not so simple. The conservatives wanted Catholicism recognized and supported as the state religion, while the radicals proposed this clause: "The State recognizes the freedom and equality of religions, as well as the separation of Church and State." Both sides were afraid to bring the issue to a vote, until General Luna broke a week-long deadlock by a balloting ruse in which the left-wing faction won by two votes. The maneuver, rather childish and not worth examining, did not increase Luna's minimal popularity with the opposition.

The split over the religious plank was duplicated by other differences along party lines; and it is interesting to note in this fledgling state the emergence of left and right political bodies so clear-cut in all democracies with but one major, modern exception. A group of "absolutists" formed around Mabini, who demanded a strong executive (at least during the current emergency) and considered the congress not a constituent assembly but an advisory body. In opposition were the "constitutionalists," who resented the degradation of the legislature to a rubber stamp. And the attitudes concerning land reform and certain types of quasi-socialist nationalization were also divided as one might expect.

The most serious schism developed over policy toward the United States. The liberals, or radicals, mostly of the middle and lower classes, believed in absolute independence. The relatively richer and more educated conservatives wanted to accept a U.S. protectorate. But what kind of a protectorate? Again the old argument flared up, and this time the conservatives were themselves divided. "Aid and guidance" was about as far as anyone dared go. Some wanted it to be temporary. Others felt that it should be restricted to protection from external dangers. The concepts were most unsophisticated. Why should the United States accept nagging responsibilities for no tangible return? The radical faction derided its opponents, who nevertheless threatened to break up the government unless the congress as a whole faced the plain reality of America's intentions. But Washington paid no attention to the argument and was scarcely aware that it even existed.

From Dewey's headquarters Mr. John Barrett wrote for the *Review of Reviews:* "By the middle of October, Aguinaldo had assembled a congress at Malolos of 100 men . . . These men, whose sessions I repeatedly attended, conducted themselves with great decorum and showed a knowledge of debate and parliamentary law . . . The executive portion of the government was made up of a ministry of bright men who seemed to understand their respective positions." Today few doubt that they would have governed the islands adequately. Theirs was the first democratic constitution in Asia. They were supported by virtually every adult Filipino in the archipelago who had even the foggiest notion of what was taking place in Malolos. Within a hundred days they had planned or created the following: an official organ, *El Heraldo de la Revolucion;* free compulsory elementary education; a system of secondary schools; a military academy at Malolos; a new fiscal and tax system; a reformed currency; a reorganized army under a regional basis commanded by Antonio Luna, numbering fifty thousand troops, of whom twenty thousand had rifles; a small navy; a diplomatic corps under the immediate supervision of Apolinario Mabini; departments of justice, courts, sanitation, and so on.

At the same time Mabini, a highly moral person, prohibited lotteries, raffles, liquor licenses, and cockpits. All these had been major sources of income to the Spaniards. He provided for civil marriages and made preparations for handing over the entire Catholic mechanism in the islands—despite his own freethought proclivities—to the native clergy. The younger generation, it is said, worshiped him even above Aguinaldo, and only below the memory of Rizal. From Manila the friars surveyed these developments dubiously. That they hoped to set the clock back is beyond question; and one of their monastic orders read as follows:

You must reject and condemn the masonic sect . . . condemn
liberty of worship, liberty of the press, liberty of thought and
the other liberties of perdition, condemned and rejected by
the Pontiff . . . reject and condemn liberalism and also modern progress and civilization . . . as being false progress and
false civilization. You must utterly abominate civil marriage
and regard it as pure concubinage . . . and reject the interference of the civil authorities in any ecclesiastical affairs . . .

On October 5, 1898, in the outskirts of Manila, *La Independencia* was born under the editorship of General Luna.
In its first issue it darkly threatened all who denied the aspirations of the revolutionary government. Circulating daily
throughout the capital and Luzon, it so aroused the people
that General Otis suppressed it the following month. Its
staff and equipment moved to Malolos. From here and later
from a dozen other places it clung to life with tenacity and
kept the revolutionary fire blazing at white heat. Yet the
Americans at Manila, even near the end of 1898, still failed
to understand why most Filipino leaders resisted United
States influence in the islands. In a talk with Aguinaldo a
high American officer asked him what on earth he expected
the United States to do. "To furnish the navy, while the Filipinos held all the country and administered civil offices with
its own people," Aguinaldo replied.

"And what would America get from this?"

"That would be a detail that would be settled hereafter."

And while in this respect, at this time, the Philippine president was somewhat on the conservative side, in matters of war
preparation he was the most radical of the radicals. Blatant
preparations for conflict, provocations within Manila, pressures and restrictions up to the very walls of the Intramural
City, had all brought General Otis to the brink of strong countermeasures. For the evolution of the most serious challenge
to the insurgents since they had been barred from the capture
and occupation of Manila we must look back several weeks.

II

When General Otis had taken up his post as commanding
general and military governor of that portion of the Philippines under United States jurisdiction, the insurgents were
showing no sign of withdrawing their forces from around Manila. There seemed, in truth, no good reason why they should.
Were they to move back, the Americans would come forward;
the two sides would still be in contact. Furthermore, if the
Americans were to abandon the islands—a possibility which
admittedly was becoming more remote by the hour—the natives would have divested themselves of many square miles
of territory and entrenchments from which they might later
resume attacking the Spaniards. They had not been allowed
to occupy Manila. Now they were practically being asked to
leave the entire province. It seemed like adding insult to in-
jury. And if they did pull back, would there not be still more
American demands?

Otis did not see matters in this light. He needed elbow
room for his enlarged force and he was aware that more
troops were en route. They were detachments of the 18th and
23rd Regular Infantry, plus more volunteers from Iowa, Tennessee, Washington, and Kansas, and would increase his establishment to 22,312 officers and men. Since the war with
Spain was over, there was little question who their potential
opponents might be. On September 8 he issued an ultimatum
to Aguinaldo which minced no words:

> The United States appreciates the services of the Insurgents
> in fighting a common enemy, the Spaniards. However, bear
> in mind that the United States has swept the Spanish flag
> from the seas, kept Spanish troops from being sent to the
> Philippines for the purpose of putting down your rebellion
> and has had Manila at its mercy since May 1st . . . Spain,
> the recognized owner, has capitulated Manila and its suburbs

to the United States; there can be no legal question as to the propriety of full American sovereignty . . . Joint occupation of the suburbs is impossible; irresponsible members of either army, careless or impertinent actions, might incite grave disturbances . . . I deplore any conflict between our forces, but find it necessary to give you notice that if your troops are not withdrawn beyond the line of city defenses, within one week, I will force you to move and my government shall hold you responsible.

Was it, as an Englishman in Manila observed, "the desire of the Americans to force a war upon the Filipinos?" More likely Otis was bluffing, for that week he wired as follows to General Corbin in Washington: "The insurgents are very strong, estimated by some to number 30,000 troops. They have been receiving a good many arms and much ammunition within the last few weeks, and I am informed have contracted with the Japanese Government for a considerable supply." On the other hand, "I shall not yield to any of their requests or make any concessions . . ."

It was not a matter of the workings of the military mind; the man's latent conviction that he would soon be fighting the Filipinos makes his position pragmatically comprehensible. But while the insurgents could not fathom his peremptory attitude, nor what they had done to deserve it, it was clear that their dilemma boiled down to a simple calculation: By placating him would it still be possible to work out an arrangement that would salvage Philippine independence in conjunction with some degree of U.S. authority? Evidently it was decided that the possibility existed. After five tense days Aguinaldo replied that his army would draw back provided that the word "demand" (used elsewhere in the ultimatum) was changed to "request." To this Otis was willing to agree, and the evacuation began on the afternoon of the fourteenth. Colonel Cailles led the way on horseback and described his exit in a message to Aguinaldo:

I inform your excellency that I have complied faithfully with your orders. The outgoing force was grand. I am at the head of a column of 1,800 men, almost all uniformed, three bands of music. As we came to the Luneta from Calle Real, Ermite, Americans and natives fell in behind yelling, "Viva Filipinos," "Viva Emilio Aguinaldo." We answered "Viva America," "Viva la libertad." The Americans presented arms and at my command my battalion came to a port.

The Pasig band played a wild, semi-oriental march. The blue-clad troops swung down the Calle San Luis. It seemed a great occasion to the enthusiastic crowds, who apparently did not realize that their army was, in effect, being driven away by the foreigners. Down the Paco road they marched, and triumphantly past the walls of old Manila, watched by morose Spanish prisoners, Spanish officers, and Spanish nobility in carriages. As they passed the Wyoming barracks they were cheered by the volunteers. It was strange, unreal; or perhaps the Americans were merely cynical, relieved to see the brown men depart.

The crisis at any rate was over. Only General Pio del Pilar's refusal to leave the suburbs of Paco and Pandacan provided a discordant note. Otis complained about it to Aguinaldo, who responded that these two important military areas south of the Pasig River had not been mentioned in the written arrangements. That was correct. Somewhat chagrined, Otis then claimed that they were part of Manila and had to be vacated anyway. Not true, replied Aguinaldo; whereupon American engineers surveyed the city and found inevitably that it had never been properly mapped; the insurgents were indeed within the capital limits. Possibly so; but weeks passed and del Pilar clung like a leech to every inch of his trenches, fortifications, and blockhouses. His lines in Pandacan were, annoyingly enough, directly across the Pasig River from Otis' headquarters in Malacanana Park. Insurgent troops kept crossing the river and raising an uproar in the American zone, almost under the window of the office wherein toiled the long-suffering general. "I had a right, a perfect right, to drive them

further away from the city," he later testified grumpily; and
one finds it possible to sympathize.

On November 16 he cabled Adjutant General Corbin for
eight thousand more Krag-Jorgensen rifles and five million
rounds of ammunition.

III

Frequently that summer President McKinley conferred with
his cabinet, which was by no means unanimous in favor of
annexation, whereas he himself had gradually moved to a
somewhat more extreme position. He seems to have been sincere in his new-found belief that annexation, if undertaken
with the aim of helping Filipinos acquire a better life and
Americans new trade opportunities, was not, as he had once
termed it, criminal aggression. The big question was whether
Americans wanted the islands. To take the pulse of the voters,
McKinley went on a long whistle-stop tour, and found that
invariably the loudest cheers came in response to probing
phrases concerning the Philippines. The president returned to
Washington convinced that the common man would back
him up at the polls in a policy of acquisition.

Unfortunately the common man entertained several critical misconceptions. He thought we had already won the
Philippines. He rejoiced, and assumed that adding them to
the American domain was another kind of Louisiana Purchase. Not one in a hundred knew of any opposition on the
part of the Filipino people. The islands were not people; they
were a geographical expression. Thus it was easy for Mc-
Kinley to drift further and further from the continental shoreline. First we went to war to protest Spain's actions in Cuba.
Then Dewey was sent to Manila; his fleet triumphed there.
Troops were dispatched; they captured Manila. Then we decided to occupy that city and harbor temporarily. Where
would it all end? Dewey and others had once thought the

Filipinos suited for self-government. But as our urge to expand itself expanded, Filipino ability to self-govern seemed to dwindle proportionally. In the words of the St. Louis *Post-Dispatch:* "The Filipino is treacherous and deceitful. Besides, we want his country." When McKinley returned to Washington, "Don't haul down the flag," "Westward ho!" and other such cries from the audience had sold him on the moral and political desirability of acquisition. Any lingering qualms were dispelled by his wife. A deeply religious invalid, she was distraught about the Igorrotes (of all people) and avid to convert them. The argument influenced him, for like practically all Americans he never seemed to grasp the fact that the great majority of Filipinos had been Christians for over three hundred years. The commercial merits of the islands also weighed heavily upon the president's mind that summer. By fall, policy had been established with a fair degree of certainty.

It was now a simple matter of ramming it down Spanish throats. The peace treaty was to be drafted in Paris in October, and while it is true that the final decision would be McKinley's, it is also evident that the character and recommendations of the American commission would be most significant. Its composition was somewhat unusual, in that three of its members were senators. This meant (as many newspapers caustically pointed out) that at a later date they would vote to ratify their own negotiations. One was an ardent jingo, W. P. Frye of Maine, who had once suggested taking Cuba by conquest and had long worked for Hawaiian annexation. Another was Senator C. K. Davis of Minnesota. His advance opinion, as stated to the president during the course of earnest talks during August and September, was that we should keep the entire archipelago except for those southern islands inhabited by Moros. Only Senator George Gray of Delaware was a Democrat and an anti-imperialist.

As to the non-congressional members of the commission, Mr. Day, a wispy little man who had resigned his office as secretary of state to head the American delegation,* was considered a moderate. And finally there was Whitelaw Reid, editor of the New York *Tribune,* mouthpiece of the Republican party, a forceful personality who had stated his views in print on many occasions. "What we shall seize we shall undoubtedly hold" summed them up. Having written and signed several articles in this vein, he could hardly be expected to retract them in Paris; and he had already remarked to Mr. McKinley, "I don't see how we can honorably give them back to Spain . . . we could not honorably desert them, and it should be extremely unwise to turn over the task of controlling them to any other power." With such a man dominating an already heavily-slanted agency, gentlemen such as Mr. Lodge were fairly satisfied and were frank to admit it. On September 16 McKinley issued secret written instructions to his emissaries. This was one day before sailing date, and his phrases rang loud in their ears as they embarked on their fateful mission. First he sounded the theme of altruism:

> It is my earnest wish that the United States in making peace should follow the same high rule of conduct which guided it in facing war.

In addition, the victor should be magnanimous in her treatment of the fallen foe; and her morality

> should not under any illusion of the hour be dimmed by ulterior designs which might tempt us into excessive demands or even into adventurous departure on untried paths.

That seemed startling. But the president was referring only to Cuba:

> The Philippines stand upon a different basis . . . without any original thought of complete or even partial acquisition, the presence and success of our arms at Manila imposes upon us obligations which we cannot disregard.

Since American arms had also been present and successful in

* His post was taken over by the ultra-expansionist, John Hay.

Cuba, should not the identical principles of settlement apply to both cases? Evidently the president did not see it that way, in view of the Teller Amendment and other considerations; for he continued along familiar lines:

> The march of events rules and overrules human action . . . We cannot be unmindful that, without any desire or design on our part, the war has brought us new duties and responsibilities which we must meet and discharge as becomes a great nation . . .

Basically it all came about, he said, because God had pre-ordained American expansion and responsibilities. On the other hand, it had to be candidly confessed that:

> Incidental to our tenure in the Philippines is the commercial opportunity to which American statesmanship cannot be indifferent. It is just to use every legitimate means for the enlargement of American trade . . .

This does not mean "large territorial possessions," he warned. All America wanted was an equal chance to secure reasonable commercial privileges in the islands. Therefore:

> In view of what has been stated, the United States cannot accept less than the cession in full right and sovereignty of the Island of Luzon.

Apparently an island the size of Illinois did not strike Mr. McKinley as "large." Still, the commissioners were instructed to accept nothing "less than" Luzon. Many a historian has joyously derided McKinley's letter; but between its lines lay other factors that call for consideration. The international situation at the century's turn in the far east was in a state of extreme flux. As to the Philippines, on September 8 the Japanese government repeated its willingness to help govern them, a task of which Spain was plainly not capable. At the same time McKinley heard a rumor to the effect that Japan would seize the islands outright if we did not. While seemingly none of this was our business, the fact is that it was our business indeed, and in a most literal sense. Without something resembling the Chinese leased ports or Hong Kong, future American trade in the Orient might be crippled. Germany's interest in the country has already been noted. As for Spain, that nation had every intention of re-establishing her despotic rule, if given the chance. That was not to be tolerated under any circumstances, all Americans agreed. And perhaps the Filipinos would not be able to resist Spain successfully, now that the mother country had been divested of Cuba and could turn her full attention eastward.

To top it all off, strong political pressures were making themselves felt. We have seen the popular reaction to McKinley's whistle-stop tour. When he came back from the middle west, he reported a widespread feeling that the United States was in a position where it could not let go. The views of the electorate, as he appraised them, could not be ignored. Senator Mark Hanna warned him in September that the Republicans might lose control of the House in November. Early voting in Maine and Vermont had already gone badly against the G.O.P. Two years later McKinley himself, as well as his party, would be up for re-election. Would the nation approve policies of withdrawal and quiescence as opposed to those of imperialism and drama? The question answered itself.

IV

His instructions to the commission may have been secret; but the men on it, and the movement of events, could be seen by all who wished to see. A barrage of comments from both sides of the fence filled the air.

"They'll give thim a measure iv freedom," predicted Mr. Dooley to Mr. Hennessy.

"But whin?"

"Whin they'll stand still long enough to be measured."

Senator Cyrus Sulloway of New Hampshire forecast uncannily what was to come: "The Anglo-Saxon advances into the new regions with a Bible in one hand and a shotgun in the other. The inhabitants of those regions that he cannot convert with the aid of the Bible and bring into his markets he gets rid of with the shotgun. It is but another demonstration of the survival of the fittest." That same Anglo-Saxon, however, observed an English journalist somewhat less reverently, "always begins by calling heaven to witness his unselfish desire to help his neighbor, but he always ends by stealing his spoons." And briskly Charles Denby wrote in the November *Forum:* "Commerce, not politics, is king. The manufacturer and the merchant dictate to diplomacy and control elections . . . I am in favor of holding the Philippines because I cannot conceive of any alternative to our doing so, except the seizure of territory in China . . . We are after markets, the greatest markets now existing in the world." And other arguments less materialistic were also expounded at length.

On the day the gentlemen of the peace commission left the port of New York, Albert Beveridge delivered one of his most famous addresses. Before an audience of thousands in Tomlinson's Hall, Indianapolis, as torches and red lanterns flared, the great orator pounded out a series of hammer-blows:

> The opposition tells us we ought not to rule a people without their consent. I answer, the rule of liberty, that all just governments derive their authority from the consent of the governed, applies only to those who are capable of self-government.

The United States would fairly judge that capability. But suppose the consent of the islanders were to be withheld? Impossible, thought Beveridge:

> Would not the people of the Philippines prefer the just, humane, civilizing government of this Republic to the savage, bloody rule of pillage and extortion from which we have rescued them?

In the final analysis, at any rate, the United States was duty-bound to rescue the natives:

> Shall we abandon them to their fate, with the wolves of conquest all about them—with Germany, Russia, France, even Japan, hungering for them? . . . It would be like giving a razor to a babe and telling it to shave itself.

The crowd roared with laughter. He observed that since 1789 the flag had marched on—to Mexico, to the Golden Gate, to Oregon—and while it was true that the Spanish isles were not part of our continental domain:

> Cuba not contiguous? Porto Rico not contiguous? The Philippines not contiguous? Our navy will make them contiguous!

A wild ovation followed these words. When it died down, he echoed the commercial sentiments of the president:

> We are raising more than we can consume. We are making more than we can use. Today our industrial society is congested; there are more workers than there is work; there is more capital than there is investment . . . Think of the tens of thousands of Americans who will invade mine and field and forest in the Philippines . . .

There was little the anti-imperialists could say that would effectively counter an array of emotional arguments like this. Senators Hoar and Vest argued dryly that under the constitution we were not allowed to acquire territory unless it could be organized into a state. Ex-President Cleveland and William Bryan, two men who in all other respects despised each other, spoke up forcefully against expansionism on moral grounds. So did the influential Speaker of the House, Thomas B. Reed, a man who had exclaimed after Dewey's victory at Manila that he should have sailed away from there at once. Several labor leaders, writers, educators, and other intellectuals denounced the peace commission as a "stacked deck." All these views—negativistic, moralistic, and self-denying in character—had no perceptible effect upon the people at large in 1898, nor upon the commissioners (who were not exposed to any of them until later), nor upon Mr. McKinley. The general mood was fatalistic; even before the Paris treaty was negotiated the Philadelphia *Ledger* asked why Uncle Sam resembled a lady throwing a stone, and replied blandly that he had aimed at Cuba in the west, and had hit the Philippines in the east.

The great debate had not yet begun in earnest, but by fall the lines of battle had been distinctly drawn up. The expansionists we know well; and they were probably backed by most of the American people. On the other side were the anti-imperialists, spearheaded by the Anti-Imperialist League. This outstanding single force opposing Philippine annexation was born on June 15 during a mass meeting in Boston's Faneuil Hall to protest the foreign policy of the administration. That evening its first act was to adopt a resolution decrying the conquest and ownership of foreign populations until such time as "we have shown that we can protect the rights of men within our own borders, like the colored race of the South and the Indians of the West . . ." The initial group consisted mostly of Democrats, old-fashioned liberals who took the Declaration of Independence seriously and insisted that no government could properly govern without the consent of the governed. Later the League also attracted important Republicans to its crusade. Some were even of the Old Guard, elderly abolitionists and their heirs, who waved Lincoln's banner of anti-slavery for Filipino and Negro alike. The organization formed in Boston spread rapidly throughout the country and changed its name to the American Anti-Imperialist League, under the presidency of Republican George S. Boutwell, former Secretary of the Treasury and once a senator from Massachusetts. All the local units merged before the year's end. Henry Cabot Lodge at first suavely categorized these developments as a comic incident.

Until now, opposition to imperialist policy had been scattered and ineffectual. The A.I.L. attracted money and brains,

LITTLE BROWN BROTHER

began mailing thousands of letters and pamphlets, petitioned Congress, and organized mass meetings. By late 1898 it represented a serious counterthreat. ("We are going to have trouble over the treaty," Lodge suddenly wrote Roosevelt.) It could never attract great numbers of followers. Its power lay in the caliber of its leadership and its influence on congress. Men like Mark Twain, Andrew Carnegie, Samuel Gompers, President David Starr Jordan of Leland Stanford University, William Vaughn Moody, President Eliot of Harvard, and William James could not be laughed off as crackpots; and their arguments were not easily dismissed. When Rome began her career of conquest, the Roman empire started to decay—this was an analogy frequently used. A callous grab of the Philippine Islands, they said, would be a betrayal of our own origins. Do not flout our own constitution, which makes no provision for colonies. The executive has no power to authorize the political and economic enslavement of a foreign population. Stop before plunging the nation into the endless sea of imperialism, which inevitably would lead to an enlarged army and navy, a European type of garrison state dominated by the military and a crushing bureaucracy.

Moorfield Storey, a stern New Englander, saw the profit system itself as the culprit; it was capital, he said, which promoted the aggression of stronger upon weaker peoples. The leadership of the A.I.L. was soon taken over by a retired textile manufacturer named Edward Atkinson. A giant of a man physically, his moral indignation was coupled with alarm over the economic consequences of acquisition. U.S. sugar and hemp producers would suffer in free competition with the Philippines, he insisted, and American workers would be undercut by Filipino labor. Retention of the islands would result in an economic loss, due to the resulting need for an enlarged army and navy.

So ran the anti-imperialist liturgy.

V

It occurred to Señor Mabini in Malolos that the time had come to deal directly with the men in Washington, and he sent Don Felipe Agoncillo there to clarify the nature of the Filipino independence movement. Surely if the American president knew the facts, which had evidently been concealed from him by sinister individuals, his deeds would correspond to his moralistic phraseology. In Aguinaldo's words: "After we had somewhat recovered from the emotional crisis caused by our exclusion from the Walled City, we were inclined to interpret the incident as a mere indiscretion on the part of the American field commanders without sanction whatsoever from their Government." Agoncillo arrived in the American capital and was granted an interview with Mr. McKinley on October 1.

A more desolate dialogue has seldom been recorded in State Department annals. McKinley asked the young lawyer to state his case. This he did (through an interpreter) by a long recital of the barbarity of Spanish rule, the revolution of 1896, the treaty of Biak-na-bato, and the reasons for the resumption of hostilities. The president listened politely; the White House clock ticked; the afternoon wore away. Agoncillo told of Aguinaldo's conversations with Dewey, Pratt, Wildman, and various American generals, and of the assurances allegedly given him by these gentlemen.

After a pause, the president inquired if his visitor had further matters to communicate. Agoncillo asked if he could be represented on the American peace commission. McKinley thought not. Could he, then, at least be heard by the commissioners? The President considered the idea impractical, in view of Señor Agoncillo's regrettable inability to speak English, and he suggested a written memorandum instead.

In composing it, the Filipino repeated what he had said

and recommended that the existing government of the Philippines be given something to say about the disposition of
the country. The document, received three days later by Mr.
McKinley, was not acknowledged; and Agoncillo left for
Paris. There the commission refused to listen to him. He only
succeeded in filing a note concerning the status of his government, one copy being handed to the Americans and another to the Spaniards. It was, he suggested, irrational to
attempt to buy, sell, barter, or otherwise manipulate the people and territory of the islands without consulting their legitimate government. The commissioners on both sides failed to
reply.

Thoroughly alarmed, Agoncillo now issued a statement to
the European press and foreign legations in which he bluntly
invalidated any resolutions agreed upon in Paris so long as
the independent personality of the Filipino people remained
unrecognized. Portions of the protest were published by a few
newspapers, but the commissioners of the United States and
Spain ignored it. They had already decided what to do about
the Philippines.

7

THE
TREATY
OF
PARIS

THE AMERICAN DELEGATION ARRIVED IN THE FRENCH CAPI-
tal on September 26, lunched with their Spanish counterparts, and were given a suite of rooms at the Ministry
of Foreign Affairs in which to conduct negotiations. On October 1 the Spaniards, headed by Señor Montero Rios, president of his nation's senate, demanded that before the talks
got under way Manila be returned to Spanish authority,
since it had been captured after the signing of the protocol.
The Americans refused to consider a proposal so palpably
unrealistic, and for the moment it was pursued no further.

For almost a month the arguments revolved around Cuba,
which Spain was more than willing to hand us, along with the
Cuban national debt of four hundred million dollars. But the
Teller Amendment made it impossible for us to accept the
island, much less its financial obligations. Furthermore, argued the Americans, the sum had arisen not through improve-
ments and capital investment in the colony but by efforts to
crush the insurrection. We were certainly not going to pay
for the very repressions which had obliquely provoked the

Spanish-American War, even though we had been coaxing Spain for years to put a stop to the disturbances there. All five American commissioners held firm, and no progress was made for two weeks. Next Señor Rios suggested neutral arbitration. That gambit was also spurned. It was ignoble; it implied that there was something to arbitrate; and if Spain happened to be correct by the tenets of international law, something was wrong with the law. Confronted by such intransigence, Rios threatened to break off negotiations and reopen the war. There was a mild flurry of alarm, for America had already demobilized except for its static posture in the Philippines. But the idea of a beaten, third-rate power again challenging the United States was not taken too seriously, and Spain's delegates soon threw in their cards. Cuba was to be delivered to the Cubans; the four-hundred-million-dollar liability would be returned to Spain; America would receive Guam and Puerto Rico—there would be something for everyone.

All this had been play-acting to some extent. Spain had expected no mercy over Cuba. Her plan, as usual, had been to put up a sham battle and then capitulate, in hopes of strengthening her later bargaining position. The Queen's diplomats were most uneasy concerning Uncle Sam's intentions in the Philippines. This was their jewel, their last Pacific colony. They knew they were about to be relieved of a certain amount of territory there, but they were determined to hang on to all they could; and it was their dream merely to cede Mindanao and perhaps the Sulus. It would be, in fact, almost a relief to get rid of those wild Mohammedans and their steaming islands, should Mr. McKinley prove innocent enough to accept them.

And technically Spain's position was good. What we held of the archipelago amounted to a proverbial drop in the bucket. The Walled City, about half of the Extramural City, and the Cavite naval base were the extent of it. On this meager basis, how much could America rationally claim? As for the first two areas, they had been captured a day after the armistice. There was really no evading these facts, and the veteran jurist Judge Day felt obliged to cable Mr. McKinley, "We have carefully examined all the leading text-writers and authorities, and find concurrence of opinion in the view that captures made after the execution of the agreement for an armistice must be disregarded and restored." The advice came as a nuisance, for in Washington it had been understood that the issue had been killed some days previously, and the president's reply was not up to his usual standards. Dewey, he said, had in effect captured the Philippine Islands on May 1, and this conquest had been "perfected" by Merritt's subsequent occupation of the capital city. But the concept was preposterous and the central fact remained: August 13 was simply and inescapably the day after August 12.

So the bickering continued, politely but monotonously, in the Quai d'Orsay—the Spaniards aloof and suffering proudly, the Americans irritable and impatient. The latter were also bickering privately. At first they held to their various original positions; and Senator Gray, as the sole symbol of traditional U.S. isolationism, dissented vigorously with his colleagues. He saw no problem concerning the Philippines, nothing to argue about or compromise. All we had to do was wash our hands of them. After they came up for intensive discussion he cabled Mr. McKinley that his attitude remained unchanged:

> The undersigned cannot agree that it is wise to take the Philippines in whole or in part. To do so would be to reverse accepted continental policy of country declared and acted upon throughout our history.

He rehearsed all the standard arguments concerning entangling alliances, the resultant need for an enlarged military and naval establishment, the competition of cheap Filipino labor and cheap Philippine sugar, added taxation, and the "menacing" church question. And regarding McKinley's

memorandum to the commission on the day the five gentlemen sailed from the port of New York:

> . . . let us not make a mockery of the injunction contained
> in these instructions, where, after stating that "we took up
> arms only in obedience to the dictates of humanity and in
> the fulfillment of high public and moral obligations," and that
> "we had no design of aggrandizement and no ambition of
> conquests," the president, among other things, eloquently
> says, "It is my earnest wish that the United States in making
> peace should follow the same high rule of conduct which
> guided it in facing war."

The Senator's phrasing, though labyrinthine, pointed up
the presidential dilemma rather accurately. Throughout October McKinley meditated. Time and again he had stated un-
equivocally that forcible annexation was criminal aggression,
that there would be no "acquisitions of territory not on the
main land, Cuba, Hawaii, San Domingo, or any other," and
so on. To make matters more perplexing, Spain's legal position was turning out sound. No one had thought of that. He
had, of course, other possible lines of action. In descending
order of palatability, they were to take only Luzon, or accept
only a naval station at Manila, or guarantee the independence
of the islands (as we were about to do with Cuba) in return
for most-favored-nation commercial clauses, or abandon
them altogether. At the moment, the American delegates
were under instructions simply to demand Luzon. He waited
to hear more from them.

They, in the interim, had been interviewing many authorities, all of whose views happened to reflect those of the
commission; not one recommended Philippine independence, and each agreed that all but a few natives yearned to
be put under U.S. control. The questioning of General Merritt was typical:

Mr. Day asked, "If the United States should say that we
shall take this country and govern it in our own way, do you
think they would submit to it?"

"Yes, sir."

"What they desire is a government for their benefit, maintained and paid for by us?"

"Yes, sir."

A condensation of this and other such opinions expressed by the general was cabled to Washington. It seemed that Merritt "did not think our humanity bounded by geographical lines." On the other hand he confessed that he "did not know that he could make out a responsibility by argument, but he felt it. It might be sentimental . . ." Sentiment aside, he thought we could hold Luzon with about twenty-five thousand troops. The attitudes were vaguely disquieting, and a majority of the commissioners found Naval Commander R. N. Bradford's testimony more to their liking. Senator Frye inquired if he thought Luzon would be sufficient indemnity. He did. And yet: "If we should adopt your line of demarcation what do you think Spain would do with the balance of those islands?"

"Sell them to Germany."

"Is not Germany about as troublesome a neighbor as we could get?"

"The most so, in my opinion."

Further interrogation of the commander also revealed a subtle shift in the attitude of Mr. Day, who had formerly recommended only the acquisition of a "hitching post" at Manila. He again posed the well-worn question and was answered "that a whole loaf is better than half a loaf" and that morally we had no choice but to accept the entire morsel. "That is," observed Day, "if one has a chance to take more, he better do it?"

"Yes. All of these islands are very valuable."

Mr. Whitelaw Reid now interposed, "If our Government once thought Cuba worth an offer of $100,000,000, what would you think the Philippine Archipelago worth?"

"Double that," replied Bradford.

That Mr. Day had veered from the middle of the road was

italicized by his dialogue with Mr. John Foreman, a thin, melancholy Englishman who had lived in the Philippines for eleven years. "Would it not be as well to take the entire property and be done with it?" And Foreman responded with a new and impressive theory: "By taking the whole of the islands, it would be a favor to Europe by setting aside all chances of rivalry."

Digests of these and other discussions were cabled daily to Mr. McKinley, who was doing some investigating of his own. General Greene, just back from the islands, predicted to him that unless the United States took them civil war would set in, in which case foreign intervention would be inevitable. On October 14 Admiral Dewey cabled warningly that a strong government had to be installed without delay. Anarchy, it seemed, prevailed in Luzon and was about to spread to the southern provinces as well. Coming from a man who had recently stated that the Filipinos were more capable of self-rule than the Cubans, the message was startling. McKinley relayed it to the Paris commission without comment.

Yet Dewey's assumptions that the natives could not govern and were not in tune with Aguinaldo's leadership were at that moment being contradicted by two of the admiral's own people—Naval Cadet L. R. Sargent and Paymaster W. B. Wilcox —who in the course of a long official journey through Luzon were finding conditions almost unnaturally peaceful. Of one province they wrote: "The Presidente and other local officials . . . are intelligent men and are extremely eager to learn news from the outside world . . . The first night after our arrival [at Ilagan] a ball was given in our honor, at which there were over fifty young ladies and an equal number of well-dressed and gentlemanly men . . . Eighty-four [captive] priests . . . appeared in good health, and we could detect no evidence of maltreatment . . . Every man, woman and child stood ready to take up arms to defend their newly-won liberty . . . We were hospitably entertained at Aparri; two balls were given in our honor . . . There are no Spaniards here, with the exception of two or three merchants. One of these, representing the company of the steamer *Saturnas*, we have met. He is pursuing his business entirely unmolested . . ."

Other passages have a familiar ring: "They desire the protection of the United States at sea, but fear any interference on land. . . . On one point they seemed united, viz., that whatever our government may have done for them, it had not gained the right to annex them." And to the military point: "The Philippine Government has an organized force in every province we visited." While the Sargent-Wilcox report was unique in being first-hand intelligence data, rather than guesswork or gossip concerning affairs in the interior, it was never seen by Mr. McKinley or the peace commissioners, nor would it likely have changed the president's mind. He was already convinced that the Filipinos could not control their society, that Aguinaldo represented less than one-half of 1 per cent of the population (he had been told this by another expert), that we must acquire not only Luzon but the entire archipelago, and that we must hold it forever. When Dewey forwarded the Sargent-Wilcox document to the Navy Department late in November, after having held it for almost a month, it was filed and forgotten.*

With Mr. Day firmly in the annexationist saddle by late October, only Senator Gray stood in opposition. But it was one against four; he began to waver; and as Mr. Reid happily wrote the president, "Senator Gray, who generally starts out on every question by stating the Spanish side of it, generally lands on ours . . . he is really doing wonderfully well . . . nobody can help admiring his honest efforts to be fair-minded . . ." Yet Gray still balked at total annexation. On the twenty-fifth, the commission asked McKinley for explicit instructions. Their cablegram crossed one from the chief executive finally advising Day that duty left him no choice but to demand the entire archipelago. And the following morning another cable sped eastward; to accept merely Luzon,

* It was eventually transmitted to the Senate on February 26, 1900.

leaving the rest of the islands subject to Spanish rule, or to be the subject of future contention, cannot be justified on political, commercial, or humanitarian grounds. The cession must be of the whole archipelago or none. The latter is wholly inadmissible and the former must therefore be required.

It had been a long journey for Mr. McKinley, and the peace emissaries had not suspected that he had so swiftly come to the end of it since bidding them farewell a month ago. They were taken by surprise and seized by reluctance to confront their Spanish friends with such an overpowering demand. What had been thus far only words were now translated into harsh reality. But even as Messrs. Reid, Frye, and Davis contemplated small compromises to soften the blow, the transatlantic cable again vibrated with a message from Secretary Hay which emphasized the decision irrevocably reached. Anticipating the crucial objection that the islands had never been captured by U.S. arms, he announced flatly that they could and would be claimed by conquest. There was to be no more argument about that. It was up to them to work it out somehow, bearing in mind that:

> It is imperative upon us as victors that we should be governed only by motives which will exalt our nation. Territorial expansion should be our least concern; that we shall not shirk the moral obligations of our victory is of the greatest . . . The president can see but one plain path of duty—the acceptance of the archipelago.

While the word "acceptance" was hardly accurate—neither Señores Aguinaldo nor Rios were pressing the islands upon us—it was the "right of conquest" theory which most troubled the commission. On November 3 Judge Day cabled McKinley that a majority considered it unsound. The president again countered that Dewey's victory was tantamount to conquest. This Mr. Day gently denied, and he reiterated that even Manila had not been captured until after the armistice. Mr. McKinley did not respond.

The argument which was thus going around in circles had not really changed since October 1, and the commissioners could not keep contradicting their own chief. While they would have preferred a more tidy claim, they had no choice but to offer what they had—whereupon the Spaniards exploded. Rios wired Madrid that it was "equivalent to proposing to Spain that she present to the United States the Philippine archipelago, doubtless as a demonstration of our gratitude for its course in the Cuban question." On November 4 he formally rejected America's demand. The London *Times* spoke up ponderously against it. So did most French papers, and in Paris a rumor gained currency that there would be no treaty. And Spain's Prime Minister Sagasta backed up his commission to the hilt, fearing that his exceedingly unpopular government might fall unless it salvaged something from the wreckage.

As the specter of a diplomatic collapse grew, in the War and State Departments there were mutters of dispatching a fleet to Spanish waters and of capturing the Philippines once and for all, and properly this time. American elections, too, were a factor. If McKinley had incorrectly assessed the popular mandate for an outward-looking foreign policy, his emissaries would lose prestige and bargaining power. On November 8, however, voting results found the Republican majority in congress cut less drastically than anticipated. The American delegates—except for Democrat Gray—took heart; and Mr. Frye unveiled the plan of offering Spain ten or twenty million dollars for the islands. Two days after receiving this suggestion, the State Department replied. It was a tolerable one, said Mr. Hay, only because we wished to avoid resuming war against a prostrate foe. He agreed that we as the victors were naturally entitled to indemnity for the cost of the war. The tone of his message dated November 13 was that of a gentleman holding his nose. Such dealings, he implied, were essentially vulgar but perhaps unavoidable in a defective world. "Willing or not, we have the responsibility of duty which we cannot escape . . . The questions of duty and humanity appeal to the President so strongly that he can find no appropriate answer but the one he has here marked out." As to the precise amount of cash, Mr. Day suggested $15,000,000; Mr. Frye $10,000,000; Mr. Gray left the figure open; Mr. Reid advised spurning the Sulu group and Mindanao (the Moros were unpopular, as usual) and accepting the balance for between $12,000,000 and $15,000,000; Mr. Davis wanted all the islands and insisted that we pay not a dime for them.

On November 21, as Señor Rios listened agitatedly, smoking cigarette after cigarette, Mr. Day offered $20,000,000 (one tenth of Commander Bradford's previous evaluation) and requested an answer within two days. Rios said angrily that he could reply at once, but already the American delegation had risen from the green felt-covered conference table. When the two sides again met, the Queen-Regent had cabled her acceptance. During a strained silence Montero Rios recited his formal reply:

> The Government of Her Majesty, moved by lofty reasons of patriotism and humanity, will not assume the responsibility of again bringing upon Spain all the horrors of war. In order to avoid them it resigns itself to the painful strait of submitting to the law of the victor, however harsh it may be, and as Spain lacks material means to defend the rights she believes are hers, having recorded them, she accepts the only terms the United States offers her for the concluding of the treaty of peace.

Work on the final draft of the treaty began on November 30. It was signed December 10. Article III had to do with the transfer of the Philippines to U.S. sovereignty. It concluded: "The United States will pay to Spain the sum of twenty million dollars ($20,000,000) within three months after the exchange of the ratifications of the present treaty."

That was all. The payment had nothing to do with any island debts owed by Spain. It was not a purchase price, nor was it a war indemnity. It was a twenty-million-dollar gift. Spain accepted it. Quite irrelevantly she handed us the Philippines. No question of honor or conquest was involved. The Filipino people had nothing to say about it, although their rebellion was thrown in (so to speak) free of charge.

The next step was legislative ratification. In Madrid, the treaty was disposed of quite briskly: the Cortes rejected it. Fortunately the Spanish constitution contained a clause empowering the monarch to override such a vote by signature. The Queen-Regent signed. Slowly but surely, with the successive elimination of one psychological and physical obstacle after another, the United States was closing its territorial embrace around the Philippines. It now remained only for the senate to legalize the adoption, and for the Filipinos to submit to it.

II

It is hard to analyze Mr. McKinley's swing to the far end of the imperial spectrum in less than a year, so diffuse were the factors which impelled him (gradually and fitfully) toward what he considered a policy of virtue. Economic profit, national honor, evangelism, altruism, racial condescension, world glory—these and other motives he had wrapped into a neat package called Duty. And by and large he believed in what he was doing; for he was a confirmed believer. He believed what he was told by men of good will, he believed intensely in God, he believed the United States had to uplift the Filipinos; and most of all he believed in his own probity. As a politician he was nearly free of cant, in the sense that there was an irreducible minimum of calculated disparity between his convictions and his deeds. To a delegation of Methodist churchmen, as they were leaving his office, he outlined with evident sincerity the steps which had led him to acquire the Philippine Islands:

Hold a moment longer! Not quite yet, gentlemen! Before you go I would like to say just a word about the Philippine business . . . The truth is I didn't want the Philippines, and when they came to us as a gift from the gods, I did not know what to do with them . . .

Having been thrust upon him by heaven, the islands had to be accepted despite practical difficulties.

I sought counsel from all sides—Democrats as well as Republicans—but got little help. I thought first we would take only Manila; then Luzon; then other islands, perhaps, also. I walked the floor of the White House night after night until midnight; and I am not ashamed to tell you, gentlemen, that I went down on my knees and prayed Almighty God for light and guidance more than one night.

The picture thus evoked of the President puttering about the hushed mansion in his sleeping robe, lost in thought, is an appealing one; and, happily, his meditations produced results.

And one night it came to me this way—I don't know how it was, but it came: (1) that we could not give them back to Spain—that would be cowardly and dishonorable; (2) that we could not turn them over to France or Germany—our commercial rivals in the Orient—that would be bad business and discreditable; (3) that we could not leave them to themselves —they were unfit for self-government—and they would soon have anarchy and misrule over there worse than Spain's was; and (4) that there was nothing left for us to do but to take them all, and to educate the Filipinos, and uplift and civilize and Christianize them, and by God's grace do the very best we could by them, as our fellow-men for whom Christ also died. And then I went to bed, and went to sleep and slept soundly.

There are, unfortunately, as many historians have pointed out, certain lacunae and misconceptions here. Virtually all the Filipinos were already devout Christians. The voice of the American voter, which McKinley took such pains to sound out during his whistle-stop tour, is not mentioned. Anarchy under Aguinaldo's government was unlikely and in any case largely irrelevant. Placing the islands under a protectorate, à la Cuba, would have satisfied ethical imperatives better than annexation. Such annexation would almost certainly have to be forcible; and this grave probability was rather well understood in Manila and Washington by November, 1898. One suspects that the president had not logically thought out the consequences of a break with historic continentalism, of the price that might have to be paid for enlarging the national mission to cover the subjugation of eight million aliens eight thousand miles away. The treaty, as Aguinaldo wrote years later, hit him like an atomic blast, and Mr. McKinley's annual message to congress delivered that week was an equal shock to the natives. Cuba, he said, would be set free as soon as possible; but he mentioned the Philippines only to observe casually that Dewey had conquered them and that this conquest had been "formally sealed" by the capture of Manila.

In Malolos the Filipino leaders cursed the hour they had agreed to deal with the Americans instead of driving them out. Another cabinet crisis ensued. Mabini advocated an immediate declaration of war but was opposed by the conservatives, including Aguinaldo, who advised moderation. It was, after all, conceivable that the U. S. Senate would not ratify the treaty. Aguinaldo, a bewildered young man, found himself pushed and pulled by embittered factions. The decision he faced was one which few persons would care to have on their consciences. Luna was in a blind rage and determined to make history by the sword. When the conservatives perceived that there would be active resistance to American terms, a course which they considered suicidal, several of their outstanding men resigned office. The defection shook the government to its foundations and practically turned it over to Mabini and the army. At this fork in the road even Aguinaldo was dispensable, and he knew it. He went along with the radicals. War now hung upon some inevitable incident.

Under the innocent name of the Filipino Club, an organization ostensibly devoted to athletic and social activities, a quasi-military fifth column took shape in the heart of Manila, its mission being to rise in force on the day fighting started. In dark little rooms behind Chinese and native shops, large quantities of bolos and insurgent uniforms were manufactured, some of which were discovered and confiscated by American military police. Bitterly the reorganized Filipino government prepared for war, understanding, if those under them did not, the unlikelihood that they could win it. Even now Otis commanded almost as many troops bearing rifles as did General Luna, and behind him stood one of the world's greatest potential military powers. The natives had no artillery, no money, no reserve matériel worth mentioning. Few of their twenty or thirty generals had ever been exposed to military science. They were mostly brave youngsters who had served as guerilla leaders against Spain and understood only rudimentary hit-and-run tactics. Junior officers and enlisted men possessed more of the same deficiencies, and many held commissions solely because they were friends of some general. In view of the nature of the terrain, any operation in the islands was certain to be a soldier's war similar to the insurrection against Spain, and in such fighting the rifle would be all-important. No Filipinos had been given target practice—an unforgivable blunder on the part of their high command, even though ammunition was admittedly not plentiful. When Luna took command he did what he could to remedy all this. Given another year he might have accomplished a good deal. As it was, by the end of 1898 he had forced a few generals to study formal tactics and strategy, some enlisted men had been taught drill and to accept commands without an argument, and a few hundred troops had received rifle training. He also put a handful of small arsenals into operation, standardized the army uniform, and nullified some of the more egregious examples of favoritism.

And while the Filipinos waited upon the United States senate and steeled themselves for what might come, the American army marked time. It was unusually warm and sticky in Manila late that year, and as the days slowly passed the volunteers, almost to a man, clamored to go home. Not unnaturally they thought the war with Spain for which they had enlisted was over and that garrison duties were the rightful property of the regular army. During this autumn 20 per cent of VIII Corps were carried on the sick list, especially since the lack of ample medical facilities made it necessary to send most ailing personnel back to the States. (Later, with the establishment of a dreary convalescent hospital on Corregidor, big enough to accommodate everyone, the percentage declined.)

Three days after the Treaty of Paris was signed the entire Astor Battery sailed hastily for New York. On December 16 almost half the Nebraska regiment departed. A flood of 427 applications for discharge came through on that date alone. In a cold fury Otis disapproved them all. But not even he could resist political pressure indirectly exerted from Washington, and after a slight pause the emigration movement continued. By the end of January all the volunteers (except a few who signed up for additional duty) had been replaced by others more innocent and willing, and by a glacier-like influx of regulars. Spirits continued low. Frank Millet of *Harper's Weekly* accompanied an inspection tour and wrote:

> One sentinel had deposited his rifle on the grass and was seated with his back against a tree smoking a cigar; another was sprawled out half asleep on a stone bench; others were familiarly hobnobbing with the natives and exhibiting the action of their rifles . . . A common sight was a sentinel on guard at a bridge or some other public place dressed in ragged trousers without gaiters, in a blue shirt which had the

sleeves cut off high up on the shoulders and a hat full of fantastic holes cut for the fun of the thing.

Trim and proud in their blue uniforms, Filipino troops prowled through Manila displaying an attitude which almost seemed to invite trouble, while the Americans cordially advised them that in due time they would be shot down like rabbits. Scuffles broke out, and occasionally the Americans turned to fighting among themselves. "The drunken brawls of the American soldiers in the cafés, drinking shops, and the open streets constituted a novelty in the colony," Mr. John Foreman later recollected, adding that both Spaniard and Filipino knew that inebriety in the Philippines was the road to death. Some men poked under houses with bayonets for the money often buried by well-to-do natives. A good deal of crap-shooting went on. Hundreds of European, Japanese, and American prostitutes had converged upon the city, boosting the venereal rate to 25 per cent of all cases on sick report. Despite outraged cries from the States, Otis took measures to register all such ladies and to have them examined weekly for disease.

Four months had passed since the capture of the place, and nothing of glory remained. Personnel engaged in paper work were few, and their duties were scarcely arduous. The Spanish Treasury Office, which formerly employed twenty-six men, was now being administered by a clerk named Greefkens between nine and five. He took two hours off for lunch. Except for his desk and files, the premises remained just as the enemy had left them. Books and papers lay strewn about, thick with dust, and no Filipino could be induced to clean up the area. Evidently Aguinaldo's order to avoid collaboration with the Americans was being obeyed to the letter. Meanwhile a squad of finance officers was trying to make head or tail out of the Spanish records. The books of the Banco Español-Filipino showed deposits, securities, and liquid assets of over three million dollars, of which two million were missing. Even by Castilian standards it had been a fine haul.

A babel of Tagalog, Spanish, English, and Chinese tongues, its broad avenues and cramped business districts drenched in sunlight, Manila stirred uneasily when news was flashed of the signing of the Paris treaty. No overt disturbances took place. Each afternoon the American military band played as usual on the Luneta bandstand facing the azure bay, before rapt audiences of Spanish and Filipino families. The natives uncovered their heads to the strains of "There'll Be a Hot Time in the Old Town Tonight." It had been rendered so often they considered it our national anthem. Wages had soared. Carpenters who formerly earned thirty cents per day now asked ninety cents; house servants demanded twenty dollars monthly instead of seven. Strikes on the horsecar lines and in factories were chronic. The price of milk jumped ten-fold; meat went to a dollar a pound. Hardly any fresh vegetables or fruits were available at any price. The insurgents continued to hold the water-pumping station, and it was understood that they would close it down whenever they chose. Except for shops catering to troops, business conditions were bad, for with Manila surrounded on land the movement of goods to and from the interior had almost ceased. Most of the carabaos having been killed for food during the siege, American soldiers had to perform coolie labor. The natives looked on mockingly as U.S. privates dragged heavy buffalo carts loaded with commissary supplies through the hot streets.

The announcement of General Otis that no volunteers would be released until senate ratification of the peace treaty was not only futile but accelerated the decline in morale. An English diplomat in Manila at the time, Richard Brinksley Sheridan, observed a fist fight between a private and his commanding officer, and also reported the following dialogue between an officer and his men:

"Stand at ease—before you dismiss, the orders for the night

are: that no man is to leave his quarters, and that every man is to be under arms." At this there was general discontent, and grumbling could be distinctly heard along the lines, and smothered expressions like: "Oh h——. I'll be d——d if I shall obey those rotten orders. It's all bosh, I'll see you in h—— first." To this the man in charge replied: "All right, boys, don't get angry with me. They are not my orders; they are from headquarters. If I had my way, it would be different."

It was a wonder that the flimsy wood-and-bamboo New City did not go up in flames. Spanish fire equipment had consisted of seven fire engines, all defunct. By cannibalizing their parts, the Americans made one serviceable. It remained Manila's entire fire department for months. Two hundred lepers had been thoughtfully released by the Spaniards from the San Lazaro Leper Hospital, and a house-to-house search had been under way since August in an effort to round them up. Garbage—which during Spain's administration had been dumped on the outskirts of town and left to rot—was laboriously hauled out to sea by *cascos* and thrown overboard. Yet smallpox, dengue fever, and dysentery continued to plague the occupying forces.

It all added up to a most inflammable and unhealthy condition, in both a literal and figurative sense. And while the Americans caroused and sulked and the Filipino soldiers strutted, while mosquitoes bred in the crumbling moat that surrounded the Old City, while Spanish newspapers in Manila joyously stirred up antagonisms between the conquerors and the natives, and while *La Independencia* stated that the Philippine people had no intention of being bought and sold like livestock, General Otis improved his defenses and worried about Iloilo.

In that town of thirteen thousand souls, the second most important port in all the islands, on the southern coast of Panay three hundred miles south of Manila, a small contingent of Spanish troops still held out against the insurgents. When a committee representing native businessmen and

Spaniards petitioned the general for protection, it placed him in a quandary. Was the United States—a nation in limbo in respect to the peace treaty with Spain—entitled to extend its military reign at the expense of the insurgent government? Dewey advised Otis to wire the War Department for instructions. The latter could send troops, he suggested—which was true; the navy could convoy them; on the other hand, snatching Iloilo from the Filipinos was not the same as taking Manila from the Spaniards, nor was it likely to be quite so simple. Otis' telegram continued, "Insurgents reported favorable to American annexation." Did he refer to the Iloilo shopkeepers? Whatever the general had in mind, Washington concluded that the important town was ours for the asking without a fight: "Answering your message December 14, the President directs that you send necessary troops to Iloilo to preserve the peace and protect life and property." The words have long reverberated throughout the annals of colonialism, but what happened was not in keeping with tradition.

For reasons not known with certainty, the above response to Otis left Washington after a ten-day delay. Therefore Brigadier General Marcus Miller's command (four transports carrying the 18th Regular Infantry Regiment, the 51st Iowa Volunteers, and a battery of light artillery, all convoyed by the *Baltimore* and a captured Spanish gunboat) did not stand out of Manila harbor until December 26. The following day, as the expedition steamed past the west coast of Mindoro, Miller learned from an advance agent that the Spaniards in Iloilo had surrendered the city to the insurgents on Christmas Eve. They could hardly be blamed for despairing —it had been over a month since they had petitioned for relief —but it made matters difficult for Miller, whose instructions were baroque. He was not to fight—but he might take the city forcibly if he had to. He was to be firm—but somehow conciliatory. Conflict with the insurgents was to be avoided —if possible. And Iloilo had to be taken—but he must use discretion.

An old Indian-fighter with over forty years in the regular army, Miller must have reviewed his orders sourly as he plugged southward. His 2,500 men anchored in the Straits of Iloilo the morning of the twenty-eighth. Scouts sent ashore found the city occupied by three thousand Filipino troops under General Martin Delgado. They also learned that the natives (and some Spaniards who had not fled) were suddenly quite content with the new order and preferred to have General Miller keep his distance. Delgado, of course, told them that he had no intention of letting American troops land. But Miller wired Otis that the insurgents would yield without much fighting; he recommended that force be used at once.

Otis tried to placate him—"foreigners have large possessions there and a great deal of money in the banks . . . remain in the harbor with your force." Unfortunately the Iowa Volunteers had been aboard the *Pennsylvania* since early October; sanitary conditions and the mood of the troops on that ship had reached the breaking point; and General Miller wanted quick action. By December 30 Delgado had further fortified the city and had been reinforced by seven thousand men. Miller was next heard asking for the Kansas regiment and twenty thousand rounds of Gatling-gun ammunition.

Two thousand more insurgents arrived the following week. While they now outnumbered the Americans five to one, Miller was not intimidated: "The city is so completely under the control of the warships of the Navy that we are indifferent as to what the insurgents do. When the time comes nothing can save the insurgents but flight . . . If we have to fight at Manila and here, I should think it better to strike the first blow here." But Otis, under orders from Washington to avoid precisely that, could only instruct Miller to sit tight and send the *Pennsylvania* back to Manila. Resentfully he did so. As late as February 3 he was still suggesting that the town ought to be assaulted and complaining about the steamers entering the port with insurgent supplies. Meanwhile Mr. McKinley had cabled Otis and Dewey: "Glad you did not permit Miller to bring on a conflict. Time given the insurgents cannot hurt us and must weaken and discourage them. They will see our benevolent purpose . . ."

Aguinaldo and his aides saw no such purpose in Miller's contemplated seizure of the city; on the contrary, tempers were running high in Malolos over the incident. In Manila Otis had heard with alarm of the native cabinet explosion. The situation was critical, he cabled, with open threats to drive the invader out. He advised the president to dispatch some civilians to attempt an understanding with Aguinaldo. McKinley was equally concerned over the turn of events; and his so-called Schurman Commission set out from San Francisco without delay. Since this mission of humanity was accompanied by six infantry regiments, it was certain to be helpful in one way or another.

Thus all was flux and menace in the Philippines. In Washington, where senate discussion of the Spanish-American peace treaty was formally scheduled to open after the holidays, clamor also reigned; for the Great Debate had begun unofficially several weeks earlier.

III

Elsewhere in the United States the Philippine problem impinged scarcely at all. The little war with Spain had been won splendidly; only 379 American soldiers and sailors had been killed, and the fact that 5,083 others had already died of disease as a result of it was not yet publicly known. Business was excellent. The conflict had stimulated it immensely; and we now owned several tropical islands which few Americans had ever heard of but which were obviously romantic and profitable. It was also a source of pride that we had rescued millions of Cubans from the forces of evil, and that with almost unbelievable altruism we were about to proffer them self-rule with but the thinnest of economic strings attached. And while New Year's Day, 1899, looked upon euphoria unique in American history, a hard core of fanatics—the Anti-Imperialist League and their scattered supporters—viewed our Philippine policy with loathing and argued that the republic was about to plumb the depths of international immorality. In Boston Edward Atkinson was conferring with his associates about publishing a weekly protest bulletin—*The Anti-Imperialist*—with which to flood the country.

Henry Cabot Lodge had fallen prey to other misgivings, for no one knew better than the genius of the Foreign Relations Committee that the treaty was approximately four votes short of senate ratification. "I confess I cannot think calmly of the rejection of that treaty by a little more than one-third of the Senate," he wrote Theodore. "It would be a repudiation of the President and humiliation of the whole country in the eyes of the world, and would show we are unfit as a nation to enter into the great questions of foreign policy." To his friend, as to most Americans, the idea that ratification was not automatic had scarcely occurred; it seemed impossible, he wrote, that men of patriotism could contemplate such an outrage upon the country. But the word patriotism may be defined in various ways, nor was it true, as Mr. Lodge complained, that the opposition consisted solely of southern Democrats, even though that party intended to use the issue as a political weapon for all it might be worth.

Almost unaware of the brewing storm, the Gay Nineties sauntered toward oblivion, exhibiting phenomena that were to become part of the national folklore. It was true that most bartenders affected handle-bar mustaches. Bicycles were really built for two:

> Daisy, Daisy, give me your answer true.
> I'm half crazy, all for the love of you.
> It won't be a stylish marriage,
> I can't afford a carriage,
> But you'll look sweet upon the seat
> Of a bicycle built for two!

Fire engines were indeed drawn by galloping steeds. Nearly every cigar store displayed a wooden Indian. Charles Dana Gibson's clean-featured young men and classically American girls were the vogue, and an entire generation was being influenced by the dress and attitudes of his characters. In mining huts, on the walls of girls' rooms, above farmhouse fireplaces, in college fraternity houses and freight-car cabooses hung the most famous illustrations of the era—"The Widow and Her Friends," "His Move," "You Are Going on a Long Journey"—and it was Gibson who brought padding to the shoulders of men's suits and consigned mustaches to oblivion.

Victor Herbert, Weber and Fields, the nickelodeon, the Katzenjammer Kids, "Gentleman Jim" Corbett—these were bywords of the times. A stein of beer was a nickel, eggs about a dime a dozen. Ladies' shirtwaists had come to stay. Mr. Kipling's *Second Jungle Book* and May Irwin's vaudeville burlesques were the rage—such as this exchange:

"Your life-line shows you are going to die of starvation among strangers."

"Shipwreck?"

"No; boardinghouse."

Buffalo Bill was in his glory, Mark Twain in his cream-white suit a sight never to be forgotten, and innocent thinkers thrilled to the beautiful truth of Ella Wheeler Wilcox's lines, "Laugh and the world laughs with you; weep and you weep alone." Cigars sold two for a nickel; they were "two-fors." There were the Floradora Sextette, buggies, sulkies, phaetons, pug dogs, the family photograph album on the parlor table. Lovers hand in hand viewed stereopticon slides. Paper collars were à la mode. General Joe Wheeler came out in an advertisement extolling Peruna. People were laughing at Mr. Winton's horseless carriage. The Memory Tablet Company of 114 Fifth Avenue, New York, was promoting its new psychological discovery—"Memory Restorative Tablets"—to galvanize tenfold the power of the human brain, and other mail-order confidence men were coining money in a thousand other regrettable ways.

As for Casey, he let the first pitch go by—a called strike. "That ain't my style," he said.

With a smile of Christian charity great Casey's visage shone;
He stilled the rising tumult; he bade the game go on;
He signalled to Sir Timothy, once more the spheroid flew;
But Casey still ignored it, and the umpire said, "Strike two!"

"Fraud!" cried the maddened thousands, and echo answered "Fraud!"
But one scornful look from Casey and the audience was awed.
They saw his face grow stern and cold, they saw his muscles strain,
And they knew that Casey wouldn't let that ball go by again.

The sneer is gone from Casey's lip, his teeth are clinched in hate;
He pounds with cruel violence his bat upon the plate.
And now the pitcher holds the ball, and now he lets it go,
And now the air is shattered by the force of Casey's blow . . .

With averted eyes we leave Casey and turn to congress, where the first voices were being raised pro and con the Spanish treaty. Senator Vest had introduced a resolution blocking annexation of the Philippines on the ground that there could be no government without the consent of the governed; since the Filipinos were not to be given American citizenship or statehood, such annexation could not be legally countenanced. Senator Hoar concurred mordantly: "Have we the right, as doubtless we have the physical power, to enter upon the government of ten or twelve million subject people without constitutional restraint?" Surely the Founding Fathers had never dreamed that their people "would be beguiled from these sacred and awful verities that they might strut about in the castoff clothing of pinchback emperors and pewter kings; that their descendants would be excited by the smell of gunpowder and the sound of guns of a single victory as a small boy by a firecracker on some Fourth of July." The

Vest resolution was derided as narrow and old-fashioned by its opponents. Furthermore, remarked Senator Nelson, it was not true that our motives were selfishly commercial; it was not the purpose of the United States to "enslave or enthrall the people of the Philippine Islands . . . We come as ministering angels, not as despots."

At Camp Merritt, as the new year dawned, eleven thousand ministering angels were being hurriedly organized into reinforcements for General Otis, who kept insisting that he required at least twenty-five thousand—preferably thirty thousand—troops for his assigned mission. ("Their army seems to be more or less excited and is considering . . . to destroy us all at once, before we can get any more soldiers. All this may be called street rumor, but it is very actively circulated. The insurgent army is becoming very tired of doing nothing and demands blood.")

Many light-years from the South China Sea, George Ade was writing his Aesopian fables in slang, oil lamps flickered in most homes and apartments, and girls' bloomers for basketball were being reviled by preachers and derided by the press. In Chicago "Bathhouse" John Coughlin was controlling the notorious First Ward. Dwight Moody, ex-salesman turned evangelist, was still stirring the people with his hymns:

> There were ninety-and-nine that safely lay in the
>   shelter of the fold,
> But one was out on the hills away, far from the gates
>   of gold—
> Away on the mountains wild and bare, away from the
>   tender Shepherd's care . . .

and "Saved by Grace" and "Hiding in Thee" and scores more in the same tenor.

Sears Roebuck's catalog was advertising a popular new musical instrument called the mouth organ. Housewives bought meat from wagons that made the neighborhood rounds accompanied by swarms of flies. Farmers and mechanics wore bright red flannel underwear. Frederick Remington was creating his nostalgic wash drawings of cowboys and Indians. With fascination people were reading Edward Bellamy's *Looking Backward*, but there were those who suggested darkly that it was nothing but a disguised Socialist tract. William Gillette was enacting Sherlock Holmes before audiences that reached the millions, and doing so with a subtlety rare for the times; and Richard Mansfield was in *Cyrano de Bergerac* at New York Garden Theatre. She of the unparalleled beauty and grace—Julia Marlowe—was playing *The Countess Valeska*, a legendary temptress who "burst upon the students of Harvard College like each one's personal dream." And there were Ethel Barrymore, Sarah Bernhardt, and a brash teen-ager named George M. Cohan in *Peck's Bad Boy. Uncle Tom's Cabin* was still the greatest money-maker of all. There were any number of traveling "Tommers," and their handbills read something like this:

A Great and Moral Play
BRING THE CHILDREN
Give Them an Ideal and Lasting Lesson in American History
HIGH CLASS SPECIALTIES BETWEEN THE ACTS
SEE The Death of Little Eva
SEE The Frolicsome Topsy
SEE Kind and Affectionate Uncle Tom
SEE The Hard-Hearted Legree . . .

And still Topsy continued to grow, Eliza crossed the ice, the hounds bayed, and Uncle Tom doggedly carried on.

Paul Dresser had written the music for "On the Banks of the Wabash," to which his brother with the name spelled correctly—Theodore Dreiser—had composed the lyrics. Other popular tunes sung and loved in 1899 were "Waltz Me Around Again, Willie," "The Girl I Left Behind Me," and "The Sidewalks of New York." Since there were no recordings, radio, or television to kill a song in a month, favorites like these could last for years. People were still speaking with awe of Jim Mutrie's sensational New York Giants. Big-time football had arrived at the Ivy League. The "Old Apple Tree Gang" (they were, in truth, a staid collection of middle-aged millionaires) was playing golf on an aboriginal course named St. Andrews near New York. That game was catching on, though most people considered its practitioners childish and jibed at those who scraped white balls through pastures into tomato-can holes.

The dime novel *Night Scenes in New York,* by "Old Sleuth," was typical of hundreds that were the rage in 1899. In a stark hotel room Adele addresses her evil-looking adversary:

"Back! Back! On your life stand back!"

To this Mr. Treadwell responds prosaically, "Adele, I love you."

"And you would prove your love by acts of violence?"

He twists his mustache and murmurs, "You are wrong. I would only persuade you to be my wife."

Adele's rejoinder contains elements of irrelevance: "Hear me, Lyman Treadwell; I am but a poor shop-girl; my present life is a struggle for scanty existence; my future a life of toil; but over my present life of suffering there extends a rainbow of hope . . . Life is short, eternity endless—the grave is but the entrance to eternity. And you, villain, ask me to change my present peace for a life of horror with you. No, monster, rather may I die at once!" And, fortunately, Mr. Treadwell failed to impose his will on Adele. Was there an analogy here to U.S.-Philippine relations?

That first day of January nobody had heard of a movie, an airplane, penicillin, or a television set. Neither chain stores, nor diesel engines, nor votes for women, nor Kiwanis Clubs, nor submarines existed. The Dow-Jones average was still to come, and so were beauty queens, Dwight D. Eisenhower, inferiority complexes, Albert Einstein, electric razors, fascism, jazz, the ICBM. It was now that Rudyard Kipling's immortal poem was published in British and American magazines:

> Take up the white man's burden—
> Send forth the best ye breed—
> Go bind your sons to exile
> To serve your captives' need;
> To wait in heavy harness,
> On fluttering folk and wild—
> Your new-caught sullen peoples
> Half devil and half child.

Almost overnight the intoxicating lines became hackneyed. Expressing as they did the hard but inescapable duty which had devolved upon our nation, they would be of much aid and comfort to the expansionists. Mr. Roosevelt recommended them to Mr. Lodge as mediocre poetry but uncommonly good sense. Henry Cabot approved them in both respects. As yet they had not come to the critical attention of Aguinaldo, Mabini, and their sullen peoples.

8

CLIMAX
IN
FEBRUARY

I T IS EASY TO BE CYNICAL AFTER THE EVENT, AND THE ARGU-
ments used by the expansionists (as they preferred to be
called) are nowadays highly susceptible to derision.
Even at the time the anti-imperialists saw their openings and
made the most of them. Their response, for example, to Treasury Secretary Lyman Gage's innocent statement that philan-
thropy and 5 per cent could go hand in hand was both joyous
and impassioned. In a Chicago speech William Bryan, for
one, suggested that the first word chloroformed Gage's conscience, while the second enabled him to pick the pocket of
the conquered. And he continued typically: "When the desire to steal becomes uncontrollable in an individual he is
declared to be a kleptomaniac and is sent to an asylum; when
the desire to grab land becomes uncontrollable in a nation
we are told that the 'currents of destiny are flowing through
the hearts of men.'"

And while few modern historians would dispute Samuel
Flagg Bemis' estimate that those years of adolescent irre-
sponsibility and the acquisition of the Philippines were a na-

tional aberration, it must also be noted that the logic of men like Bryan (such as in the above passage) was often over-simplified. The claim that the Philippines were incapable of self government and needed Uncle Sam contained a kernel of truth. Assuming that one characteristic of sovereignty is the capacity for self defense, the expansionists felt that the Filipinos would be helpless against the encroachments of such a nation as, say, Germany. Since we had helped rescue the islands from Spain, could we morally allow another country to seize them? For, unfortunately, a liberator's debt always goes beyond mere liberation. This brings up the protectorate alternative. We have seen that of all possible lines of action it was the most impractical, involving heavy costs, risks, and philanthropic commitments without even a 5 per cent return. It was not like sheltering Cuba, a few miles from Florida.

Then, too, few congressmen understood that the islands could hardly be returned to Spain, for the reason that she probably did not have the physical power to reconquer them. The unawareness of Filipino military potential and the extent of the collapse of Spanish authority in the islands was nearly total among the imperialists. Spain could regain control with ease, they assumed, should the United States pull out. This implied that she would do so with our approval. The idea that we would take responsibility for deliberately handing the islands back into her anachronistic grip was repellent to both factions; but since it rested upon a misconception it was vulnerable. David Starr Jordan, president of Stanford University, exposed it succinctly. We cannot acquire title to the Philippines even technically, he said, until "the actual owners have been consulted. We have only purchased Spain's quitclaim deed to property she could not hold and cannot transfer. For the right to finish the conquest of the Philippines we have agreed on our part to pay $20,000,000 in cash, or $2 apiece for each man, woman and child." Nonetheless if we abandoned the islands, Spain certainly had a right to re-enter them and might try to do so with the not inconsiderable means at her command. A canary that flies the coop remains the property of its owner, who may go to considerable lengths to repossess it.

The commercial aspirations of the imperialists were also valid in the sense that the controversy did not exist in a vacuum but in a hard world. A nation acts in self interest, and McKinley was correct in saying that legitimate means of increasing America's foreign trade were all to the good. The word legitimate, of course, called for definition. A hundred times the expansionists repeated that they fully intended to combine commerce with decency. Senator Nelson, in a speech similar to many others, insisted that we would religiously uphold the best ideals of the republic, in harmony with justice and the highest civilization.

That would have been splendid if the Filipinos had agreed to being annexed. But here the imperialist banner found itself impaled upon a dilemma, for by January, 1899, it was generally known that the native government (at least) wanted no part of us. The painful fact having sunk in that there was to be no consent of the governed, the American Declaration of Independence became an integral part of the dispute. It said nothing about states or continental boundaries, nor did it put colonies on a separate shelf. By implication it referred to all people under U.S. jurisdiction:

> We hold these truths to be self-evident, that all men are created equal; that they are endowed by their Creator with certain unalienable rights; that among these are life, liberty, and the pursuit of happiness. That, to secure these rights, governments are instituted among men, deriving their just powers from the consent of the governed; that, whenever any form of government becomes destructive of these ends, it is the right of the people to alter or abolish it . . .

To counter this mandate, administration spokesmen modified it. The governed people as a whole did not have to consent, said Senator Platt—only some of them. He defined this minority as intelligent, educated Filipinos who knew what was good for them, in contrast to the ignorant masses who did not. "'Consent of the governed,' indeed!" exclaimed Representative Gibson in a House address. But the Democrats, Populists, and Republicans of the old school who opposed the treaty claimed that the moment we annexed the Philippines the constitution would apply in full force. We would have to make every Filipino a citizen of the United States—the Negrito dwarf as well as the Tagalog statesman—with all the rights of other citizens. Legally and financially, the islands would have to be treated like a state, subject to the same imposts and taxes; on this point the constitution was quite clear.

Senator Platt, who was carrying the burden of speechmaking for his side, simply denied everything. The Philippines did not have to be awarded statehood. Their people did not have to be made citizens. Congress would decide at its leisure about how and when to accept Filipinos and their products into this country. In other words, there was no law which estopped us from creating a pure colonial system. Providence had put it upon us, he said, and we proposed to execute it.

The debate waged in January was as vitriolic as any in American history. In a way, the issue was even more clear-cut than that of slavery. We were about to absorb the Philippines against the wishes of her people (in this respect the annexation of Guam, Puerto Rico, and Hawaii was not comparable), whereas slavery had been present in the American colonies for hundreds of years before the republic was even born. The prospect puzzled many thoughtful men in and out of congress, especially since our country had been founded upon diametrically opposite principles of law and ideology. The utterances of the opposition, printed and spoken, are filled with despair. Bryan asked if "thou shalt not steal upon a small scale" was to be substituted for the law of Moses. Round-faced, clean-shaven Senator Hoar burst out that the Monroe Doctrine was defunct, that if Uncle Sam sank to this deed he would be nothing, after all, but "a cheapjack country, raking after the cart for the leavings of European tyranny." The vulgar allegory indicates the state of mind of this ordinarily self-possessed orator. And even Theodore Roosevelt's close friend, Henry Adams, late in the month penned these lines in a private letter: "I fully share with Hoar the alarm and horror of seeing poor weak McKinley . . . plunge into an inevitable war to conquer the Philippines, contrary to every profession or so-called principle of our lives and history. I turn green in bed at midnight if I think of the horror of a year's warfare in the Philippines . . . where . . . we must slaughter a million or two of foolish Malays in order to give them the comforts of flannel petticoats and electric railways."

Prophetically Andrew Carnegie had written in a magazine article that the Philippines would be to the United States precisely what India was to England—a nation of incipient rebels. His communications to senators and cabinet members increased in volume, and it was he with his untold millions in wealth who almost singlehandedly financed the organized anti-imperialist movement. "Andrew Carnegie really seems to be off his head," Secretary of State John Hay wrote Whitelaw Reid. "He writes me frantic letters, signing them 'Your Bitterest Opponent.' He threatens the President, not only with the vengeance of the voters, but with practical punishment at the hands of the mob."

But Carnegie could only scurry around Washington on the periphery of the argument and probably had little effect upon members of the world's most exclusive club. In still another secret speech upon the senate floor Orville Platt reiterated that the right to acquire land under territorial status was already established; he alluded to New Mexico, which after forty-eight years was still a territory. But, said Mr. Hoar, the cases were not comparable. New Mexico wanted to be a state. The Philippines did not want to be a state or a territory or any other kind of American appendage. "You have no right," he declared, "at the cannon's mouth to impose on an unwilling people your . . . notions of what is good."

As January dwindled, however, a small tide seemed to be running in favor of ratification. Mr. Lodge, at any rate, thought things were looking up, although the anti-annexationists were also counting noses and had decided tentatively that the treaty was doomed. Bleak, snowy weather settled over the northeast coast most of the month. In Cuba the last Spanish troops departed for home, while the native provisional government commenced taking over political control of the island. From Manila General Otis continued to cable views of a fairly optimistic nature; their implication was that the Filipinos would accept U.S. sovereignty—grudgingly, perhaps, but they would accept it. Advice of this kind comforted the administration, for it cast doubt upon the accusation that in ratifying the treaty the senate would throw a new war into the country's lap. Henry Lodge redoubled his mighty efforts behind the scenes, bringing all his power and personality to bear upon those who might still be swayed. Sixty of ninety senators had to vote affirmatively, which meant quite a few Democrats. The senate roll-call breakdown was 46 Republicans, 34 Democrats, 5 Populists, 2 Silverites, and 3 Independents. With several Republicans and practically all the Populists and Silverites against the treaty, Mr. Lodge and his aides had no easy task, especially since their political influence outside their own party was close to nil.

Some borderline senators, it must be said, were bribed by promises. McEnery was promised that he would be allowed to name a federal judge of his choice. McLaurin of South Carolina was told that he could select all his state's postmasters. More discreditable tactics were used on Kenney of Delaware, who was in a serious personal legal squeeze and was virtually threatened into voting for ratification. As the month went on, lobbying became somewhat more blatant; and the Democrats exerted equal and opposite influence when and where they could. "It's an outrage the way Hanna and his friends are working this treaty through the Senate," wrote

Senator Arthur Gorman of Maryland to a friend. "If an honest vote could be taken, I doubt whether there is a bare majority for the treaty; but all the railroad influence, which is being worked through Elkins, all the commercial interests . . . are bringing pressures on Senators in the most shameful manner."

Not one had ever visited the Philippine Islands. Few knew much about them even at second hand. The debate was therefore conducted with much heat and little light. Among the outward-looking senators only Mr. Lodge really understood the Philippines, their people, and their military and economic ramifications; but he had not yet addressed the senate. Senator Caffery of Louisiana, in opposition, was another exception who had somehow dug up most of the background and current facts. He predicted serious military trouble from the insurgent army and also contended that the Philippines would be a commercial headache, since tropical countries always export more than they buy. And several times he and Mr. Hoar skirted another conception, the future significance of which they could not yet fully grasp—that the islands would become a military liability in years to come (America's heel of Achilles, Theodore Roosevelt was to term them), and that we would have to overextend ourselves strategically to defend them.

Kipling's poem in *McClure's*, February issue, had begun to circulate early in January. As soothing as it was to the imperialists, it also provided a satirical target for their opponents, so that on balance it is hard to know which side it benefited most. Almost immediately parodies such as this, burst into print:

> Pile on the brown man's burden
>   To gratify your greed;
> Go, clear away the "niggers"
>   Who progress would impede;
> Be very stern, for truly
>   'Tis useless to be mild
> With new-caught sullen peoples,
>   Half devil and half child.

> Pile on the brown man's burden,
> And if ye rouse his hate,
> Meet his old-fashioned reasons
> With Maxims up-to-date;
> With shells and dum-dum bullets,
> A hundred times make plain
> The brown man's loss must ever
> Imply the white man's gain.

One unusual argument used by a few southern Democrats was that it would be bad to incorporate "a mongrel and semi-barbarous population into our body politic . . . inferior to, but akin to, the Negro." Senator Teller, whose resolution had freed Cuba, was asked whether it did not also apply by moral inference to the Philippines. It did not, he replied startlingly. The latter islands must go through a testing period (he gave no time limit), after which the United States would decide whether to set them free or accept them as a state. The rebuff stunned those who had been counting on Teller for support. At the University of Chicago Carl Schurz spoke exclusively about the Philippine problem in a convocation address, thousands of copies of which were distributed by the Anti-Imperialist League. This excerpt was quoted in senate debate:

> It is objected that they are not capable of independent government. They may answer that this is their affair and that they are at least entitled to a trial. I frankly admit that if they are given the trial, their conduct in governing themselves will be far from perfect. Well, the conduct of no people is perfect, not even our own. They may try to revenge themselves upon their Tories in their Revolutionary War. But we too threw our Tories into hideous dungeons . . . we, too, have had our civil war which cost hundreds and thousands of lives and devastated one-half of our land; and now we have in horrible abundance the killings by lynch law . . . They may have troubles with their wild tribes. So had we, and we treated our wild tribes in a manner not to be proud of. They may have corruption and rapacity in their government, but . . . Manila may secure a city council not much less virtuous than that of Chicago.

But why, asked Senator Lodge reasonably, all these fears about America doing harm to the Filipinos? For what reason would we oppress them? The United States government had, unlimited power over the senator's own life, children, property, and human rights. It was not abusing them, nor would it abuse those of the Filipinos. The contention was sharply attacked by the isolationists. With no exceptions, they replied, every colonial system in history had been foisted upon natives by some degree of terrorism. India and Algeria were cited most frequently. The Populist Senator, General J. B. Weaver, was one of many who quoted Abraham Lincoln to the effect that no man was good enough to govern another without the other's consent.

So the storm raged, and by the latter part of January, informed sources in Washington calculated that the treaty remained two or three votes short of ratification. There had been some switches toward administration policy, but one or two men had decided to vote against it. During the entire month, Mr. McKinley had not spoken a word in its support.

II

Apparently confident that the treaty would be ratified, the president had not intruded upon the senate debate (which was being waged in executive session) either by formal speech or by comment for publication. During the month his only move relating to the Philippines had been to legitimatize the U.S. occupation by a proclamation extending the authority of General Otis in time and space. In itself this was no surprise, for the Treaty of Paris was no secret. What rather shocked General Otis was the president's phrasing. It was not only that "the future control, disposition and government of the Philippine Islands are ceded to the United States," apparently in perpetuity. The new sovereign would determine the "private rights and relations" of its wards. Those who refused to co-operate would be whipped into line "with firmness, if need be." Local offices might be held by natives, "provided they accept the supremacy of the United States by taking the oath of allegiance." America would take over "all the public property and the revenues of the state." And while the mission was "one of benevolent assimilation . . . there must be sedulously maintained the strong arm of authority."

A wiser man than when he had first arrived in Manila, Otis visualized uneasily how the febrile new cabinet at Malolos would react to such a document. He showed it to several Filipino *pacificos* in Manila, who agreed that it would be a major mistake to publish it. Yet Otis was under instructions to do so, and his next step took courage for a man who cherished his commission. He eliminated the more provocative statements, inserted others to the effect that native participation in the process of government would be more extensive than Mr. McKinley had indicated, and then released the new text via newspapers and posters. Even so, the results were discouraging. Most natives ridiculed it. Within twenty-four hours every placard had been torn down. General Luna, writing under his own name in *La Independencia,* assailed it as a subterfuge to quiet the people until the United States could institute a reign even more odious than Spain's had been. To make matters worse, McKinley's unexpurgated proclamation was released in Iloilo by General Miller, who was still sulking on his transport in that peaceful southern bay. The reason for the *faux pas* was simple. Unknown to Otis, the War Department had also sent an enciphered copy to Miller for informational purposes. The latter assumed it was meant for distribution, and he published it in both Spanish and Tagalog translations. The differences between his original and the gloss rendered by Otis were noticeable and significant.

Three days later Aguinaldo responded with his *Otro Manifesto del Sr. Presidente del Gobierno Revolucionario,* which was close to a formal declaration of war. It protested the gratuitous assumptions that Otis was the ruler of the Philippine Islands and that the United States owned them; reviewed the entire course of revolution against Spain; cited earlier promises by various American commanders; accused them of double-dealing; and ended with these harsh sentences:

> My nation cannot remain indifferent in view of such a violent and aggressive seizure of a portion of its territory by a nation which has arrogated to itself the title: champion of oppressed nations. Thus it is that my government is disposed to open hostilities if the American troops attempt to take forcible possession.

> I denounce these acts before the world in order that the conscience of mankind may pronounce its infallible verdict as to who are the oppressors of nations and the tormentors of mankind.

> Upon their heads be all the blood which may be shed.

The American proclamations had been most inept. For one thing—a technicality, but to the natives a galling one—the senate had not yet confirmed the treaty. More important, the documents were marked by indifference and arrogance. They gave the Filipinos no chance to nourish their dignity, and this applies to the Otis version almost as much as to the original. McKinley took no interest in native rights except those which he condescended to grant them. Nothing was said about their long fight for independence, nor of the sufferings they had experienced under Castilian rule. He did not acknowledge their ability for self government. He merely said, in sum, that we were taking them over and hoped to treat them well. Even conservative Filipino elements were saddened by the attitudes expressed.

Since the Manila cable was being censored by American authorities, the Filipinos had to get their viewpoints out of the country by way of the *Junta Patriotica* in Hong Kong, whence a cry of distress now issued forth: "Are the Americans our friends?" they asked. "Any moment a shot may be

fired by an irresponsible American or Filipino soldier . . .
After remaining a month on the outskirts of the city, where
we had been stopped . . . we were ordered away. Did we
not cheerfully obey?" They denied that they were savages
who would murder, loot, and burn. They complained that
Dewey had confiscated their little fleet late the previous year
"because of foolish rumors that we would attack the Americans. We asked for an explanation . . . were not even given
an answer." The Spaniards were being shown every consideration, while they, the Filipinos, were being treated like foes.
Why had this turnabout taken place? "Does this satisfy
American ideas of justice?" While they had been capturing
all of Luzon outside of Manila, the Americans recognized
and encouraged them. Now that America held the capital
city she turned her face away. "Is this just?" The catechism,
addressed to the world at large and to President McKinley
in particular, went on for two thousand words and elicited
much sympathy from Bryan and his cohorts. In Washington
it was not acknowledged.

Affairs at this stage in Manila were unbearably tense. A
dogfight in Binondo caused some gunplay which was mistaken for an uprising; an American call to arms actually followed. Across the neutral zone soldiers of both sides yelled
taunts and obscenities. Knifings became a nightly matter.
Americans never walked the streets alone and always carried
a loaded weapon. Most male natives kept a small knife or
bolo hidden under their clothing. Early that month Otis had
cabled Corbin in the War Department, "City very quiet. Great
suppressed excitement. Families leaving." Thirty thousand
Filipinos fled the capital during the first week of January.
Spectacular as always, Colonel Cailles wired his secretary of
war at Malolos: "An American interpreter has come to tell me
to withdraw our forces in Maytubig fifty paces. I shall not
draw back a step, and in place of withdrawing, I shall advance a little . . . I said that from the day I knew that
Maquinley [sic] opposed our independence I did not want

to have dealings with any American. War, War, is what we want. The Americans after this speech went off pale."

To which Aguinaldo himself replied, "I approve and applaud."

Most routine Filipino complaints had to do with U.S. soldiers searching houses without warrant and brandishing their guns too freely. The American authorities replied that this was necessary in view of obvious plans for revolt. Something had to be done, after all, to confiscate the thousands of bolos being manufactured and sold by Chinese metalworkers. Native shopkeepers protested that troops were taking their wares, promising to pay later, and not doing so. Some Americans gravely settled their debts with Confederate money, and Otis insisted that this type of larceny had to be stopped—if necessary by deductions at the monthly pay table. Americans called all Filipinos niggers, dagoes, yuyus, or gugus. But John Bass cabled (*Harper's*, January 27) that the Tagalogs were the chief cause of trouble: their impudence had become intolerable; they were shoving U.S. generals off the sidewalks and threatening to cut every invader's throat. The American health officer in Manila, Dr. Frank Bourns, in a personal letter agreed:

> As an American acquainted with Oriental ways, I was so ashamed of myself the last month or two that I hated to leave the house. Our soldiers received and submitted to untold insults from the insurgent troops, and bore them patiently, all because of the most stringent orders from headquarters to avoid trouble, if possible, without actual sacrifice of dignity.

On January 10 Aguinaldo received this note from a secret agent in the Old City: "Otis has received a telegram from his Government ordering him not to open hostilities . . . he is awaiting 15,000 regular troops, and Congressional action on peace treaty . . . yesterday three Americans were boloed advanced line Santa Ana."

To the commander at Caloocan Aguinaldo telegraphed,

"Tell the Filipino soldiers that they must keep on good terms
with the Americans, in order to deceive them . . . since the
hoped-for moment has not yet arrived."

When one Filipino captain neglected to remove his pistol
while strolling near an American outpost, the sentry shot and
killed him. An entire party of American engineers, mapping
an area near Santa Ana, was captured and thrown into the
Malolos jail. General MacArthur caused the Filipino telegraph office in Manila to be seized and its equipment confiscated. Yet the insurgents were perhaps more provocative
than the white troops, largely due to the fact that General
Miller had been forced to back down at Iloilo. Still General
Otis, glued to his desk at headquarters, entertained relatively few qualms. On January 11 he wired Washington that
the immediate danger would pass in a few days. Three days
later he reported that conditions were positively sedate. On
January 15 he conveyed to General Miller views still more
astonishing; conditions were improving, he thought, and the
Malolos government was slowly disintegrating. Later in the
month he advised Washington once again that the excitement
was lessening. His illusions, however, were largely the result
of conferences then taking place between Aguinaldo's representatives and his own. Hostilities, he felt, could not commence during negotiations. Unfortunately they broke down
on January 27, the date of his last message paraphrased above.

The talking had started January 9 at the suggestion of
Señor Mabini, who was being goaded by the remnants of the
native peace faction. Six meetings took place between three
Filipinos and three U.S. army officers; and the attitude of the
head of the American team, Brigadier General R. P. Hughes,
is best expressed in his own words:

> We were very very sorry, at least I was, to have the confer-
> ences stopped, because I was trying to prolong them until
> General Lawton's ship could get there with four battalions,
> which we needed very much. But we could not stretch it out

any longer. The papers had begun to attack us, and stated
absolutely in words that we were doing nothing but trying to
gain time . . .

It would be fruitless to do more than recapitulate the
squabbling. The Filipinos asked that America bring in no
more reinforcements and occupy no more territory until
some kind of *modus vivendi* could be worked out. They tried
to get some concessions bearing upon their independence, or
at least an American protectorate arrangement; but such
hopes were pure fantasy. Only two possibilities existed: Philippine submission or war. It was the same old dilemma. U.S.
military commanders in the Philippines could not make policy; on the other hand, Washington refused to negotiate with
or even listen to the Filipinos. As for Otis, he never advised
Washington how threatening matters were—quite the contrary; therefore the War Department, the State Department,
and the White House saw no need for making the slightest
compromises to save face for Aguinaldo's cabinet. The reports
sent by Otis to the War Department are so sketchy as to be
nearly meaningless. Only once did he drop a casual hint
that the natives might accept qualified independence under
American protection. This phrase, if pursued to a diplomatic
conclusion, might have averted war, for it opened the door
to any number of verbal or ritualistic solutions. Not until
eighteen months later, in his annual report for 1899, did Otis
admit the all-important fact that the insurgent representatives had never stopped pleading for some concession which
would satisfy their people. Thus in Manila there was rigidity
and drift; in Washington indifference and ignorance of the
facts; in Malolos total disillusionment. When Otis told the
Filipinos that the Schurman commission was en route to deal
with them, Mabini cynically replied that this was an ingenious scheme to kill time and muddy the waters, amounting to
nothing in practice.

"I beg you to leave Manila with your family and come here

to Malolos," Aguinaldo wrote to a friend in the Walled City,
"but not because I wish to frighten you . . . it is not yet the
day or the week." Feverish last-minute preparations for conflict took place within the insurgent camp. All provincial
presidentes were officially alerted by telegraph. Teodoro
Sandico, a youthful propagandist who had become director
of diplomacy under Mabini in the revolutionary cabinet, advised Aguinaldo that as soon as the Filipino attack began
the Americans should be driven into the Walled City, which
should then be set afire. On January 20 the Philippine Congress, in a dead giveaway, voted Aguinaldo authority to declare war at any moment he saw fit. The man was at the
zenith of his power. Where not revered he was feared. His
congress was pliant. All provinces were represented by men
who followed his dictates to the letter. From afar he even
dominated Manila; for example, on December 30, the anni-
versary of Rizal's death, he had ordered the day to be honored as a holiday, whereupon every native stopped work and
business was paralyzed.

By the end of January some forty thousand natives had
fled the capital city, mostly northward or directly to Malolos.
Jammed with women and children, the one Philippine railway running north from Manila lost all resemblance to a military transport system; and General Luna, in despair, had
abandoned trying to utilize it strictly for troops and supplies.
With civilians hanging out the windows of the coaches, and
even riding the flatcars and the caboose, the train resembled
a cartoon trolley *sans* merriment. Some of the more solvent
natives took passage by sea to Hong Kong. All roads leading
from the capital were a chaos of ponies, carriages, and heavy-
laden pedestrians. To his "fifth column" (Sandatahan) in
Manila Aguinaldo issued final instructions for the day of attack:

> The chief of those who go to attack the barracks should send
> in first four men with a good present for the American com-
> mander. They should not prior to the attack look at the Amer-

icans in a threatening manner. To the contrary the attack . . .
should be a complete surprise and with decision and courage.
In order to deceive the sentinel, one should dress as a woman
and take care that the sentinel is not able to discharge his
piece.

At the moment of attack, the Sandatahan should not attempt
to secure rifles from their dead enemies, but shall pursue
slashing right and left with bolos until the Americans surrender.

The officers shall take care that on the tops of the houses
along the streets where the American forces shall pass there
will be placed four to six men who shall be prepared with
stones, timbers, red hot iron, heavy furniture, as well as boiling water, oil, and molasses, rags soaked in coal oil ready to
be lighted and thrown down on passing American troops.

In place of bolos or daggers, if they do not possess the same,
the Sandatahan can provide themselves with lances and arrows. These should be made so that in the withdrawal of the
body, the head will remain in the flesh.

These primitive methods were considered necessary because few Filipinos in the American zone possessed firearms.
By the end of January virtually all rifles in Manila had been
smuggled to the native army in wooden coffins supposedly
containing corpses for burial outside the city limits. But of
the thirty thousand *insurrectos* surrounding Manila a third
were still without rifles. One Filipino unit (in reserve, fortunately) consisted of Negritos armed with spears. Another
rear "battalion" was of children whose duty was to throw
stones at the enemy.

At this time the insurgent army roughly numbered eighty
thousand men, half of whom possessed rifles. The bulk of this
strength was concentrated in Luzon, but fairly substantial
forces also existed in Mindora, Panay, Leyte, and Samar,
with a sprinkling further south. Its main problem—one that
neither side as yet recognized—was that few knew how to

aim a rifle. For generations the normal aiming pattern taught to army recruits of Western nations had been this:

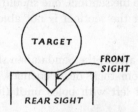

Natives who did not understand the rear sight often removed it as a nuisance. Aiming vaguely along the barrel and pointing only the front sight at the target, they invariably fired high. They had not been taught the trigger squeeze, and jerking at the trigger accentuated the error. They had beaten Spain anyway. Could they repeat against the legions of North America?

Numerically those legions were not too impressive as of January 31, 1899, when the reported total was just under twenty-one thousand officers and men. Deducting those at Cavite and Iloilo, and those engaged in administrative duties, left fourteen thousand combat troops in Manila. Another three thousand also had to be subtracted—members of the provost guard whose job it was to quell any interior uprising and efforts to set the city afire—so that only eleven thousand troops were on front-line duty. The length of this front was sixteen miles. (Seven hundred men per mile of front compares with an average of nine thousand in World War I.) Otis made no attempt to form a continuous line. He assigned each regiment a sector containing one outpost, or observation post, of which there were twelve. Behind them, each respective regiment was quartered in reserve. Other floating reserves had been spotted further back. Tightly knit to headquarters and to each other by telegraph, this system gave Otis the opportunity of reshuffling his hand rapidly during the course of an engagement.

The Pasig River, as we have noted, was not fordable. Split-

ting both forces in half, it worked to the disadvantage of the
insurgents, who would have to cross it by boat in order to
move north or south. The Americans, however, operating on
interior lines, could pass easily from one zone to the other
over three good bridges. We shall return later to the tactical
situation and to the role of Dewey's fleet; but a few other
existing factors may be noted here. In contrast to the dedicated Filipinos, the American army was one of the more undisciplined ever placed in the field by this nation. There are
many reasons why this was so. They were mostly volunteers,
they had been marking time for almost six months, the climate had taken a good deal out of them, the war with Spain
was over, the prospect of fighting natives halfway around the
world for no clearly understood reason was not enticing, and
so on. Whatever the causes, the majority of them wanted to
go home. Most officers called most men by their first names.

The number of saloons in Manila had multiplied twenty-
fold since last August. The volunteers hated their .45-caliber
modified 1869 Springfield rifles, single-shot monsters of short
range which kicked like a mule and caused the shooter to
flinch when he fired it. The food was still poor. Very little
cured bacon ever arrived unspoiled. Bread was either hard as
a rock or a doughy mass during humid weather. Because of
rapid deterioration in the tropics, fresh meat was scarce. As
for the dehydrated vegetables furnished in enthusiastic quantity, they had no taste to speak of. No American army has
ever complained so much and so bitterly—to each other, to
their officers, and to their families and congressmen back
home.

It remained to be seen whether the low spirits of this expeditionary force would be translated into low military effi-
ciency. Meanwhile, in other respects all was satisfactory. So-
called Hong Kong cotton khaki uniforms had replaced the
former heavy woolens. There was more than enough food,
such as it was. Against a profound scarcity of native artillery,
the Americans had ample field guns. They included 3.2-inch

breech-loading rifles and 1.65-inch mountan guns. Deadliest
of all were Gatling and Hotchkiss machine guns practically
unknown to the *insurrectos*.

All in all, the prognosis for the Philippines was unfavor-
able. In their hearts, most officials at Malolos knew that a
child could not whip a man, especially one of the world's
strongest. However disgruntled and listless it may have
seemed, the American army probably would fight very well,
if the time came. With the breakdown of the January conferences, only one slim hope remained: that the Treaty of
Paris would be rejected by the United States senate. The vote
thereon was set for Monday, February 6.

III

The news from the Philippines, filtered through the skimpy
dispatches of General Otis to the War Department, then
through the Department of State, and finally even more mea-
gerly to the White House, to congress, and to the press, was
thin gruel indeed; but its essential flavor was plain. We were
about to annex the Philippines against the wishes of its native
government (although the exact amount of support enjoyed
by that government was veiled in some obscurity); and as a
political issue all this had been a boon to the Democrats ever
since the treaty had been signed in Paris. The scorn which
they heaped upon it was not confined to the senate. In the
House young John Sharp Williams of Mississippi, a sardonic
orator, delivered a blast which evoked laughter and applause:
"We are not bound to have the Philippines! Why, six months
ago men who talk that way did not know where the Philippines are!" And concerning our alleged obligation to preserve
them from ruling themselves inadequately he sneered, "Who
made us God's globe-trotting vice-regents to forestall mis-
management everywhere?"

As January crept into history and a brave new month was

born, it was the beginning of the end of the Gay Nineties in a happy, prosperous nation. But via the Associated Press, the Filipino Junta in Hong Kong issued another of its ceaseless complaints; the ineffable Americans, it seemed, had raised the Spanish poll tax from two dollars to five dollars for the poor, and from thirty-seven to one hundred dollars for the rich. In the New York papers little had been said for weeks about the Filipino insurgents. One gets the impression that if they existed at all they were somnolent. Most of the news centered about the ratification of the treaty. Professor S. A. Knapp, just back from the Philippines as confidential agent for (quite incomprehensibly) the Department of Agriculture, confided to an Associated Press interviewer that the issue there was not at all critical. Perhaps it really was blowing over. But who on earth was Professor Knapp? In the senate debate soared to a new high of intensity. Senator Rawlins of Utah inquired if the Philippines were desired "in order to send thither swarms of office-holders, carpetbaggers, to riot among them like slimy worms, eating out their substance?" And biting words were directed by Senators Hoar and Caffery against clergymen who had been advocating a holy war to Christianize the Filipinos. How, they asked, could good come from evil, Christliness from despotism? But Senator Foraker derided arguments such as these as cheap melodrama; he announced coolly that he knew of no man who wished to acquire the islands by force against the will of their populace. That was true, in a sense; nobody wanted to take them by force if they could be taken without force.

Don Felipe Agoncillo, Mabini's minister plenipotentiary who had suffered so many slings and arrows in Paris, was now in Washington on the last leg of his lonely quest. An epic in futility, it may be summarized starkly. On January 5 he requested in writing an audience with the Secretary of State. Mr. Hay did not answer. A week later he tried again, suggesting that the menacing situation in the islands seemed to call for preventive measures. Mr. Hay did not reply. On January 24 he dispatched another note in which he pointed out that since a *de facto* state of war existed at Manila, some understanding ought to be reached quickly. Mr. Hay did not respond. He next called a press conference at which he disclosed the series of snubs for publication. A few newspapermen who checked at the State Department were told that none of Señor Agoncillo's letters had arrived there.

He next produced copies of his correspondence to Mr. Hay, but since no record of them appears in the archives of the State Department the modern reader can only guess who was lying. At any rate, most of the press turned irritably against Agoncillo as a fraud who represented a nonexistent government and was interfering in Uncle Sam's private affairs. It was even suggested, for reasons not made clear, that he be arrested; and after addressing one last protest to the Secretary of State for transmission to the senate (it was not transmitted), the frustrated Filipino entrained for Montreal on February 3. It was, no doubt, a coincidence that he left the country that particular evening.

IV

Ever since the declaration of war against Spain, William Jennings Bryan had been in assorted difficulties. A dedicated pacifist, he had first joined the army as a private. Having recently run for the presidency of the United States, he and his gesture were laughed at. Commissioned a colonel in command of the 3rd Nebraskans, he was next assailed for accepting such a post and amateurishly endangering the lives of his men. (A picture of him taken at a training camp lends some support to the thesis: in his tight uniform and long hair he looks nothing like any soldier who ever lived.) When he resigned from the army in order to oppose the Paris treaty, the newspapers derided him for cowardice in the face of the

Filipinos. Everything he did was wrong; he would rather be wrong than be president, it was said.

His next move, which had an effect upon both the Philippine Islands and the United States which may be fairly described as unparalleled, was to descend upon Washington to instruct his people to vote in favor of the Treaty of Paris. "It will be easier, I think, to end the war at once by ratifying the treaty, and then deal with the subject our own way," he observed. Consternation followed. Senator Pettigrew accused him to his face of rank hypocrisy. Mr. Bryan did not understand. He explained blandly that his intention was to saddle the Republicans with a *fait accompli* which would ruin them at the polls in 1900. Members of his party begged him to fold his tent and silently steal away before he consummated a political catastrophe; but Bryan stayed on, and before returning to Omaha persuaded several Democrats to vote for ratification. His reasoning combined fact with fantasy. Free silver as an issue was dead; it would never get him into the White House. He also calculated that ratifying the treaty would not bind us to hold the islands but would merely sever them from Spain, and after that we would surely let them go. An integral part of his plan, therefore, was an amendment (which he concocted with Senator Bacon) along the lines of Senator Teller's masterpiece concerning Cuba.

It was, all in all, one of the most pathetic thrusts in American political history. The Washington correspondent of the Boston *Globe* reported that Mr. Bryan had been amazed at the favorable reception to McKinley's expansionist speeches: "It is believed here that Mr. Bryan saw the handwriting on the wall, interpreted it correctly, and as a result advised Democrats of the Senate not to oppose ratification." Another factor of importance was that he did not foresee the impending new Filipino insurrection, which, through one of the ceaseless ironies of history, would be touched off by a regiment of his own state. He sympathized with hundreds of Nebraska wives and parents who were beseeching him to get their menfolk home. Thus he had several reasons for affirming the treaty; unfortunately, they were not good ones and a false thread ran through them that anyone could see. "One word from Mr. Bryan would have saved the country from disaster," wrote Andrew Carnegie, who was also in Washington, but for opposite purposes. "I could not be cordial to him for years afterward . . . a man who was willing to sacrifice his country and his personal convictions for party advantage."

How many votes Bryan swayed is uncertain, but it is a fact that by the first week of February the treaty was still a single vote short of the needed two-thirds majority. Had the Great Commoner's move failed? Yet Henry Lodge felt sure that over the weekend he could induce at least two senators, who were sitting on the fence, to climb down on his side. And, at any rate, "They'se wan consolation," Finley Peter Dunne summed up; "an' that is, if th' American people can govern thimsilves, they can govern anything that walks." And from London, the magazine *Truth* addressed to this country a cheery warning widely reprinted in newspapers hostile to the annexationist cause:

> We wish you much joy of the islands
> Which you have so easily won.
> But the troublesome part of the business
> Has only, we fear, just begun.
> You will find how exceedingly ungrateful
> Your new fellow subjects can be,
> Compelling you even to shoot them
> Before they consent to be free.

In sorrow and anger the last words of debate were uttered. Senator Platt painted a harrowing picture of the results which would follow if U.S. troops were to be withdrawn abruptly from Manila. What would the Filipinos do, anxiously asked Mr. Joseph Choate (soon to be ambassador to Britain) if we pulled out? In reply Speaker Reed drawled, "Well, I don't suppose they would pursue us farther than

San Francisco." Senator Lodge had been unusually busy behind the scenes, but shortly before the day of decision he
arose to deliver one of his most compelling addresses. The
anti-imperialists, he said, had chosen to peg their arguments
on the highest possible moral level. He would therefore meet
them there and would say nothing about the commercial advantages of acquisition. He would speak only of facts, logic,
and the simplest of international proprieties:

> In our war with Spain we conquered the Philippines, or, to
> put it more exactly, we destroyed the power of Spain in those
> islands.

Let us suppose, he said, that the senate does decide to ratify
the Treaty of Paris.

> The Islands pass from the possession of Spain into our pos-
> session without committing us to any policy. I believe we can
> be trusted as a people to deal honestly and justly with the
> islands and their inhabitants thus given to our care.

Now assume that the treaty is rejected, or that the clause relating to the Philippines is stricken out.

> That will hand the Islands back to Spain, and I cannot con-
> ceive that any American should be willing to do that. Sup-
> pose we reject the treaty, what follows? Let us look at it
> practically. We continue the state of war . . . we repudiate
> the President and his actions before the whole world, and the
> repudiation of the President . . . brands us as a people in-
> capable of treating affairs or of taking rank where we belong
> as one of the greatest of the world powers.

It was a majestic effort and a final one. By Friday, February 3, the tumult and the shouting were over; nothing else,
it seemed, could affect Monday's outcome; and the New York
Times complacently reported:

MANILA NEWS NOT ALARMING

Otis and Dewey Believed to be Able
To Control the Situation

That morning the stock exchange, for some reason, went through a period verging on the panic stage, but closed strong after irregular trading. The Los Angeles *Times* in a little editorial remarked, "The auto-mobile vehicle has passed the test of practicability. It is a mechanical success." And concerning the peace treaty:

JUST A VOTE SHORT

PEACE TREATY'S FRIENDS NEED MORE
THAN FAITH

They Have a Feeling of Renewed Confidence,
But the Basis of It is Not Plain

The members of congress recessed until Monday. Silence settled over the halls and offices and cloakrooms of the capitol. Mr. and Mrs. McKinley retired early, as was their custom, while the homes of many legislators were hubbubs of preparation for Saturday-night parties. From coast to coast the nation settled down for a normal weekend.

V

In Luzon, too, conditions seemed relatively normal, considering the chronically deplorable relations which had been existing there for some time. Generals Noriel and Ricarte were away on leave. Only General Pantaleon Garcia, among the higher officers stationed near Manila, was at his post some ten miles to the north of the capital. Colonel Cailles was attending a private party that evening. No special alert orders were in effect. General Luna, director of war, was far distant in San Fernando, Pampanga Province. Colonel San Miguel, commanding insurgent troops facing the 1st Nebraska Volunteers to the east of Manila, seems to have been in Malolos.

The Nebraskans had recently moved from barracks in the damp Binondo district to high, sandy ground near Santa

Mesa where, it was hoped, the healthier climate would alleviate the regiment's unusually high sick rate. It was commanded by a young, tough West Pointer named Colonel Stotsenburg, who had been warned by General MacArthur that his position was extremely exposed and more vulnerable to attack than any other along the American perimeter. Nonetheless the former had lately advanced his outpost a trifle and had been having especially vehement arguments with Colonel San Miguel during the past few days. Late in January he had called for additional artillery, and two guns of the Utah battery had been emplaced three hundred yards behind the San Juan Bridge.

On the warm, moonless evening of February 4, at eight-thirty, Privates Grayson and Miller, on patrol near their regimental outpost, had cautiously worked their way into the advance area as far as the bridge when they heard a Filipino signal-whistle on their left. It was answered by another from the right. Directly ahead, from the native blockhouse designated as Number Seven, a red lantern unaccountably flashed. The two Americans froze. Four Filipinos loomed up on the dirt road. "Halt!" Grayson shouted. The natives stopped. *"Halto!"* replied their lieutenant derisively . . .

9

THE
FIRST
SHOCK

ALL AMERICAN TROOPS NORTH AND WEST OF THE PASIG-SAN
Juan river conjunction were commanded by General
MacArthur; and except for elements of the 3rd Regular Artillery (fighting as infantry), this 2nd Division was
composed entirely of volunteers. From west flank to east in
a four-mile arc that rested on Manila Bay, these regiments
were the 20th Kansas, the 3rd Artillery, the 1st Montana, the
10th Pennsylvania, the 1st South Dakota, the 1st Colorado,
and the 1st Nebraska encamped in the San Juan River bend—
of which last unit Private Grayson was now the most noteworthy member.

The disposition of Filipino forces has never been ascertained with certainty. Colonel San Miguel, as we have seen,
was definitely the local commander in the Santa Mesa area
where the first shots were fired. General Pantaleon Garcia
seems to have been in command on San Miguel's right, and
may have been the colonel's superior. General Luna himself
had taken over the entire northern defense tier, featured by
seventeen former Spanish blockhouses and a maze of new
and old trenches. In the Santa Ana area, insurgent forces

were led by the rather unsavory General Pio del Pilar; both
he and the bulk of his men were suspected of having been
former bandits (*ladrones*) in Manila province. Covering his
left near Pasay were some five thousand riflemen and bolomen probably under Generals Mariano Noriel and Artinio
Ricardo, neither of whom was then at the front.

In the bay slumbered Dewey's warships, lately reinforced
by the ironclad *Monadnock* and her murderous ten-inch
guns. Otis and the admiral had already worked out arrangements for bringing fleet units within a half-mile of the shoreline to enfilade insurgent lines north of Tondo and south of
the San Antonio fort. Within Manila proper, provost guards
were reasonably prepared for sabotage, arson, and armed uprising. At the front, junior American officers knew by heart
the detailed defensive plan issued from headquarters—"The
Palace," as it was called. The *Laguna de Bay,* an ex-Spanish
riverboat which had been armor-plated, was warped to her
berth near the mouth of the Pasig. Under the command of
former steamboat skipper Captain Grant of the Utah Artillery, she carried two three-inch guns, two 1.65 Hotchkiss revolving cannon, a few Gatlings, and sixty infantrymen who
were able to fire from her deck behind armor protection. This
remarkable contraption ("a formidable and ugly-looking
craft," General Otis affectionately called her) drew only four
feet of water, could cruise unopposed up and down the Pasig,
and was considered worth a regiment of infantry. General
plans had been worked out for offensive operations. Two key
objectives were the waterworks eight miles to the east and
rebel headquarters at Malolos. The feeling was that, if war
came, two violent blows by MacArthur and Anderson respectively would end it quickly.

There is no evidence that the Filipinos, on the other hand,
had evolved any scheme beyond that of merely holding their
positions, creating an uproar within the capital, and charg-
ing the American line at random. Their trenches and blockhouses were half-empty. A throng of half-naked Igorrotes,
armed with bows and arrows, had been given "the post of

honor" opposite the Utah Battery. In little nipa-hut villages that dotted the plain, *insurrectos* dozed, talked, and oiled their guns. Galvanized by the initial firing near Pandacan, they rushed to the front.

The Americans also moving forward, mostly youngsters in their late teens who had never seen a battle, were silent and tense. Like a wave that breaks diagonally against a curving shore, the roar of small-arms fire had meanwhile spread from the Nebraskans westward to the Kansans under Colonel Frederick Funston near the waterfront. Two insurgent Krupp guns opened up. Within a few minutes MacArthur's entire command was engaged; but with both sides firing only at each other's rifle flashes casualties were few. Now the Utah field pieces began to pound enemy positions east of the Chinese cemetery. Even in the chaos, Mauser bullets could be heard spatting into the nipa shacks and bamboo thickets, while the ancient Springfields roared and set the night aflame with enormous muzzle flashes. Already the striking power of their heavy, slow-moving slugs had awed the natives, and many a head had been nearly torn off at impact. The first Filipino charge—a headlong dash against the 10th Pennsylvanians—took place shortly after nine o'clock. The picket line wavered, and reinforcements hurrying into position almost failed to close a gap which had been temporarily opened. An hour later the insurgents tried again in the same sector and were thrown back more easily.

There were no more massed assaults until 4 A.M., when Colonel Stotsenburg of the Nebraska volunteers telegraphed that his unit was nearly surrounded and needed help. At that moment, a third enemy attempt to cross the Santa Mesa stone bridge was being barely stopped. When reinforcements arrived, the crisis was over. A native officer there wired his superiors in Malolos: "No change; everyone is holding his post with enthusiasm. The second zone continues silent. I hope for orders." All night long rifle exchanges continued and occasional light attacks were driven off by Americans holding their outposts by firing blindly into the blackness. Gradually the shooting subsided. Breakfast and coffee were brought forward as a brilliant sun climbed out of the eastern hills and stared upon a hushed, motionless, almost idyllic scene.

The first phase of the first battle in what was to be the bloodiest conflict in Philippine history, including World War II, was over. As yet neither side had advanced its line; nothing of much importance had happened; and despite the expenditure of some two million rounds of rifle ammunition hardly anyone had been killed or wounded.

II

Over the centuries, fighting between Filipinos and Spaniards had followed a fairly set pattern, in that the engagements (raids would be a more accurate word) usually occurred at night, with both sides retiring at daybreak. The natives were therefore astounded to find themselves under attack on Sunday morning, February 5, by the 3.2 guns of the Utah Battery, which had been hauled up to the outpost line to shell the blockhouses facing MacArthur's right. Behind this modest barrage, the Nebraskans, Coloradans, and South Dakotans swept forward across the river, chased the natives into the hills, and captured the water reservoir. Now the Nebraskans pivoted south along the east bank of the Pasig and stormed their way to a point just opposite Santa Ana. It was all over by late morning, and this fact, more than the ground captured or casualties inflicted, was especially significant from an insurgent standpoint. The Americans were aggressive and they moved fast.

Elated and perhaps surprised at the ease with which affairs had proceeded thus far, MacArthur committed the rest of his force at noon. This time the story was somewhat different, for the terrain better suited the defense and the area was dominated by strong enemy forces entrenched on La Loma Hill. Two miles of broken, swampy country sloped toward it; at its base lay a large cemetery crisscrossed by barbed-wire fences and exasperatingly dotted by thousands of headstones. Atop the hill the Filipinos had converted two stone churches—Chinese and Catholic—into fortresses; and near them they had emplaced a few muzzle-loading cannon. After a brief bombardment by the Utah guns, the Pennsylvanians, Montanans, and 3rd Artillery moved ahead cautiously. The last regiment, bogged in a morass, suffered twenty-five casualties before even reaching the cemetery. Meanwhile the Pennsylvanians, swept by a torrent of fire from the Chinese church, were also going down in substantial numbers. For two hours they and the Montanans were stopped, until the regulars on their left swarmed up the hill from the east and occupied both churches.

During these operations, which indicated that the war might, after all, assume a serious aspect, the Kansans under Funston were working their way through a bamboo jungle under covering fire from the *Charleston* and *Callao*. Short of the Lico Road they halted. "It was an impossible situation," wrote the Colonel. "The enemy in his excellent trenches were [*sic*] pouring into us a fire that we could not hope to overcome by merely firing back at him." He decided to charge the position with bayonets. The five companies, stumbling and jogging along west of the railway, closed with the enemy and forced him back in a panic. Most native dead had taken bullets in the head, as they stood up in their trenches. The majority of wounded had been carried away by retreating comrades.

As the survivors fled with their wounded, the Kansans pursued them for two miles. It was an old picture: white men efficiently pumping bullets into the backs of little brown men floundering through the underbrush in search of cover. Belatedly Funston now advised his brigade commander where he was and why his command had exceeded its assigned objective. He was told to fall back to the Lico Road. In so doing, this regiment came under fire from the *Concord,* which had just relieved the *Charleston;* but no one was hit, and by late afternoon a talkative, exhilarated body of foot soldiers was munching hardtack and bacon and preparing to bivouac for the night.

The volunteers had proved themselves, and MacArthur's division had done an excellent day's work. By nightfall the new front had been shoved slightly ahead of the old line of Spanish blockhouses. General José Alexandrino, hurrying down from Malolos, was met by General Luna. For once the latter's harsh, contemptuous demeanor had deserted him. "Our enemies are too strong!" he burst out. His own northern line, which he had drilled, inspected, and exhorted personally for weeks, had nearly collapsed; and for a brief period his nerve did the same. Was this to be the pattern of the new war? Were the Americans so much stronger than their predecessors, the Spaniards, that resistance might be hopeless? A chill of apprehension touched the Filipino hierarchy. And the news from the south was even worse.

In contrast to MacArthur's command, almost half of General Thomas Anderson's First Division was composed of regular army personnel. Running in a quarter-circle from Fort San Antonio Abad on the waterfront through Pandacan, they were the 1st North Dakota volunteers, the 14th Regular Infantry, the 1st California volunteers, the 4th Regular Cavalry (dismounted), the 1st Idaho volunteers, two batteries of the 6th Regular Artillery, the 1st Washington volunteers, and one battalion of the 1st Wyoming regulars. Except for a few random shots fired back and forth, this division had played no part in the evening's events. At 7:48 Otis telegraphed Anderson to attack, cautioning him not to advance too far, and to look out for his flanks and the *Monadnock.* Along with lesser craft, the monitor steamed slowly to a point opposite Panay during the early morning hours. When the advance began at 8 A.M. Sunday morning, using brand-new telescopic sights she began firing her ten- and four-inch guns and rapid-fire weapons just ahead of the American line, the forward position of which was constantly indicated by a red flag. The five-hundred-pound shells crashed into positions occupied by the natives and stunned them. They had never experienced anything like it; and long before the North Dakotans arrived they had begun pouring out of their trenches and barricades. In hot pursuit along the beach, the Dakotans also found themselves under fire from the ironclad. They dived for cover while frantic shore-to-ship signals fluttered, and then continued their advance.

Anderson's center had encountered problems caused by heavy vegetation along its line of march, but as the day wore on a ragged line was established through Pasay and San Pedro Macati, a suburb four miles southeast of the Old City. It was on Anderson's left, where Washington and Idaho volunteers converged for an attack against Pio del Pilar's arrogant and hated troops, that the most devastating blow was struck. What ensued makes it clear that insurgent officers were not tactically capable of dealing with the Americans in an orthodox frontal engagement.

With cowboy and Civil War rebel yells, the volunteers burst out of Pandacan, dislodged the insurgents from their trenches, and hustled them against the Pasig. Del Pilar had never expected to retreat, nor had his men, and suddenly they were trapped. Their natural impulse was to swim back across the river. The usual story handed down since that day was that it was like shooting fish in a barrel. The volunteers, most of whom had been marksmen since boyhood on the plains and mountains of their western states, thronged the west bank of the river and leisurely selected their targets. By ten o'clock the episode was over, the river was pink with Filipino blood, and del Pilar's brigade had been virtually wiped out. This is why the Nebraskans, arriving somewhat later, found such negligible resistance to their swing southward after crossing that stream, and why it was possible for the

Californians to capture Santa Ana and San Pedro Macati with so little difficulty. In so doing, they also fell upon several tons of rice, over thirty thousand cartridges, eight cannon, and seventy-eight rifles—all of which had been incredibly stockpiled less than a mile behind the front. During all these events, Anderson's center and left flank had been assisted by the *Laguna de Bay*, which had demoralized and dislodged the insurgents whenever she steamed past their positions, firing like a demon.

And if the battle had gone badly for the Filipinos at the front, the Sandatahan were thwarted by the provost guards and accomplished very little behind the U.S. lines. Along with about a hundred Filipinos who had infiltrated the fighting zone, they managed to fire portions of the New City and kept cutting the fire hoses. Six men caught doing this were shot on the spot. Bamboo thickets around the suburbs were touched off several times, and fire-fighting Americans silhouetted against the flames were sniped at and occasionally hit. Sniping fire from within part of the Paco district became so intense, in fact, that all nipa huts there had to be burned down. Fifty-three unarmed civilians innocently emerged. A hundred more were dislodged from the Paco Church by artillery fire which necessarily demolished that structure. Over fifty natives, all in all, were killed in the Manila area, and several hundred captured to await army trial.

For twenty-four hours between 8 P.M. on February 4 and 5 respectively, Manila was a city gripped by hysteria and resounding with clamor. It burned in all directions, and only the lack of wind prevented a real catastrophe. In the Oriente Hotel wives of American officers bolted their doors and in small, white-faced groups prepared for the worst. At street corners trigger-happy American sentries challenged everything that walked and each carriage which clattered by. All British residents in Santa Ana had congregated in one house, and throughout the evening the men shielded the bodies of the women while bullets whipped through the walls and wounded soldiers groaned outside. Later that day, when the Americans occupied the place, one Englishman commented ingenuously to a U.S. officer concerning Dewey's part in the fight: "This is not war; it is simple massacre and murderous butchery. How can these men resist your ships?"

"The Filipinos have swollen heads; they only need one licking," was the reply; "and they will go crying to their homes, or we shall drive them into the sea, within the next three days."

There was some looting on the part of all nationalities concerned, especially the Chinese residents, who were neutral and entertained the least possible affection for both sides. Many *barrios* were set afire for no good reason by excited American troops, causing General Otis to issue an order which read, "The burning or looting of houses . . . the abuse of unarmed citizens . . . will be punished with the utmost severity known to military law. Individual soldiers detected . . . will be promptly arrested, and in case they attempt to escape will be shot." In the fires and pandemonium the timid water buffalo went wild, and no power could hold them back. They ran blindly into buildings, picked themselves up dazedly, and charged again. By dusk, many of them had found refuge in the bay and rivers; there they stood, with only their noses showing, until the city was quiet.

Late in the day Admiral Dewey, on the *Olympia,* finally found time to scrawl out for cable transmission the following message, which arrived at 8:05 Sunday morning, February 5, Washington time:

> Secretary of the Navy, Washington:
> Insurgents have inaugurated general engagement yesterday night which is continued today. The American Army and Navy is generally successful. Insurgents have been driven back and our line advanced. No casualties to Navy. In view of this and possible future expenditure request ammunition requisition doubled.
>
> DEWEY

And subsequently from Otis to the War Department:

> Action continues since early morning. Losses quite heavy.
> Lines badly cut at first. Communications now satisfactory. Ev-
> erything favorable to our arms.

American casualties had been 59 killed and 278 wounded.
A writer in the *Independent* estimated Filipino losses as high
as five thousand. An infantry officer, Frederick Herman, put
the figure at five hundred. General Otis reported that his own
men had buried seven hundred of the enemy on the field, and
thought their total casualties came to about three thousand.
It is now known that some field commanders had exaggerated
their reports. For reasons mentioned earlier, however, it is
certain that the natives proportionally suffered far less
wounded than the Americans—probably not many more than
those killed outright. A fair guess would be that casualties
went against the insurgents four or five to one. In any event
it was clear that they had taken a serious beating and that
projecting the figures forward indicated a short, sharp war
of subjugation surely ending before the rainy season.

III

The news of the outbreak of still another war, so close upon
the heels of the Spanish conflict, came as a bitter, anti-
climactic shock to the American people, if the newspapers of
the day accurately reflected public opinion. It was really going too far; there was a limit even to America's patience.
Since the Filipinos had started it, they, cried the Washington
Star, "must be taught obedience and must be forced to observe, even if they cannot comprehend, the practices of civilization." It was maddening to contemplate yet another
military campaign in the tropics, but what else was to be
done? Our prestige was at stake; the islands had to be pacified. Even many newspapers favoring Philippine independ-

ence agreed that since we had been attacked ("as wanton,
wilful, and gross a violation of law as was ever committed,"
in Senator Spooner's words), we had no choice but to restore
order by force.

Upon hearing the news, Mr. Bryan observed maliciously
that destiny was no longer as manifest as it had recently
seemed. But the New York *Times* was furious:

> The Filipinos have chosen a bloody way to demonstrate their
> incapacity for self-government . . . the insane attack of these
> people upon their liberators . . . To commit to their unsteady
> hands and childish minds political powers . . . would be to
> give a dynamite cartridge to a baby for a plaything.

Fortunately:

> It is not likely that Aguinaldo himself will exhibit much stay-
> ing power . . . It seems probable that after one or two col-
> lisions the insurgent army will break up.

As for "Aguinaldo's Allies in Boston," who were demanding
the immediate cessation of hostilities:

> The Anti-Imperialist League might go one step further. It
> might send rifles, Maxim guns, and stores of ammunition to
> the Filipinos . . . it would be more openly and frankly
> treasonable.

Sixty years later one finds it hard to believe that the editorial
columns of the *Times* could employ language such as this:

> . . . these babes of the jungle from Aguinaldo down . . . are
> veritable children. They show the weaknesses and the vices of
> the resourceless and unmoral human infant. Aguinaldo is a
> vain popinjay, a wicked liar, and a perfectly incapable leader.
> His men are dupes, a foolish, incredulous mob.

It was not then known that the fighting had started in an
area (Pandacan) which, by General Otis' prior admission to
Aguinaldo, was beyond the city's suburbs. Thus, in a sense,
American troops were there unlawfully. (Not until some

months later was Private William Grayson to utter his much-publicized remark that it was "the damned bull-headedness" of his officers in encroaching upon insurgent territory which had led to the shooting.) From Montreal, Señor Agoncillo pointed out to an Associated Press correspondent that since many Filipino troops and officers had been captured in Manila theatres after the outbreak it seemed hardly likely that their side had instigated the attack. And in the senate, after the Monday-morning headlines had jarred the nation like so many thunderclaps, gray-haired old Ben Tillman of South Carolina gave voice to a thought which was already haunting some minds. Was it happenstance that war had started just before the final vote on the treaty? "Time alone will tell whether this battle was provoked by the Filipinos . . . or by the Americans for the purpose of endeavoring to sway men in this Senate."

The inference was preposterous, unworthy; and even as the senator spoke a few of his colleagues were subjecting their former stand to an agonizing reappraisal. Who could have dreamed that the insurgents would reply to "our mercy with a Mauser," to use the startled words of President McKinley? It was, in truth, an "insult." "The dignity of the government" had been bruised, and those responsible had to be "thoroughly thrashed." In this vein the Salt Lake *Tribune* suggested that these "misguided creatures" needed "their eyes bathed enough in blood to cause their visions to be cleared." The end result, intoned the Reverend Doctor Dix, was so beatific that it had to be achieved peacefully if possible, but by the sword if necessary. Since war was already raging, his advice seems somewhat belated. Representative Brosius simply called the process "rough surgery."

Even as debate resounded in congress hour after hour, extra after extra was pouring off the nation's presses, black with headlines both soothing and stirring to the patriotic reader . . .

OUR TROOPS ARE STEADILY ADVANCING AGAINST THE FILIPINOS

GENERAL OTIS HAS THE SITUATION WELL UNDER CONTROL

GENERAL OTIS THINKS THERE IS NO DOUBT ABOUT HIS
SUBJUGATING THE FILIPINOS AFTER AWHILE

THERE WAS ON YESTERDAY A SHARP ENGAGEMENT BETWEEN
OUR TROOPS AND THE FILIPINOS, WE LOST FIFTY MEN,
THE FILIPINOS LOST HEAVILY, BUT NUMBER UNKNOWN

GENERAL OTIS IS PREPARING TO MAKE A MORE VIGOROUS
ONSLAUGHT AGAINST THE STUBBORN FILIPINOS

It was against this background—a potpourri of amazement,
wounded pride, martial spirit, and resentment—that the afternoon showdown vote on ratification approached. Senator
McEnery of Louisiana introduced a resolution which would
not bind the U.S. to offer citizenship to the Filipinos, since
we did not intend to annex their islands permanently but "in
due time" to dispose of them in the best interests of both
nations. Hooted down by Bacon and Hoar as a veiled annexation scheme with the added intent of shielding Louisiana
sugar-growers from Philippine competition, it was tabled.
Senator Gray had retreated in full cry from earlier principles.
Now that the Filipinos were shooting at us, he exclaimed,
concessions or retreat were out of the question. The treaty
which he had helped forge must be ratified if only to give
them the great boon of liberty. Liberty? sneered Thomas
Reed. We were merely buying ten million people at two dollars per head. And the early afternoon hours slipped by.

At two-thirty, one doubtful senator joined those of the
wider outlook. Five minutes before the hour another moved
hesitantly into Mr. Lodge's camp. The roll call was taken at
three o'clock sharp. Of eighty-four senators voting, fifty-
seven said "yea"—one more than the required two-thirds. The
war of words, if nothing else, was ended. "Until the fight was
over," Mr. Lodge wrote Theodore, "I did not realize what a
strain it had been, but for half an hour after the vote was an-

nounced I felt exactly as if I had been struggling up the side of a mountain . . ." The Republican majority (minus only Hoar of Massachusetts and Hale of Maine) had been joined by fifteen assorted Democrats, Populists, and Independents. "It was the hardest, closest fight I have ever known, and probably we shall not see another in our time where there was so much at stake." This was perhaps true, although not in the sense that Mr. Lodge intended; and he continued, "We were down in the engine room and do not get flowers, but we did make the ship move." To give credit where due, he might also have cited Private Grayson and William Jennings Bryan. Yet it had been a close call, and the senator was rightly proud of his generalship. A carping person might have pointed out, however, that his dice were loaded. The treaty was all or nothing. To decline the Philippines was to kill the treaty, and this the upper house was unwilling to do. Everyone, including Henry Lodge, knew that if the key issue could have been voted upon alone the islands would have been set free. "There is something deeply pathetic in today's telegram," observed the Singapore *Free Press*. "The steed having been stolen, the American Senate locks the stable door."

A few days later, Senator Bacon brought forth his resolution—perhaps one of the more fateful in blood and treasure acted upon by the congress of the United States—to the effect that we would transfer control of the Philippine Islands to the natives as soon as they demonstrated the efficacy of their own government. A 29–29 deadlock resulted. Vice-President Garret A. Hobart, a man otherwise lost to posterity, killed it by a casting vote. Next the McEnery joint resolution was dusted off and again put to the test. It passed by a lackluster 26–22 margin, with almost half the senators abstaining. The margin by which Senator Bacon had been defeated indicates that the Philippine clause could not have stood on its own feet under the two-thirds rule. The manner in which the McEnery amendment was passed is similarly noteworthy, including the further fact that the House re-

232   LITTLE BROWN BROTHER

jected it. Complicated by extraneous factors, perhaps una-
voidably so, the essential fact was nonetheless inescapably
plain, and was so stated by Charles Denby, the most forthright member of McKinley's Philippine Commission, in the
February 1899 *Forum:*

> . . . the cold, hard, practical question alone remains. Will the
> possession of these islands benefit us as a nation? If it will
> not, set them free tomorrow, and let their people, if they
> please, cut each others' throats . . .

IV

Military extremists among the Filipinos may have welcomed the outbreak, but others—especially responsible civilians—were exceedingly alarmed and wished to nip it in the
bud. It fell to Judge Florentino Torres of Manila, who had
been a member of the recent Filipino negotiating commission, to make peace overtures. On Sunday evening, February
5, he was received by General Otis at U.S. headquarters.
The fighting had begun accidentally, he said, and Aguinaldo
was willing to end it. He suggested an armistice and the establishment of a neutral zone between the armies, of any
width General Otis might desire, during the peace negotiations.

Otis, in the words of his provost marshall, General Reeve,
"sternly replied that the fighting having once begun must go
on to the grim end."

Torres, somewhat nonplussed, next asked permission to
send a certain Colonel Arguelles to Malolos further to sound
out Aguinaldo and Mabini. Otis agreed, and Arguelles was
passed through the American lines next morning. At Malolos
the colonel was told by the two top Filipinos that they had
no objections to negotiations and an armistice. He returned
to Otis with this overture. The general's response is summarized by his dispatch to Washington dated February 8:

"His [Aguinaldo's] influence throughout this section destroyed. Now applies for cessation of hostilities and conference. Have declined to answer."* After this rebuff, the war got under way in earnest.

The broad plains of northern Luzon comprise a fertile farmland worked by thousands of peasants who ship their excess produce mainly to Manila by road or rail. To throttle such traffic, to close quickly and on level ground with the enemy, to utilize the roads and Manila-Dagupan railway for military transport, the American high command from the beginning made this smooth, rolling basin the primary theatre of war. The first requirement was to capture Caloocan, several miles north of the capital, in which were located railway maintenance shops, roundhouses, and rolling stock. MacArthur moved against it on February 10 after a heavy bombardment of insurgent lines by the *Monadnock*.

Observers from La Loma hill were treated to a textbook military operation. On the swampy left the Kansans pushed around the insurgent flank, while on the center and right other regiments, deployed in a long line of squads, could clearly be seen (as in a child's picture book) moving fanwise against the pleasant little tree-filled town. Major Jones of the quartermaster department stood out dramatically, riding his horse (against orders) at the head of the 3rd Artillery firing line. "These fellows can't shoot!" he kept shouting exuberantly. "As long as they aim at us, we are all right." Amid din and smoke which resembled a forest fire, the insurgents found themselves outflanked and began to retire. The Americans entering the outskirts, firing and shouting as they scrambled along, found heaps of Filipinos dead in trenches and along the roads. With a rush, they entered the heart of the village, captured the old stone church, and began routing the enemy out of house after house. Later, Captain William Bishop of the Kansans was charged with killing unarmed cap-

* Under Senate interrogation, he later referred to his cable as "hasty" and "misleading."

tives taken during these actions; it was to be the first in a
depressing series of similar charges.* What with Americans
burning the nipa huts to dislodge sharpshooters and the insurgents firing the town on general principles, there was very
little left of Caloocan by late afternoon. Officers galloped
through the fiery main street with their faces covered. Bamboo huts and branches burst and crackled like rifle reports.
Back in Manila that evening after a long, thrilling day with
the forward troops, Mr. Bass wrote, "Homeless dogs ran
howling through the streets. Motherless broods of chickens
peeped helplessly. As we rode back to town over the battle-
field, the doctors were still wandering about in the darkness,
calling into the night from time to time to make sure that
they had left no wounded on the field." This was a kind of
war which no one in the islands had anticipated. With
Caloocan taken, the U.S. left flank now swerved upward in a
northwesterly direction along the bay.

The remorseless tide of victory early that week also continued south and east of the capital. The water pumping
station, a vital target, was captured after a sudden attack led
by Colonel Stotsenburg. Unfathomably the insurgents had
left it intact except for cylinder heads and piston rods. When
these parts were found hidden in a coal pile, the pumps were
put to work again. To the south the California volunteers
had pushed far past Santa Ana to the small town of Pasig.
There they sat, out of touch with the rest of their division
and under heavy fire from reinforced Filipino troops, until
Otis insisted that they return to Santa Ana before being cut
off.

These various actions early in February were characterized by a pattern not clear to American commanders at the
time, but which had been an ancient story to Spain. The

---

* Bishop denied the charge and was backed by Otis. But Colonel Crowder
(later Judge Advocate General of the Army) endorsed the Otis report thus:
"I am not convinced . . . that Private Brenner has made a false charge against
Captain Bishop . . . [however] considerations of public policy . . . require
that no further action be taken in this case."

white troops of the western powers had won, it seemed, large and decisive victories. They had driven the natives away from Manila and (so ran the communiqués) had slaughtered them in vast numbers. The latter were apparently demoralized, penniless, and without sufficient armament to continue resisting. The Spaniards, however, sensed that it was the end of the beginning rather than vice versa. If asked, Spanish officers in Manila might have told Otis and his staff that they had been winning victories of this type since 1551. They could have predicted that before the native dream of independence could be thoroughly crushed a massive campaign would have to be instituted not only in central Luzon but throughout the archipelago. They could have reminded Otis that the Filipinos were accustomed to formal defeats, but that they could recover and reorganize quickly, and that under Emilio Aguinaldo they had a leader with infinite patience, total support of the peasantry, and an affinity for harassing operations.

The Americans did not consult the cynical Spanish officers still in Manila; and with the valor of ignorance Otis now commenced a series of attacks preliminary to his plan of swallowing the *insurrecto* force in Luzon. As yet the hopelessness of such tactics and the impossibility of surrounding the shifting, mobile native army (which could move twice as fast as the Americans) had not dawned upon the phlegmatic commander in "The Palace." All winter and spring his battalions, like tenuous threads of chromatin, advanced while the natives retreated, so that by summer the United States army held several outposts far from its original Manila nucleus.

At last General Marcus Miller received orders from Otis to capture Iloilo in co-ordination with the navy. While preparing to disembark his men, he was astonished to hear shells from the *Petrel* and *Baltimore* crashing into the town. Before he could get a man ashore the marines had landed, the insurgents had set fire to the outskirts, sailors had captured the fort and hoisted the Stars and Stripes, and it was all over.

"No arrangement or agreement with the senior officer of the Navy," he reported icily, "was made that he should open the attack without conferring with me." After the two branches of service had co-operated in saving about half the city from going up in flames, a military garrison was established. Completely surrounded on land by a Tagalog force, it resembled a miniature Manila ante bellum.

A newcomer to the Philippines who had commanded a portion of the southern line during the February 5 fighting, Brigadier General Lloyd Wheaton was assigned the task of clearing the area immediately south of Manila, where insurgent harassing fire had been mounting in volume during February and March. This gaunt, black-bearded, cloaked, long-legged Civil War veteran had won the Congressional Medal of Honor in 1864 and had spent twenty-five years as a captain in the Regular Army. Despite his temporary rank as brigadier general of volunteers, his military mentality was still that of a company officer. He was seldom seen anywhere but at the front lines. The fighting thus far had established him as the leading theatrical personality of the U.S. high command, both in appearance and in the booming cadence of his language. In the rice paddies around Manila he had risen among his crouching men like an elongated ghost. "Action!" he screamed. "Step out! Do you think those —— —— will wait to give you a fight? Be hounds, not snails! Catch 'em!"—and so on. Like Otis, he had insomnia and kept awakening his staff for conferences in the dead of night. Once at 2 A.M., after a dismal breakfast, one officer ventured to ask, "What are we to do now?" Wheaton roared, "Stay awake, dammit, what are soldiers for?" On another occasion a correspondent remarked during mess, "But one thing we will all admit, General, the Filipinos are brave." Wheaton slammed his fist on the table. "Brave! Brave! Damn 'em, they won't stand up to be shot!"

A provisional brigade under his command—"Wheaton's Flying Column"—moved southeast from Manila along the

Pasig River on March 10. Within a week it had reached the
Laguna de Bay Lake, twenty miles from Manila, and had
opened the full length of the Pasig to traffic. After the expedition had burned all villages on the west bank of the lake, detachments of the 1st Washington volunteers were left behind
to nail down the three largest towns, while the rest of
Wheaton's force returned to Manila. Again what had been
accomplished was not clear, for overnight these points also
became little more than islands in a hostile sea, attached to
the capital by a single line of communication. And Mr. Bass
wrote:

> In this region the road along the lake is lined continuously
> with houses, where stores of rice were found. For four or five
> miles along this road we burned the houses and stores of rice.
> It was a very desolate picture as I rode between the charred
> ruins of former homes. Nearly all the people had fled. Occa-
> sionally a woman with her children or an old man sat dis-
> consolately near a heap of smouldering ashes; as I rode
> through mile after mile of this desolation the conclusion
> forced itself upon me that our government, with its weak,
> vacillating policy and want of tact, and Aguinaldo and his
> followers, with their nagging trickiness and their misrepre-
> sentations of our every act, would both be called to account
> for all this destruction when historians, in cold blood, should
> write the truth . . .
>
> There still remains a month and a half before the rainy season
> begins. At present we hold only the province of Manila and
> the town of Cavite.

Wheaton reported thirty-six American casualties against
twenty-five hundred Filipinos killed and wounded—a ratio
of seventy to one. Even the general's exaggerations were in
the grand manner. Another toehold had been established
in a southerly province. But instructions from Otis virtually
to abandon the entire area which had been briefly under
Wheaton's control puzzled and exasperated officers in the
field and those at "The Palace." Why the caution, the timid-

ity? Experienced veterans, who had calculated on the basis of the wild happenings of February 5 that the campaign could be wound up by June, began to wonder about their commander in chief. General Miller had been explicitly instructed not to budge from Iloilo. Most of his command was shipped back to Manila Province. Was central Luzon the only area which interested Otis? If so, these other excursions seemed irrational.

Infantry units were shipped hundreds of miles south to the islands of Cebu and Negros, where without difficulty they occupied the respective capital cities. Instantly Filipino raiders began to organize in the adjacent mountains, instigated by Tagalog agents who soon had both islands in a revolutionary fervor. More troubles were plainly impending here. The campaign would have been logical with adequate forces. As it was, the tiny garrisons merely invited retaliatory attack. Was VIII Corps big enough to win and hold far-flung territories and at the same time to whip the main *insurrecto* force under Luna?

As affairs were going, everyone but Otis could see that reinforcements were likely to be required far in excess of recent estimates. Since the beginning of time military leaders have begged for more soldiers, but the Governor-General kept repeating that thirty thousand men were all he needed. To him the rebellion was a local Tagalog affair, and after the first deceptive victories around Manila he believed (and advised Washington accordingly) that it would collapse in short order. Nor was he alone of this opinion. In a *Harper's Weekly* article (March 11) even the astute Frank Millet wrote that it was "impossible to believe that the campaign will be a long one." (The most efficient way of winding it up, he thought, was simply to bribe Aguinaldo.) On April 20 Otis cabled Corbin that thirty thousand men would still be ample. Next month, when offered more, he doggedly repeated his magic figure and remarked that the entire native army was down to six thousand men. However, he now inserted the new word "effectives." This meant about forty thousand total Americans. When his volunteers began to depart under the six-month arrangement, he reluctantly asked for another ten thousand troops. At this point he was prodded by the War Department. Some gentlemen there did not share his optimism; and he was asked for a new estimate which would, if anything, "err on the safe side." Perhaps feeling that large troop requests would reflect upon his ability to quell what was, by his own admission, a trivial uprising, the general hemmed, hawed, and finally on August 15 asked for a total of sixty thousand. He had now doubled his original requisition. Meanwhile congress had passed an act authorizing an increase in the regular army to one hundred thousand men, plus three cavalry regiments. The 3rd, 4th, 17th, 20th, and 22nd regular infantry regiments reached Manila before the end of March.

Returning to the war early in the spring of 1899, we find on the scene a new and exceptional individual: Major General Henry W. Lawton. Six feet three inches tall, with hard, pleasant features beneath a crop of iron-gray hair, he too had won the Medal of Honor in the Civil War, where he had fought in twenty-eight major battles. In 1886 he had topped a peerless reputation as an Indian fighter by capturing Geronimo, the Apache chief. When the war with Spain broke out, he was promoted major general of volunteers, fought in Cuba at El Caney, and was sent to the Philippines to replace General Anderson as commander of the First Division. Ordinarily a man of character and restraint, he held in check a monumental temper. When it exploded, his staff discreetly disappeared for a time. Some hidden instability prodded the man. He was known to have been drinking heavily in Cuba, and largely for that reason had been removed as military governor of the Santiago district. The reason given had been "ill health." Before sending him to the Philippines, Mr. McKinley had personally lectured him on the evils of drink and had made him swear that he would be temperate in his new command. The pledge was honored. In his large white helmet, which he was constantly implored to abandon, Lawton was a perfect target. He held no animosities against any man, white or brown. Shortly after arriving in the islands he was shot at by a native in ambush, who missed and was immediately killed. "The little fellow had a good nerve," observed Lawton, "sticking it out behind the bush after his comrades had run." His first big assignment was to lead an April expedition into Laguna Province and capture the important city of Santa Cruz. This was accomplished in three days, whereupon Otis telegraphed him to return to Manila with his entire force. As he did so in puzzlement, the insurgents reoccupied the city and adjacent area.

Compared to these rather haphazard operations, the campaign to the north stands out as the only one of serious military significance. It was led by MacArthur and its primary aims were two: to crush the main insurgent army under Luna, and to take the native capital of Malolos. After a week of steady fighting which cost the Americans 534 casualties, the city was occupied, although attempts to surround the rebel forces failed. As usual, Otis directed MacArthur to stop where he was and to abandon a plan to drive the natives eight miles north to the line of the Rio Grande Pampanga. With the capture of Aguinaldo's capital city the war was as good as over; so calculated General Otis.

But by spring several subtly disquieting factors, from a U.S. standpoint, had emerged. First of all, the campaign thus far had been fought in the dry season. MacArthur's movement had even enjoyed the advantage of utilizing the one Philippine railway. Would campaigns such as this prove feasible during the four or five months of torrential rain soon to come? If not, the job of pacifying the islands would have to carry over until October. And the biggest question-mark was Otis himself. Was he the man for the job? Many thousands of miles away, Mr. Roosevelt had begun imploring Mr. McKinley to replace him by General Greene. The root of the matter was

American casualty

Jolos aflame

MacArthur's force entering Malolos; standing at ease in front of Aguinaldo's former headquarters

Malolos in ruins

U.S. firing line advancing on Antipole, June 3, 1899

A fieldpiece in action south of Manila

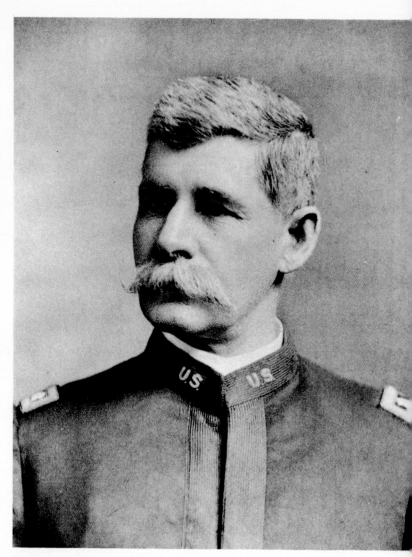

General Henry W. Lawton

Filipinos captured at Pasay and Parañaque

Hauling supplies by carabao

General Lloyd V. Wheaton

ansas troops at a street barricade

Washington Volunteers near Pasig

President McKinley and Cabinet

California infantry being towed to their transport: destination Ne

Otis' faulty conception of the nature of the rebellion, which led to his optimistic views, which in turn led to his paradoxically conservative mishandling of the campaign. Time and again (in the major drives mentioned thus far, and in lesser forays through May) he had forced field commanders to return to Manila with all or most of their forces, after they had reached their objective. Over and over he reported to the War Department that the natives had been "scattered." But as soon as the Americans left, the rebels moved back in. Soon another expedition had to be laboriously fitted out to quell them.

"The loss is usually given in the ratio of twenty to one. The twenty is guesswork," wrote Albert Robinson for the New York *Evening Post*. And in another cable: "But what of these 'glorious victories'? Wherein lies the 'glory' of killing 'niggers'? It seems to take very little nowadays to make a 'glorious victory' . . . There are towns here which have been 'captured' again and again, each time with a 'glorious victory.' Today it is unsafe for an American to go even ten miles from the city of Manila." He and other correspondents seethed under the censorship which Otis had imposed. One high officer in the Philippines confided to Robinson that Filipino losses were being deliberately puffed by ambitious U.S. field officers, and he complained that the tactics employed by Otis always led to assaults against chosen, fortified positions. The general had become increasingly surly of late. In conferences he was maddening—either uninterested or peevishly sarcastic. He was still using the same defective maps. In June Mr. John Bass, writing for *Harper's Weekly*, slipped past the censor, via Hong Kong, a blistering four-thousand-word dispatch which, in its entirety or as quoted fragmentarily, aroused much uneasiness throughout the States:

He [Governor-General Otis] has never been out on the lines, and I venture to say that he is the only American officer of the original army in the Philippines who has not seen a fight or a skirmish. He knows the country only from such imperfect maps . . . as he has been able to pick up from Spanish sources, and even the work of English commercial houses . . . In fact, they are not military maps at all . . . The criticism is freely made here that, under these conditions, relying on hearsay evidence merely, it is impossible for a general to make intelligent plans, and the fact that we have been floundering about in the wilderness for months without accomplishing anything is the result of the efforts of one man . . .

Since the 4th of February various expeditions have taken place, principally in the island of Luzon. These expeditions resulted in our taking from the insurgent government certain territory. Some of this territory we have occupied; the rest we have returned to the insurgents in a more or less mutilated condition, depending on whether the policy of the hour was to carry on a bitter war against a barbarous enemy, or to bring enlightenment to an ignorant people, deceived as to our motives.

. . . Why is it that the American outlook is blacker now than it has been since the beginning of the war? . . .

First, the whole population of the islands sympathizes with the insurgents; only those natives whose immediate self-interest requires it are friendly to us . . .

The second cause is that our army is ill-equipped and unwieldy in its management.

The third reason is that the plans of campaign followed are not adapted to the nature of the country, the climate, or the people . . .

. . . the half-past-eight-o'clock rule is still on in Manila, and everybody must be in-doors, because the authorities are still afraid of an uprising in the town.

The sooner the people of the United States find out that the people of the Philippines do not wish to be governed by us, the better . . .

To chase barefooted insurgents with water-buffalo carts as a
wagon-train may be simply ridiculous; but to load volunteers down with two hundred rounds of ammunition and one
day's rations, and to put on their heads felt hats used by no
other army in the world in the tropics, in order to trot these
same soldiers in the broiling sun over a country without roads,
is positively criminal. Out of as strong and robust an army as
ever wore shoe leather, there are five thousand men in the
general hospital . . .

Pasig, the second largest town in this part of Luzon, was
looted and burned; the villages for miles along the southern
shore of Laguna de Bay were laid waste. The barbarous native should be taught how terrible war waged by American
soldiers was. Then came a period when sometimes a town
was burned and sometimes it was not . . . The insurgents
are a good deal like children, and they imitated us; instead
of leaving their towns for us to burn, they burned them
themselves . . . Now there has been a great hue-and-cry
made because the insurgents mutilated two of our dead by
cutting off their ears, and yet one or two of our own scouts
made a practice of cutting off the ears of the insurgents they
killed, and preserving them as trophies.

. . . The insurgents came back to Pasig, and their first act
was to hang the presidente for treason in surrendering to the
Americans. Presidentes do not surrender towns to us any
more. When we returned to Pasig we found the place well
fortified, and we suffered some loss in retaking it. This process
might go on indefinitely . . .

Of the many villages taken by Lawton in his march northward, only Baliuag has been retained. San Isidro is again the
capital of the insurgent government. Santa Cruz and the
other towns on the lake were abandoned to the insurgents
after a body of 1500 men had been taken in *cascos*, at great
expense, to the spot, and many lives had been lost; one hundred insurgents were killed. The object of the whole expedition was subsequently explained to be the capture of a
few launches, which, from their blockaded position in the

river, were practically useless to the enemy. These expeditions, lacking the purpose of holding the land conquered,
alienate population already hostile, encourage insurgents,
teach them true methods of fighting us, and exhaust our men.

. . . Unless the insurgents fall to pieces by natural disin-
tegration—and I believe the authorities have counted on this
process more than on the force of arms—the insurrection will
prosper for some time to come.

From minutely supervising paper work it was natural for
Otis to supervise minutely all field operations. A major general commanding as many as ten thousand men could not
move a company without express orders. Should he advance
too fast, Otis would slow him down, or stop him, or even
make him retreat. Apart from Otis, supply was the major
stumbling block. Central Luzon was a network of streams,
hardly any of which were crossed by bridges which would
accommodate heavy transport. During the rainy season they
all became torrents most of the time. The rice paddies were
hard going for infantrymen, almost impassable for field guns.
Then, too, would there be more easy victories without artillery support? On the ubiquitous *muy malos caminos* buffalo-
drawn wagons could traverse five miles per day at best, and
this in the dry season.

Beyond the rolling Luzon plains lay ranges of towering
mountains. The prospect of fighting a full-scale war in them
was bleak. How were wounded men to be evacuated through
swamps and thickets, if they lay miles from the nearest road?
With dysentery germs abounding in every river and well,
the water problem was a major one. Heat exhaustion had already taken its toll. During Lawton's May offensive in Laguna
province, hundreds of U.S. troops had fallen out during the
march and were unable to rejoin their companies until evening bivouac.

Speed was the answer to most of these difficulties, in the
sense that it may have been barely possible for an aggressive

commander to win the war between early February and June. But whatever his other assets Otis was hardly a man attuned to daring; and as the campaign flickered aimlessly during the first quarter of 1899 it became clear that a fast victory was slipping away. Otis remained (or pretended to remain) placid. The rainy season, he wrote Washington, would not hamper him at all. "Present indications denote insurgent government in perilous condition. Its army defeated, discouraged, and shattered; insurgents returning to their homes . . ." The truth of this appraisal remained to be seen.

V

If it was dawning upon most white men that the war might be long and laborious, their brown opponents were even more disconsolate. Mabini himself admitted that there was really nothing to do but harass the invader until a negotiated peace could be worked out which would afford the Filipinos their basic, inalienable rights; outright victory was out of the question. Though he had been discouraged for a time, General Luna disagreed violently. Discipline would check the rot. He personally stripped dozens of negligent officers, including generals, of their rank, and had some of them thrown into jail. As complaints poured into his headquarters after each battle, with different brigades blaming each other for what had happened, he turned vicious. He visited various field officers and told them to shut their mouths and fight. When a group of newcomers volunteered for action, he sneered, "Tell them to go to hell." They were weak sisters who would only break and run, he predicted. His own brother, Dr. José Luna, who tried to effect the release of an Englishman imprisoned for a minor offense, was warned, "If you come to intercede for the Englishman, don't talk, because if you utter one word I will throw you in the same place he is."

When he instituted a single punishment—death—for any

number of trivial violations, he was given the nickname "General Article One." He demanded that every able-bodied native who had served in the Spanish militia, regardless of age or health, be delivered to him for combat duty. And as he threatened colonels, disarmed troops who had failed in action, slapped and drew his gun on generals who resisted his authority, military morale sagged and his own position became precarious. Soon he was hated more than the Americans. In a quandary, the cabinet feared to back him up; yet he was the best commander they had. Popping up anywhere without warning, he terrorized the peasantry and other noncombatants. If they aided the Americans, Luna had them shot as collaborators. If they refused to do so, they stood a chance of being mistreated by white men who wanted food, water, and information, and were determined to get them in one way or another.

Moral armchair attitudes concerning brave resistance are one thing, but performing them interminably with no hope of victory is another. The burning of innumerable *barrios* and towns had already created sorry conditions around Manila. Sickness and near-starvation were mounting in Luzon's southern and central provinces. Thousands of homeless refugees streamed after their soldiers in various directions; some even trickled into Manila to try their luck under the grim *norte americanos*. When the flow of farm produce stopped, all of Luzon became a potential poorhouse. In Manila Filipinos were treated with indifference, especially those previously connected with the native government. Police, firemen, sanitation supervisors, clerks, veterinarians, tax collectors, and tram conductors were all U.S. troops. American military law, in those early days of the war, was often slanted against Filipino defendants. In one case, a native's horse stopped to urinate on the Santa Cruz bridge, whereupon its owner was arrested for blocking traffic and fined twenty-five dollars. Each time he tried to explain, the judge raised the fine five dollars. After it reached fifty dollars, the Filipino subsided.

When some members of the cabinet (which had moved to

San Isidro after the loss of Malolos) suggested working out a compromise with the Americans, Luna knocked Foreign Secretary Buencamino to the floor. He then arrested him and other like-minded officials on grounds of treason. It is significant that Aguinaldo released them only after Luna had left for the front; the man was becoming unmanageable. On June 4 he curtly telegraphed Aguinaldo that he was coming to see him. Perhaps by a coincidence, the presidential guard on duty on June 8 was a unit which earlier had been disarmed by Luna for alleged cowardice. In search of Aguinaldo, Luna entered the convent-headquarters. Shots were fired. The general reeled out, bleeding from bullet and bolo wounds. As he swayed in the center of the village square, members of the guard walked over and killed him with another volley.

Thus was America relieved of her most dangerous military opponent, Aguinaldo of his most ominous rival. Responsibility for the crime remains a mystery. After a personal investigation, Luna's brother absolved the Philippine president. Except for its aftermath the question is academic. A new congressional and military crisis flared up, out of which emerged yet another cabinet, even more subordinate to Aguinaldo. Upon also being appointed commander in chief of the army, however, he turned most civil functions over to Apolinario Mabini. All spring and summer Aguinaldo toyed with the idea of abandoning Luna's concept of head-on, massed resistance to the United States. The Filipino could not match the American in tactics, marksmanship, artillery, naval support, ammunition, and rifles; but there was another way, more in keeping with Aguinaldo's temperament and experience. This was guerilla warfare on an organized, elaborate scale. But it was not yet the moment; there would be plenty of time during the wet months to think it over and to await developments. And the war went on . . .

The Iowa volunteers entered San Fernando in May. Out of 4,800 combat troops in that area, 2,160 were then on sick report. Seventy per cent of one regiment were in the hospital. Stomachs refused to hold food, nerves were taut, many men could not sleep. "The sun, field rations, physical exertion, and abnormal excitement from almost constant exposure to fire action . . ." were the reasons given by MacArthur. In an advance against del Pilar's regiment, General Robert Hall lost three men killed and ten wounded—and eighty-four casualties through heat prostration. "All Gugus look alike to me," the men said; and they sang:

> Damn, damn, damn the Filipino,
> Pockmarked Khadiak ladrone!
> Underneath the starry flag
> Civilize him with a Krag
> And return us to our own beloved home . . .

The Nebraska volunteers, in a grand charge during which Colonel Stotsenburg was killed, stormed and captured Quingua, and then in the face of hostile fire crossed the broad, swift Rio de Pampanga. One hundred and eight new cases of malaria showed up a few days after Lawton's reconnaissance of Candaba Swamp. Otis offered fifteen dollars for each insurgent rifle surrendered to the Americans. The response was poor. When recalled from his May campaign, Lawton stormed into "Palace" headquarters with a serious, almost insulting proposition. Give me two regiments and a free hand, he said, and I will end the insurrection and deliver Emilio Aguinaldo dead or alive within sixty days. General Otis literally laughed at him. During leisure hours the troops hunted chickens and ducks, and captured little monkeys for pets.

On June 10, in the isthmus between Manila Bay and Laguna de Bay, three thousand natives under generals Ricarte and Noriel fell upon four thousand U.S. troops and caught them in a crossfire. Out of water, prostrated by heat, an entire American division disintegrated. As 898 men (many never to return) staggered off the trail and disappeared into the countryside in search of water and shade, they discarded their clothes, their rations, even their rifles. Angrily Lawton dispatched Brigadier General Samuel Ovenshine with reinforcements. Next day they caught the enemy on the west bank of the Zapote River. "We are having a beautiful battle, hurry up ammunition, we will need it," Lawton wired Otis. "We have the bridge. It has cost us dearly." And once more the insurgents were thrown back with heavy losses.

American battle casualties since February 4 were now approaching the two-thousand mark, not counting those sick and those already dead of disease. Then and later, most bodies had to be buried in the islands, for as Otis cabled Adjutant General Corbin:

> Impossible to embalm and ship bodies now. Experiment failure; weather warm, decomposition rapid. Process of embalming immediately after death unsuccessful. Of twelve bodies already sent to U.S. doubtful if some reach port.

An enormous Negro named Fagan deserted the U.S. army, taking with him all the revolvers he could carry, and was commissioned a captain in the insurgent forces. One day, after he had requested the custody of several American prisoners, shots were heard. He explained that he had to kill them all when they tried to escape. He was never again left with white prisoners. Fagan drank heavily, played a guitar, fought like a wildcat, and lived in camp with a native woman. His life was to be short but interesting. Troops under General Hale dislodged the enemy from Maycauyan, the general being wounded in the process. The 23rd Infantry took Bustos. When three men were killed and one wounded in a squad of five near Longos, the remaining man, Private Thomas Sletteland, won the Congressional Medal "by his cool and unerring aim successfully holding the enemy back until reinforcements came."

Starting in June, the 6th, 16th, 19th, 24th and 25th infantry regiments arrived in the islands, while the last disillusioned volunteers left for San Francisco or New York. A few light showers had begun to fall upon west-central Luzon in May. The first cloudburst of the season struck the area precisely on June 1.

10

*For there's many a man been murdered in Luzon
and Mindanao . . .*

RAIN
AND
REACTION

EXCEPT FOR THOSE WHO HAD BEEN AT MANILA A YEAR EARlier, the Americans had never seen such rain. Between May and October seventy inches fell (as much as the California enlistees had experienced in the last seven years); and it seemed to descend almost in semi-solid masses, not with normal gravitational speed but as though flung down by a furious god. Most of the Manila-Dagupan railroad was washed out; little bridges over various rivers collapsed. In Manila, during even a moderate downpour, the narrower streets became canals. Low areas and rice paddies merged into broad stretches of artificial lake. From Laguna de Bay to Manila Bay the Pasig was generally swollen and unnavigable. A good deal of higher ground escaped flooding but turned to mud. It was not, as the *Review of Reviews* gravely explained to its readers, the best time of year for marching. And in a long cable to Adjutant General Corbin, Otis confessed that there would be a short delay in the project at hand. Twelve per cent of his command were ill. Personnel from the Cuban campaign, he reported, were suffering from a recurrence of Caribbean fever. Some of the new men were homesick, and with touching military innocence were clamoring to break their twelve-month contract with Uncle Sam. The native high command was regrouping and reinforcing its army. And while the Governor-General concluded, as usual, that the insurgent cause might collapse at any time, yet "I am not sanguine." It was all rather depressing and contradictory.

Few men were any longer housed in barracks or other semi-permanent shelters; in scores of scattered outposts they were exposed to sudden cloudbursts that drenched them and their equipment on the ground. There was no mosquito netting, and a good night's sleep was fairly impossible. The insects bit through shirts and trousers and brought blood which dried up into small scabs. When scratched, these became open sores. The despised canned "goldfish," accumulating month after month, was a real problem of storage and transportation. Men forced it down only when absolutely necessary, and one wrote that it was "a personal hazard for anyone to mention the subject."

During this quasi-truce, Otis permitted no extension of the U.S. lines. Lawton hated the growing atmosphere of extreme depression and suggested in June that offensive actions were necessary if only for morale purposes. At his insistence the maximum possible amount of raiding and scouting went on. In August San Mateo was captured after a sharp fight. Next morning Major Parker, who had led the assault, was handed direct orders from "The Palace" to evacuate the town and return to his original lines. When he reported to Lawton, the latter said, "Well, you have got me in bad with Otis!" "How is that?" Parker asked in astonishment. "Why, by going ahead and taking San Mateo; Otis will hardly speak to me."

Until well into October a confused series of attacks, captures, counterattacks, evacuations, and recaptures took place, the net result of which approached the infinitesimal. On both sides casualties were slight. Except when the insurgents attacked—such as at San Rafael, Porac, Imus, Bacoor, the Zapote Bridge, and Angeles—they showed little disposition to fight in strength. They faded away when the Americans appeared, returned when their enemy left, cut telegraph wires, ambushed supply trains, tore up the American-held section of the railway, and provided other minor annoyances. From current rebel headquarters at Tarlac Aguinaldo issued another proclamation in which a new note was sounded:

> In America there is a great party that insists on the United States government recognizing Filipino independence. They will compel their country to fulfill the promises made to us in all solemnity and faith, though not put in writing . . . the great Democratic party of the United States will win the next fall election . . . Imperialism will fail in its mad attempts to subjugate us by force of arms.

As fitful skirmishes continued that sodden summer, the fighting began to take on unique and regrettable aspects. The Filipinos developed a nasty habit of putting out white flags and luring the Americans into death traps. The Spanish word for friend became a bitter mockery. All insurgents without rifles, it seemed, were *amigos. Amigo!* they cried: *mucho amigo!* When captured, they were *amigos*. When released, they returned to shooting and boloing Americans. Who was a noncombatant? By late summer few insurgents any longer wore their proud gingham uniforms. To the Americans all gugus were indistinguishable anyway, and the dilemma was solved by a simple, sinister slogan: *"There are no more amigos."*

War in the tropics has never been noted for chivalry, and by 1899 the Philippine affair was a model of its kind. "I don't know how many men, women and children the Tennessee boys did kill," a Missouri infantryman reminisced concerning one sortie; "They would not take any prisoners." Americans were found badly mutilated, and there was evidence that some wounded U.S. prisoners had been tortured, or assisted, into a speedier oblivion. Captured white men could look forward to varying degrees of mistreatment, and one thing was certain: their diet would approach the starvation level. The Americans, on their part, became specialists in the "water cure," usually administered to elicit information. A blend (in the words of an observer) of Castilian cruelty and American ingenuity, it consisted of forcing four or five gallons of water down the throat of the captive, whose "body becomes an object frightful to contemplate," and then squeezing it out by kneeling on his stomach. The process was repeated until the *amigo* talked or died. Almost invariably he talked. When the refugee problem began to be alleviated by the first small reconcentration camps, the circle was complete. What Otis was now doing to the Filipinos was almost what "Butcher" Weyler had done to the Cubans; and the paradox was all the greater since we had gone to war with Spain to put an end to just such abominations.

As yet the American people knew next to nothing of these developments. Enlistments for subduing and uplifting the natives were heavy, especially as everyone knew that the insurgents consisted of little more than a few hundred cannibals and *ladrones;* the amusing little fracas would be over unless one joined up quickly. In the islands, it is true, some volunteers were deserting, but the cases were hardly publicized, and those who did manage to reach Hong Kong were picked up by the British and returned to Manila. The campaign had turned out to be no picnic. Field rations were skimpy and unpalatable—usually hardtack, "goldfish," and canned tomatoes. Each man was his own chef while fighting or on patrol. It was hard to build a fire from damp wood. Green water from ditches and holes often had to be used for cooking and drinking. The wet ground made shoes fit badly; some men carried them rather than wear them over their blisters. "Last night one of our boys was found shot and his stomach cut open," wrote Private A. A. Barnes of the 3rd Artillery to his brother in Indiana. "Immediately orders were received from General Wheaton to burn the town and kill every native in sight;

which was done . . . I am probably growing hard-hearted, for I am in my glory when I can sight my gun on some dark skin and pull the trigger . . . Should a call for volunteers be made for this place do not be so patriotic as to come here."

The first tales of church desecration began to filter back to the States. They were denied by Otis—the Chinese and *insurrectos* were responsible, he said—but as the volunteers poured home, so did the evidence: crucifixes, vestments, candlesticks, chalices, ostensoria, and other holy articles made of gold. The 1st Colorado Company from Cripple Creek, reported the Boston *Pilot*, got off the boat at New York with enough church goods to fill a large store. The press made much of the issue, and most Americans varied between anger, disbelief, and a desire to hush up the affair. Even Frederick Funston (now a brigadier) was denounced for having appropriated a silk robe with gold ornaments thereon.

But in Manila, despite the rain, time passed pleasantly enough. Champagne and other wines were not taxed and living was cheap. Scores of officers' wives had come to stay. There was horse racing and betting near Pasay. Handsome victorias carrying army belles, drawn by tiny ponies and driven by natives, dashed through the streets. A luxurious Army and Navy Club had been set up a year ago, almost immediately after the city's capture. High-ranking civilians joined its swank counterpart, the University Club. Others of less status entered the American Club and set to work planning a swimming pool, a gymnasium, a library, and a schedule of social events. An enormous amount of entertaining went on, weather permitting. There were gala lunch parties up the river, gatherings on the flagships at Cavite, much drinking, dinner-dancing, and sight-seeing. Caste lines were drawn with machine-like precision. "In the American and European life of Manila, the Filipino is a small quantity, and there is scarcely any social communication between the two races," wrote Charles Ballentine of the Associated Press. Yet it was more or less comprehensible, for their countrymen were fighting ours; they were, in short, the enemy.

From the suburbs of the capital one might still occasionally hear the muffled, somewhat chilling, crackle and boom of distant gunfire. Within an amorphous zone between ten and thirty miles from the Walled City, the war went on.

II

The civilian members of the so-called Schurman Commission —chairman Jacob Gould Schurman (president of Cornell University, who had resisted the appointment through opposition to McKinley's Philippine policy and had been told, "Oh, don't let that bother you; I didn't want the Philippines either . . . but in the end there was no alternative"), Charles Denby (former minister to China, a dedicated imperialist), and Professor Dean C. Worcester (University of Michigan scientist who opposed Philippine independence)—had been appointed to head off the war, but arrived in the islands weeks after it broke out. They therefore had "no status," as General Otis frequently pointed out. He resented their mission and tried to get the War Department to recall them. Negotiations with insurgent leaders, he protested, cost American lives and prolonged his difficulties. But the commissioners spoke to no insurgents. They confined their harmless interviews to British, Spanish and Filipino men of position and property who were unanimous in asking Uncle Sam to annex the islands; and the first of their hastily issued "regulative principles" read as follows:

> The supremacy of the United States must and will be enforced throughout every part of the Archipelago, and those who resist it can accomplish no end other than their own ruin.

Next they listed a dozen reforms and blessings which would flow from America's rule, including a measure of autonomy

and self-rule. But there was to be no independence; as for the
war, truce negotiations had to be preceded by the surrender
of the native army and its weapons. The cart being in front
of the horse, nothing moved. Everywhere the proclamation—
like McKinley's earlier one—was torn down or defaced. From
rebel headquarters Aguinaldo announced that any native
found reading it would be executed. A few days later Mabini
circulated a counter-manifesto exhorting his countrymen to
fight to the death against the invader. "Annexation in whatever form it may be adopted will unite us forever with a nation
. . . which hates the colored race with a mortal hatred," he
observed. But the battle of words was noted with contemptuous detachment by the two military members of the commission, Otis and Dewey, who knew that they had more
decisive means of promoting manifest destiny. Neither attended a single meeting with the civilians.

For several frustrating months the acting commissioners
toiled on, permeated by a conviction that the rebellion had
arisen solely because of the sinister ambitions of its leaders,
in the words of McKinley's last message to congress. Living,
as it were, in a dream world, they were ignored both by the
U.S. military and the *insurrectos*. After gathering three volumes of data and statistics, they departed for New York in
August, unmourned and unsung. In due time they issued a
report which asserted that the Filipinos had deliberately
started hostilities, that all Filipinos of wealth and intelligence
were opposed to the war, that anarchy everywhere prevailed,
that "enthusiasm ran high" for U.S. civil control, that "the
primary object of this struggle is not, as is pretended, the
liberty of the Philippine peoples, but the continuance of
[Aguinaldo's] own arbitrary and despotic power," that the
"tribes" were incapable of self government, and "that a war
was never more humanely conducted."

These remarkable tidings were doubtless received by Mr.
McKinley with satisfaction, underscoring as they did his own

convictions to the letter. Ignoring senatorial cries of "white-wash," he prepared to launch still another commission—this one more of an administrative body, however, for according to General Otis the insurrection was as good as over. Judge William H. Taft, calculated the president, would make an excellent chairman.

In the meantime the insurgents, who seemed to have no understanding of the futility of negotiating from weakness with a man like Otis, continued to annoy him with peace overtures not involving total surrender. His response was unusually brusque. A scheme delivered by Colonel Arguelles to call a fifteen-day cease-fire so that his government could "justify itself before the people as having employed all the means in its power to avoid the ruin of the country" was rejected as a ruse to give the rebels time to replenish their ammunition. There was much discouragement when Arguelles returned. For the nth time the cabinet fell, and Señor Mabini departed angrily for a vacation at Balungaw's hot springs, where he hoped to find a cure for his paralysis. His place as secretary of state was taken over by Pedro Paterno, of Biak-na-bato fame. He organized a new body to deal with Otis, who repeated (with the dutiful backing of the Schurman Commission) that the first condition of peace was the disbanding of the native army and the surrender of its rifles. But not even Paterno could stomach such terms.

Late in September Aguinaldo made his last attempt to secure an honorable peace. Three of his army officers came to Manila under a flag of truce and requested not an armistice but the formation of a joint committee merely to discuss ways and means of approaching one. When Otis turned this down also, the emissaries toured the city, were wildly cheered by the natives, and returned empty-handed to Tarlac.

There would be no more peace overtures. Otis was convinced that his fall campaign would win the war. The rebels were sure that the Democrats would win the 1900 U.S. elections and revoke the annexation program—an interesting concept debatable to this day. Apparently all they had to do was hang on. Meanwhile they determined to stop begging the Americans for crumbs. Thus, by a quirk of events, the insurgent government returned to the same extreme policy previously advocated by Mabini and Luna which had cost the one his job and the other (indirectly) his life. Any chance that the insurrection might have been peacefully terminated that summer now fell to the ground. "The first blow was struck by the inhabitants," Mr. McKinley said sternly in a Pittsburgh speech; "They assailed our sovereignty, and there will be no useless parley, no pause, until the insurrection is suppressed and American authority acknowledged and established." But if the president's understanding of how the war had started was incorrect, if his definition of sovereignty was open to question, his concept of the nature of the rebellion was even more delusive. Only a man who had turned a deaf ear to dozens of warnings could have said as he did in Fargo, North Dakota: "We never dreamed that the little body of insurgents whom we have just emancipated . . . would turn upon the flag that had sheltered them against Spain."

Admiral Dewey had just told him so. For the conquering hero had come home at last—to the greatest ovation ever awarded an American thus far in history, to parade under a massive Fifth Avenue victory arch of gleaming white plaster (soon to be quietly demolished) followed by Governor Theodore Roosevelt on horseback, while the flags of the fleet fluttered in the North River, to accept from the president a $10,000 jeweled sword voted him by congress, to speak to the multitudes words that few could hear but which were hysterically applauded, to receive a Tiffany loving cup of solid gold embossed with sketches of his victory. Over cigars, in the quiet of the White House study, the admiral and the president spoke of the Philippines; and McKinley's handwritten notes survive:

. . . Talk with Dewey
     Oct. 3/99—

Self-govt—are they capable?
No & will not be for many many years.
The U S must control and supervise, giving
     Philipinos participation as far as capable.
What does Ag represent?
He has no more than 40000 followers
     of all kinds out of 8 or 10 millions
What is our duty?
     Keep the Islands permanently
     Valuable in every way.
How many troops needed?
     50000
Have we ships enough?
     Ought to send some more. Recommends
     that Brooklyn go and smaller vessels
Should we give up the Islands?
     Never—never
The stories of church desecration and inhumanity

The phrase trailed off into nothingness. And as the nation's
two foremost gentlemen conversed in Washington, General
Otis perspired and planned in his office overlooking the Pasig.
For his was the practical problem and the duty, and his hand
grasped the sword of righteousness.

III

At the moment he had under his command 47,465 officers
and men; 16,018 more were en route and would arrive before
the end of the month. When they did, the rains and typhoons
would be as good as over, and cool breezes would render general operations possible. There was no longer any reason to
delay the decisive stroke. Its goal was to run the insurgent
army northward, trap it, and (in the words of a volunteer
officer) "to capture Aguinaldo, the head and front of the
whole business, the incarnation of the aspirations of the Filipino people." A vast encircling movement had been planned,

involving nothing less than the occupation of all north-central Luzon, the capture of every significant port, and the stretching of an armed barrier across the central plain to cut off escape to the south. Three divisions were to act as independent pincers under generals MacArthur, Lawton, and Wheaton.

The all-important railway ran through fertile valleys and populous cities to Dagupan. MacArthur's task was to follow it through Tarlac and drive the enemy force toward the Lingayen Gulf.

At the same time, twenty-five hundred men under Wheaton would sail by transport to Dagupan, land there, occupy the coast road and western port towns, join hands with Lawton's advance guard, and squeeze the insurgent army against MacArthur's column—a grand strategic concept involving the transversal of a coastal range as wild and rugged as the American Rockies.

The huge Candaba swamp lies east of the railroad. Running through it north-northeasterly, the Rio Grande de Pampanga skirts the eastern edge of the plain. Lawton's division was to move up that river, garrison the towns en route, and occupy all mountain passes opening into the valleys of northern Luzon. Most crucial of all was the need for closing the circle through contact with Wheaton's force.

These three movements would encompass the main body of *insurrectos* in a square some one hundred miles on each side. The difficulties of terrain were manifold and the snail-like pace at which the columns would move had been regretfully taken into account. Still, the concept was impressive, and the army was ready and anxious to get the job done. The native high command had some knowledge of its broad outlines and had fortified certain key positions, such as the entrance to Dagupan. Smugglers and legitimate agents from Yokahama and Singapore had spent the summer delivering additional rifles and cartridges. Through taxes, the marketing of natural products, and the sale of bonds, the Filipino government had raised several million dollars for the war effort since February. Estimates varied wildly (between forty and two hundred thousand) as to the numerical strength of its army; but by October it was certainly at its all-time peak. These men could live and fight on very little; a sip of water, a few mouthfuls of rice and fruit and sometimes fish, and they were ready for another day's work. They had lost some of their confidence, they feared the burly American sharpshooters, but they were as loyal as ever to Emilio Aguinaldo.

On the American side, the large, stolid figure of General Otis inspired no such devotion. To everyone's surprise he had somehow evolved this elaborate scenario, but few officers and newspapermen considered him capable of actually staging it. These doubts were aggravated by his rigid control of outgoing dispatches. In February most reporters had written that the Americans had fired first, whereupon Otis had altered their copy to say that the Filipinos had started hostilities by an unwarranted attack against the American lines. "My instructions are to shut off everything that could hurt McKinley's administration," the censoring officer explained. By July the newsmen had reached the end of their rope. They appointed Oscar Davis, John McCutcheon, Robert Collins, and John Bass to secure an interview with the Governor-General. It lasted for three stormy hours. Otis did not deny suppressing the facts. He had to do it, he insisted, to shield the people from distortions and sensationalism. Bass and Davis reminded him that they all had carefully avoided transmitting sensations which they had personally witnessed, such as American soldiers bayoneting wounded *amigos,* the looting of homes and churches, and so on.

If they persisted in challenging his official line, Otis replied, he would demand their expulsion. They smiled, and Mr. Collins of the Associated Press referred to a remark made by Otis' man: "Of course we all know that we are in a terrible mess out here, but we don't want the folks to get excited about it. If you fellows will only keep quiet now we

will pull through in time . . ." Were they really to keep
quiet? The Governor-General denied that such a preposterous statement had been uttered. It seemed very much to him,
he snapped, as though the Associated Press were in the pay
of the Filipino Junta in Hong Kong. After a stunned silence
Mr. Davis handed the general their "round-robin" protest
and asked permission to cable it home. Otis read it. In a high
falsetto quivering with emotion, he stated, "You have served
a paper on me—a most extraordinary document. Are you
aware that this constitutes a conspiracy against the government? My first thought was to put you all off the island. My
second thought is to summon a general court martial and
have you tried for conspiracy." The newspapermen watched
him sardonically and Davis repeated his question. Could they
transmit it? Otis refused. It was sent to Hong Kong by mail
and there cabled to the States. Signed by eleven correspondents, it read:

> The undersigned, being all staff correspondents of Ameri-
> can newspapers stationed in Manila, unite in the following
> statement:
> We believe that, owing to official despatches from Manila
> made public in Washington, the people of the United States
> have not received a correct impression of the situation in the
> Philippines, but that these despatches have presented an
> ultra-optimistic view that is not shared by the general officers
> in the field.
> We believe the despatches incorrectly represent the exist-
> ing conditions among the Filipinos in respect to internal dis-
> sension and demoralization resulting from the American
> campaign and to the brigand character of their army.
> We believe the despatches err in the declaration that "the
> situation is well in hand," and in the assumption that the in-
> surrection can be speedily ended without a greatly increased
> force.
> We think the tenacity of the Filipino purpose has been
> under-estimated, and that the statements are unfounded that
> volunteers are willing to engage in further service.

The censorship has compelled us to participate in this misrepresentation by excising or altering uncontroverted statements of facts on the plea that "they would alarm the people at home," or "have the people of the United States by the ears."

The document was reprinted in most U.S. newspapers and created a sensation more or less along party lines. For example, the Philadelphia *Record* commented, "The administration might score a point by lifting the silly censorship established at Manila by an incapable military martinet whose accidental elevation to unrestrained authority has been, in truth, the worst blow yet inflicted upon the prestige of the government at Washington." The New York *Times* countered that newsmen with an army at war had no rights at all. But "it is pretty evident that things are worse in Manila than reported," said the Augusta *Chronicle;* ". . . the public is getting very restive under the censorship that equals deception . . . the bulk of the people are sick of the whole Philippine business." The St. Louis *Globe Democrat* suggested, however, that all "these absurdly pretentious and officious" reporters be kicked out of the islands. "Otis is a failure," blared the Philadelphia *North American* contrarily —a man who tried to win wars with the pen instead of the sword. There had not been such an uproar, such an insurrection, since Colonel Roosevelt's round-robin letter a year ago, in which he had gone over General Shafter's head to demand that the army be withdrawn from Cuba before yellow fever destroyed it.

One wonders if Otis was, after all, completely at fault. With a war going on, he could hardly be expected to encourage the enemy by permitting tales of woe to emanate from U.S. headquarters. The extent of sick casualties had indeed been minimized; but was the Filipino high command entitled to know the correct figure? Furthermore, everyone realized that many so-called heat-prostrated soldiers were

simply combat stragglers, and that others in the hospital were
malingering. Did Aguinaldo have to be informed that his opponents were in military difficulties? Yet the newsmen considered it their duty to transmit the unadorned facts, as
though they were reporting a fire or a robbery. They wanted
to explain why there were so many U.S. stragglers, malinger-
ers, and sick, and so few military results to date. "Every fight
became a glorious American victory . . ." wrote Mr. Collins,
"and we were drilled into writing, quite mechanically, wholly
ridiculous estimates of the numbers of Filipinos killed."

But the controversy went deeper than censorship; it was
grounded in a general mistrust of Otis as a commander. To
this end, the correspondents also peppered their complaint
with a series of quotations contributed by men in the field.
"His reports always end with 'Troops in the best of spirits,'"
said Corporal Charles Green; "You ought to hear the boys
cuss when they read it. They are all tired and sick of this and
want to go home." Stated Corporal William Hurder: "General Otis is not fit and never was fit to command . . .
Repeatedly we have cornered the Filipinos . . . These advantages have always been neglected, on account of counter
orders . . ." Private R. H. Misenheimer called Otis an old
grandmother. "Washington or Otis held the men back," ob-
jected Private John Warren; "At Ballanig we could have captured the enemy's supply train and also have captured
thousands of natives, but a halt was ordered." In the considered opinion of Private John Grieve, Otis made a better
clerk than a general.

One may not place excessive faith in these lowly expostula-
tions, but they made pleasant reading for those who questioned the administration's imperial policy or who resented
Otis' dictatorial attitude toward the press. He remained taciturn and unmoved; flatly he refused to share his facts, figures,
and plans with the war correspondents, most of whom were
hard-drinking craftsmen not over-reverent concerning military secrets. They had let the cat out of the bag several times

before. For example, when Wheaton was relieved of his command at Angeles and assigned to the Dagupan expedition the news was leaked to the local papers, and thence to America, long before Wheaton even got his twenty-five hundred men aboard the transports. Some writers had even divulged (by mail) that only a tiny fraction of volunteers were re-enlisting. Otis was now being worriedly interrogated by the War Department, and doubtless he fumed at this monitory note from Alger: "Some newspapers report you are about to be relieved. Pay no attention . . ." He threw up his hands. For his part, he replied in effect, the damned newspapermen could henceforth cable anything they pleased. On September 9 he announced that the office of censor (a Captain Greene) was being abolished. But the revisions and deletions continued under the guise of correcting factual errors; nothing really changed; the news continued to reflect the harried optimism of the monarch in "The Palace."

Relentlessly Mr. Roosevelt, from his own mansion in Albany, continued his backstage vendetta against this man who so plainly lacked the military virtues in which his Rough Riders had abounded. In August he wrote his civil-service reform friend in Iowa, Lucius B. Swift: "The President has a profound belief in General Otis and believes the Philippine business is well in hand. Merely as an outsider I doubt this . . ." He was now imploring McKinley to give Lawton the supreme command. In a stream of letters to Cecil Spring Rice, George F. Becker, Elihu Root, and the president, he reiterated his uneasiness. Otis was painstaking and hardworking, he admitted, but was he capable of executing a crushing campaign against the natives? Mr. McKinley still thought so, but even he conceded that everything hinged upon impending military events.

And if the general's light had dimmed since February, the innocuous Secretary of War was already a casualty of that summer's resentments and apprehensions. Ever since April 1898 he had been accused of appalling inefficiency; the "em-

balmed beef" scandal and others were laid at his door; and
long had Mr. Roosevelt been trying to cut him down. When
he told McKinley that the overwhelming majority of Americans considered "Algerism" a national curse which was im-
periling the administration, the president listened gravely;
and although he liked Alger he finally implied that the man
might have to go. To simplify matters, Alger announced his
candidacy for the senate with the backing of Governor
Pingree of Michigan, a tireless critic of the administration.
With a clear conscience McKinley now asked him to resign.

Next the president telephoned a New York corporation
lawyer named Elihu Root and offered him the War Department. Mr. Root responded in surprise that he knew nothing
about war. Fine, said Mr. McKinley; "I don't want a man
who knows about war and the army. I want a lawyer to handle the problems of the new islands." Mr. Root accepted the
job. He was later to prove adept at army reorganization and
colonial administration, but at the moment his misconceptions of the Philippine crisis were considerable. At the Mar-
quette Club in Chicago he bared them in his first official
speech:

> Well, whom are we fighting? Are we fighting the Philippine
> nation? No! There is none. There are . . . more than sixty
> tribes . . . all but one ready to accept American sovereignty.

Emilio Aguinaldo he dismissed as a military dictator who
had surrounded himself with a band of brigands—a man who
had attained power by murdering General Luna. As for the
U.S. legal position:

> Gentlemen, the title of America to the island of Luzon (*sic*)
> is better than the title we had to Louisiana . . .

And in conclusion:

> The American soldier is different from all other soldiers since
> the world began, and today I am prouder of him for what he

is doing . . . than I ever was for the greatest victory he ever won.

This, then, was the handsome, imperative man who would henceforth dominate war and peace in the Philippines.

IV

Momentarily something had somehow gone wrong with the great crusade. Mr. McKinley, Mr. Root, Mr. Lodge, and Mr. Beveridge might speak sonorously of God, glory, and duty, but any child could see that we were at war with the Filipinos, whose territory we demanded from a distance of eight thousand miles, while we were not fighting Cubans nor coveting their island scarcely a stone's throw from the Florida Keys. How to explain this discrepancy? By summer 1899 a certain uneasiness, a pang of conscience, had drifted subtly across the land. Sampled sixty years later, pro-administration speeches and journals seem evasive and defensive in flavor, much like the Spanish assurances concerning Cuba in 1895: The rebels are brigands and already in flight; their movement will soon collapse; their evil aims have no relationship to the sane aspirations of the vast majority of law-abiding natives; after deftly dispersing the bandits, the mother country will restore order and prosperity. But was this old, familiar catechism for once true? Some people wondered; and many more wondered after the Otis press scandal in July. Even Mr. McKinley is said to have woefully remarked that if Dewey had only sailed away when he smashed the Spanish fleet, "what a lot of trouble he would have saved us" —a sentiment which the Boston *Transcript* reiterated in poesy:

> O Dewey at Manila
> That fateful first of May,
> When you sank the Spanish squadron
> In almost bloodless fray,

> And gave your name to deathless fame;
>   O glorious Dewey, say,
> Why didn't you weigh anchor
>   And softly sail away?

In a normal organism reaction follows and is equal and opposite to hysteria. The little war with Spain had been thrilling indeed. Now there was this repellent, confusing Philippine affair to swing the pendulum back with a vengeance. And the excuses given therefor were vaguely unsatisfactory. We would not haul down the flag under fire—this was basic. But why (it was asked) were not the Cubans also firing at us? Because (it was confessed) we gave them independence. And not the Filipinos? They will get it too eventually. Why not now? Why was the Bacon amendment defeated? No matter; we will uplift the Filipinos even more than the Cubans. Suppose they prefer not to be uplifted by us?

The dialogue took many forms and exhausted millions of words, but on the basis of the coming 1900 elections one may assume that more people were in favor of expansion, despite reservations and regrets, than those opposed to it. In congress, however, the proportion was reversed. Philippine annexation would have been decisively defeated had it been voted upon on February 6 as a single issue, and surely few senators had changed their minds half a year later. But if the anti-imperialists were outnumbered in the nation as a whole that summer, they were by no means out-talked. Tactically their climactic assault was launched a year too soon to influence the 1900 voting, and mere words would scarcely induce Mr. McKinley to call off General Otis. But from the pen of William Vaughn Moody came the anguished classic, "An Ode in Time of Hesitation":

> Lies! Lies! It cannot be! The wars we wage
> Are noble, and our battles still are won
> By justice for us, ere we lift the gage. We
> Have not sold our loftiest heritage.

The proud republic hath not stooped to cheat
And scramble in the market-place of war . . .
Ah no!
We have not fallen so . . .
Tempt not our weakness, our cupidity!
For save we let the island men go free,
Those baffled and dislaureled ghosts
Will curse us from the lamentable coasts
Where walk the frustrate dead . . .
Oh ye who lead,
Take heed!
Blindness we may forgive, but baseness we will smite.

These were stirring lines, although two years were to ensue
before Mr. McKinley would be coincidentally smitten; and
they were echoed by Hoar of Massachusetts in the upper
chamber. All men within the sound of his voice, he declared,
would be fighting for their liberty, were they Filipinos, and
would despise others not doing the same. And from the
south Senator Tillman taunted the holier-than-thou Republicans. Who were they to wring their hands over the limitation
of Negro suffrage? "Your slogans of the past—brotherhood
of man and fatherhood of God—have gone glimmering . . ."
Stung by such accusations, supporters of the war called
it sacrilege to utter the names Aguinaldo and Washington
in the same breath, and denounced as treason the encouragement of insurgents who were trying to shoot down
the Stars and Stripes. They denied that it was practical
or moral to deliver self-government to a chaotic mixture of
"tribes" eight million in number and devoid of experience
in law, order, and self-defense. Stubbornly they continued
to insist that the only proper thing to do was first to conquer
them and then, slowly and patiently, to lead them along the
paths of education, local autonomy, sanitation, law, and military aptitude.

In the process we too would be uplifted, but in a different
way. "From a nation of shopkeepers we become a nation of

warriors," thundered the famous editor of the Louisville *Courier-Journal*, "Marse" Henry Watterson.

We escape the menace and peril of socialism and agrarianism, as England has escaped them, by a policy of colonialism and conquest. From a provincial huddle of petty sovereignties held together by a rope of sand we rise to the dignity and prowess of an imperial republic incomparably greater than Rome. It is true that we exchange domestic dangers for foreign dangers; but in every direction we multiply the opportunities of the people. We risk Caesarism, certainly; but even Caesarism is preferable to anarchism. We risk wars; but a man has but one time to die, and either in peace or war, he is not likely to die until his time comes. In short, anything is better than the pace we were going before these present forces were started into life. Already the young manhood of the country is as a goodly brand snatched from the burning, and given a perspective replete with noble deeds and elevating ideas.

It was, of course, Mr. Kipling rephrased; and even as U.S. youths in Luzon performed their noble deeds and pondered elevating ideas, new parodies on that gentleman's ballad poured from many a pen . . .

> Take up the sword and rifle [wrote Bertrand Shadwell]
>   Send forth your ships with speed,
> To join the nations' scramble,
>   And vie with them in greed;
> Go find your goods a market;
>   Beyond the western flood,
> The heathen who withstand you
>   Shall answer it in blood . . .
>
> Take up the sword and rifle,
>   Still keep your conscience whole—
> So soon is found an unction
>   To soothe a guilty soul.
> Go with it to your Maker,
>   Find what excuse ye can—

> Rob for the sake of justice,
> Kill for the love of man.

By now the imbroglio had attracted attention throughout the western world. It was not only that America was doing precisely what the British, the French, the Spanish, and the Dutch had been doing for centuries; nor was it that the Americans were probably mistaken about trade and political trends in the Far East, the commercial value of the Philippines, and the assumed glories of colonialism; it was that U.S. imperialists seemed really to believe what they were saying. This was incomprehensible to Europeans accustomed to operating with the minimum of fanfare and self-deception. Their ironic comments were often used as ammunition by the anti-imperialists. As for the claim that the Filipinos had to pay for their follies and misdeeds, Mr. Pulitzer's editorialist inquired, "Of course Aguinaldo's punishment should fit his crime, but what is his crime?"; and in another issue the *World* (now anti-imperialist) also asked:

> We've taken up the white man's burden
> Of ebony and brown;
> Now will you tell us, Rudyard,
> How we may put it down?

Tempers soared with the temperature and debate became more acrimonious. Once a Republican high mogul, Carl Schurz called McKinley a contemptible rascal and was in turn abused for his terminology. Andrew Carnegie frenziedly wrote, spoke, and donated his treasure to the cause, and he too was pilloried; for was he not sweating immigrant workmen twelve hours daily on near-starvation wages in his Pittsburgh blast furnaces?

The administration and its followers attacked William Jennings Bryan most of all, conveniently forgetting that he alone had insured ratification of the Paris treaty by his defection last December. Now he was vilifying the Republicans again with ruthless oratory (according to his plan) and asking for the military defeat of his own country. It was really too much for the opposition to bear, and a murderous counterattack was launched against him. The cover of the pro-Republican magazine *Judge* showed Aguinaldo with his foot upon a dead American soldier; below the colored drawing was the caption: "What Is Behind Aguinaldo, That Fiend Who Has Slain Many American Soldiers?" A die-cut flap, when lifted, disclosed the smiling face of Mr. Bryan.

For five months there had been little fighting and no real progress in the islands, nor could honeyed announcements from "The Palace" entirely disguise the fact. Restlessness increased week after week. Admiral Dewey, asked to comment on Admiral von Diederichs' removal as commander of the German Pacific fleet, stated that he had been removed because "his time was up, not as a concession made in friendliness to the American government . . . Our next war will be with Germany." Official circles were dismayed, but the general public laughed and applauded their hero. Mr. Lodge was returned to the senate by a party vote of 190 to 72, and waspishly Henry Adams wrote, "Cabot smiles because he has got his re-election, and all the world knows how great and good he is." His friend, Theodore, attended a Rough Rider reunion and noted that he had been received by the crowds exactly as if he had been a presidential candidate. He had 1904 very much in mind; the problem was whether he should make himself available for the vice-presidency next year, and he and Cabot discussed it in anxious correspondence all summer long.

At sixty-two Admiral Dewey took a Catholic bride of forty-nine, whereupon the whispering started: the admiral was a fool to remarry at his age; the house (a gift from the American people) which he had promptly deeded her would become the official Washington seat of the papacy; Mrs. Dewey's gowns and jewels were excessively grand, almost ostentatious; and so on. It had been seventeen months since the admiral's victory—slightly too long for supreme glory to en-

dure. Mild jokes began to be heard about him; his presidential
bubble had been ever so slightly pricked.

To Whitelaw Reid came a bitter letter from Andrew
Carnegie: "It is a matter of congratulation that you seem to
have about finished your work of civilizing the Filipinos. It
is thought that about eight thousand of them have been completely civilized and sent to Heaven." But Mr. McKinley
contemplated the course of recent events with something resembling awe. "And so it has come to pass," he mused one
autumn morning (while his secretary transcribed the words
for posterity), "that in a few short months we have become a
world power; and I know, sitting here in this chair, with what
added respect the nations of the world now deal with the
United States and it is vastly different from the conditions
I found when I was inaugurated."

It was certainly true that the trend of American history
had swerved sharply, more so than even Mr. McKinley suspected; but still the strange new war went on—the only cloud
on a glorious sunrise. The nation awaited the autumn campaign that would stifle the insurrection—so they had been
told time and again—and Mr. Dooley summarized it all for
Mr. Hennessy:

> . . . We say to thim: "Naygurs," we say, "poor, dissolute, un-
> covered wretches," says we, ". . . ye mis'rable, childish-
> minded apes, we propose f'r to larn ye th' uses iv liberty . . .
> We can't give ye anny votes, because we haven't more thin
> enough to go round now; but we'll threat ye th' way a father
> shud threat his children if we have to break ivry bone in y'er
> bodies. So come to our ar-rms," says we.
>
> But, glory be, 'tis more like a rasslin' match than a father's
> embrace . . . An' there it stands, Hinnissy, with th' indulgent
> parent kneelin' on th' stomach iv his adopted child, while a
> dillygation fr'm Boston bastes him with an umbrella. There it
> stands, an' how it will come out I dinnaw. I'm not much iv an
> expansionist mesilf.

The gentlemen from Boston to whom Mr. Dunne referred

had embarked upon their most provocative venture. For
some time they had been showering the troops in the islands
with terse letters and leaflets of advice—"Boys, don't re-
enlist. Insist immediate discharge"—exasperating enough to
the authorities; but meanwhile even more dangerous doings
were afoot. The second of Edward Atkinson's pamphlets had
rolled off the presses in June: "I. THE COST OF A NATIONAL
CRIME. II. THE HELL OF WAR AND ITS PENALTIES. III. CRIMINAL
AGGRESSION: BY WHOM COMMITTED?" This hundred-page masterpiece of anti-imperialist invective and reasoning was
loaded with documented atrocity stories, death and disease
statistics, culled quotations from the record showing the alleged perfidy of U.S. diplomacy, and other facts and figures
tending to discredit the war effort.

Three generations later one thumbs through its cheap,
grayish pages with a slight sense of shock. A volunteer writes
that even the Spaniards are appalled at American cruelty.
Mr. Atkinson predicts that eight thousand U.S. troops will die
the first year. Sergeant Vickers demands to know what he is
fighting for. Another volunteer claims that men like him are
buried and forgotten, with only regular troops mourned and
replaced when they fall. The London *Economist* states soothingly that Otis has no need to hurry; after all, it took the
British five years to subjugate upper Burma. Various soldiers
are quoted as disgusted with the war and tired of shooting
down "little black boys." Mr. Atkinson analyzes the fiscal figures and concludes that within two years the war will bank-
rupt the country. He beseeches that no youth volunteer or
enlist in this so-called criminal enterprise. A horrid tale is told
of what happened to the French when they undertook to
civilize Madagascar: "In ten months 4,200 of these men died
. . . The French are now trying to maintain troops under a
sick and death rate that they are afraid to have published
even in their own country." A Nebraska mother calls McKinley a pure and simple murderer. From India, it is said, about
eight thousand Englishmen return home yearly with some

form of venereal disease. There are hints that The League is helping to smuggle arms and money to the Filipinos.

This sort of thing in wartime was dynamite, and even as the government was pondering what to do about it Mr. Atkinson brought matters to a head by requesting permission of the Secretary of War to mail copies of the pamphlet to the Philippines. Receiving no reply, he mailed them. The War Department now came to life, labeled the material seditious, and instructed Otis to destroy it upon arrival at Manila. Steps were also taken to intercept the pamphlets at San Francisco. But Atkinson (who had been under no illusions) had made his point: while engaged in suppressing the insurrection, the government would also suppress freedom of opinion at home. Many expansionist publications defended him. The Boston *Journal* advised the government that it was wrong to gag an honored patriot like Atkinson. The Springfield *Republican* thought his pamphlet no more seditious than any newspaper or speech criticizing the administration, and predicted gloomily that the next step would be to stamp out freedom of speech within the borders of the United States.

The angry cry which went up is hard to fathom by today's more cautious standards. Rightly or wrongly we were at war with the Filipino people, and the sentiments Mr. Atkinson had disseminated to our fighting men were ruinous to morale —perhaps even traitorous. It was as though similar propaganda had been mailed to U.S. troops in Korea half a century later. That war, too, was controversial and distasteful, but not even its most ardent opponents dreamed of urging army and navy personnel not to fight. In Luzon American officers were beside themselves with fury. Men like Atkinson, they said, were giving aid and comfort to the enemy; thus they were instrumental in killing American boys. Not without logic General Lawton remarked that if he were to be shot by a Filipino bullet it would be the same as a bullet from an American whose words were prolonging the war. And there was no question but that a good deal of The Anti-Imperialist

League's material was also reaching the enemy, for copies of it were captured in the field and Señores Mabini and Paterno had long been quoting from it *ad nauseam.*

Essentially the question was one of ethics. Could the anti-imperialists be allowed to encourage the official enemies of the country, and thus waste American lives; or must they keep silent and allow evil (as they saw it) to be perpetrated without a murmur of dissent? At no time during the course of the insurrection was this dilemma ever solved.

On October 17 The League convened in Chicago and among other flourishes laid down this fundamental principle:

> We hold that the policy known as imperialism is hostile to liberty and tends towards militarism. We regret that it has become necessary in the land of Washington and Lincoln to reaffirm that all men, of whatever race or color, are entitled to life, liberty and the pursuit of happiness . . . We demand the immediate cessation of the war against liberty, begun by Spain and continued by us . . . We propose to contribute to the defeat of any person or party that stands for the forcible subjugation of any people.

That week VIII Corps finally crashed against the rebel armies in central Luzon.

11

*For there's many a man been murdered in Luzon
and Mindanao
and in Samar . . .*

THE
GUERILLA
WAR

BRIGADIER GENERAL "FIGHTING JOE" WHEELER, LEE'S SENIOR
cavalry general in the Civil War, had served in congress from 1881 to 1898 as a representative from Ala-
bama, resigning to become a major general of dismounted
cavalry in the Cuban campaign. The evening before Las
Guasimas he had perceived that darkness enabled him to
outflank his superior officer (who happened to be General
Lawton), assault the Spaniards ahead of schedule with his
first brigade, and thus confound the regular infantry. When
the Spaniards abandoned their entrenchments, his excited
cry—"We've got the damn Yankees on the run!"—became the
classic line of that war; but his unexpected dawn attack almost provoked a catastrophe. Furiously Lawton had advised
him that this was no political campaign but a war; he (Lawton) was in command of the advance "and he proposed to
keep it, even if he had to post a guard to keep other troops
to the rear." When Wheeler, however, continued to show little inclination to obey orders, General Shafter himself was
forced to order him "very positively" to remain where he was

and to cease fighting without specific instructions. Upon the end of the Cuban campaign, Wheeler was demoted one grade, transferred to the Philippines, and placed under Major General Arthur MacArthur, who thus had more than one headache to contend with en route to the Lingayen Gulf.

Shortly after MacArthur's force started up the railway, unscheduled and unprecedented rains washed away long sections of track, while the insurgents blew up bridges and instituted harassing attacks against working parties trying to keep the supply line open. Slowly the Americans moved toward Capas, a small town fifteen miles south of the rebel capital at Tarlac. There Wheeler was told to pin down the main enemy force while two other regiments worked around its flanks. Highly indignant, he requested permission to launch a full-scale attack. When MacArthur reiterated his original order, Wheeler deployed his brigade and charged anyway. Now MacArthur sent a messenger to bring the wiry little brigadier to him personally. Wheeler galloped to the divisional command post, reined his horse on a dime, and was ordered to recall his men. He saluted impassively, returned to the front, and proceeded to throw the rest of his command into the attack. In the melee which followed, the U.S. brigade became disorganized. Again MacArthur recalled "Fighting Joe," and reprimanded him in terms that must be left to one's imagination. Despite this small imbroglio, Tarlac was reached and occupied on November 12, while the insurgent government was retreating slowly, evacuating one "capital" after another.

Active resistance from troops operating along the railroad under generals Alexandrino and Concepcion melted away. The capture of President Aguinaldo, who was not many miles away, would have been simplified by information concerning his whereabouts, but not a man, woman or child brought before MacArthur's officers would talk. They had no idea where he was, they said, although they were delighted by the arrival of the American army and longed to co-operate with it. All the natives, in fact, were exceedingly friendly. Everyone was an *amigo*. Gratified at the reception he was receiving, MacArthur continued methodically up the railway. By this time it had broken down, and gangs of men had to push the cars between Capas and Tarlac. Beyond the latter point it was all but discarded as a supply artery.

As for "Fighting Joe," he was fighting mad. For several days he had been assigned to construction chores in the rear, and he wrote MacArthur that if he were being discriminated against for being an ex-Confederate, such humiliation was contrary to Washington's philosophy of Boys in Blue and Boys in Gray fighting arm-in-arm against the common enemy. To this dramatic plea MacArthur merely responded: "Do not attempt to move forward until further orders. No enemy in front between here and Bayambang and none in that town." General Wheeler had fought his last battle in the Philippines.

On November 20 the expedition reached Dagupan, defeated the *insurrectos* there, captured much war material, and occupied the important coastal town of Santa Cruz. Mac-Arthur had done his job effectively and on schedule; and he wired Otis: "The so-called Filipino Republic is destroyed. The congress has dissolved. The President of the so-called republic is a fugitive as are all his cabinet officers, except one who is in our hands. The Army itself as an organization has disappeared . . ." He went on to outline a unique plan for ending the insurrection; after an "early date" it would be proclaimed null and void, and any native who shot an American soldier would be dealt with as a murderer. But the estimate was, as events proved, quite inaccurate; and the recommendation not only contradicted international rules of warfare but disregarded the fact that many American soldiers had been captured.

The fate of U.S. prisoners, virtually hostages, is illustrated by an incident at Mabalacat. Here four Americans searching (as always) for chickens were surrounded by rebels who killed one and captured the others. For six weeks, during which playful Filipinos sometimes pointed cocked pistols at their heads and then pulled the triggers on empty chambers, they were abused and underfed. At last a detachment of the 25th Infantry approached the insurgent camp. Before departing, the natives shot the prisoners down and hacked them with bolos. While several dozen other Americans were being held by the enemy, MacArthur's plan was out of the question. But if Wheaton and Lawton were fulfilling their end of the bargain, perhaps the insurrection was in its last throes: Draconian measures would be needless. What was happening to the other two expeditions?

On Lawton's part, a reasonable amount of speed was necessary if Aguinaldo were to be taken. First of all, the various mountain passes leading eastward had to be closed. Secondly and even more vital, the top loop of the circle had to be completed in order to block egress into the vast reaches of northern Luzon. The sense of urgency which accompanied the drive along the eastern edge of the plain was therefore heightened by fantastic difficulties which Lawton encountered. Seemingly the Rio Grande de Pampanga furnished an ideal line of communications; but in fact it turned out worthless from San Isidro northward—either so flooded that the swift current racing down from the mountains halted the launches and their laden *cascos* in tow, or (between cloudbursts) so shallow that they went aground on sand bars. Men trying to pull the barges upstream with ropes from the shore became exhausted and accomplished nothing. After two hours of hauling, one *casco* was found to be further downstream than before work began. Meanwhile sniping by insurgents concealed on the riverbanks was causing steady casualties. After ten days Lawton's column was still milling around San Isidro. Food and ammunition were piling up, but with no way of moving them the troops were stalled.

When the river rose on October 27 after a rain, Lawton decided to dispatch a mobile force north, regardless of risk, with a mere ten thousand rations. From this date on, Brigadier

General Samuel Young with some artillery, two cavalry squadrons, and a battalion of the 22nd Infantry dominated the expedition. Surrounded by the rest of his infantry, Lawton devoted his time and energies to the transport problem; he had become, as he wryly admitted, his own supply officer. From San Isidro he bombarded Otis with complaints concerning the quartermaster department in Manila. Those oafs had no conception of his dilemma, he wrote; they kept sending him tons of stuff, half of which he didn't need and none of which could be brought up the Rio Grande. Where were the shallow-draft launches he had been asking for? "All boats sent to me draw too much water," he explained patiently. "The question of supplies is the only serious one confronting me and this should have been solved long since."

He placed his division on half rations and sent a Colonel Howard back to Manila to stir things up. When his launch was ambushed from the shore, the colonel was killed. Lawton fired off another emissary. At this juncture a captured proclamation indicated that Aguinaldo and his government were leaving for Bayombong in Nueva Viscaya. Since the document was several days old, its news was distinctly alarming. Should Aguinaldo slip through the mountain passes, Lawton's labors would be largely in vain. On the other hand, it was hopeless to chain the division to its motionless supply train. Sam Young, some distance ahead, now asked permission to leave his wagons behind, live off the country, and try to intercept the Filipino president by a headlong dash into wild country never before seen by a white man.

The proposition raised a question in the form of General Otis. He would never sanction such a lunatic scheme if he knew about it. Also he was at odds with Young personally. Six feet four and 250 pounds, General Young had commanded III Corps in Cuba. When reassigned to the Philippines he had perpetrated the *gaucherie* of suggesting to the War Department how the Philippine campaign could be wound up and in what manner Otis was mishandling it.

Washington helpfully passed the document on to Otis, who became most wroth and (in Young's opinion, at least) made subsequent efforts to ruin the latter's career. Did Lawton dare to release him? Reluctantly (perhaps enviously) he did so. Cut off from Otis, Lawton, the telegraph and his supply base, Young and eleven hundred men were now on their own. By November 8, after hardships and fighting so incessant that they are best glossed over, Young reached San Jose and learned that the Filipino party—which included Aguinaldo, his wife, child, mother, members of his cabinet, and an armed guard several hundred strong—was still south of the mountains. The Americans, who had been using primitive sledges to drag cartridge boxes through the mud, now abandoned them. Henceforth each man carried a bandolier of ammunition and little more.

All roads were morasses. With some exceptions, horses and foot soldiers were shoeless. The field guns had long since been left behind. On several occasions the infantry caught up with and passed the cavalry which, during periods of rain, was averaging a mile or two a day. The troops had been campaigning for five weeks,

> and had been on half rations for two weeks. Wallowing through the hip-deep muck, lugging a ten-pound rifle and a belt filled with ammunition, drenched to the skin and with their feet becoming heavier with mud at each step, the infantry became discouraged. Some men simply cried, others slipped down in the mud and refused to rise. Threats and appeals by officers were of no avail. Only a promise of food in the next town and the fear that if they remained behind they would be butchered by marauding bands of Insurgents forced some to their feet to struggle on.

By now Young's main body had reached a point twenty miles east of Dagupan. He sent scouts groping westward for Wheaton's force, which presumably had landed nearby. At first no contact was made, and apprehensively Young wrote Lawton that Aguinaldo's chance of eluding him was good

unless Wheaton connected with him. When his scouts uncovered a rumor that Wheaton's transports had indeed arrived, the remnant of Young's command hacked its way
toward the gulf in an effort to close the trap. Aguinaldo was
nearby; of that there could be no question, for on November
14 a cavalry column had run into his rear guard. Frantically
Young pressed forward to the next town along the road which
blended into the last pass separating the insurgents from salvation. Led by a native guide, the Americans reached it.
Were they in time? Unfortunately they were in the wrong
village; and as General Young commented: "The only reason
that the guide who had led us to Manaoag instead of Pozorrubio was not shot was because he could not be found."
The expedition commanded by Lawton and spearheaded by
Young had in six weeks traversed 120 miles of frightful military terrain, fighting much of the way, had garrisoned every
town and mountain pass along the east fringe of the central
Luzon plain, had turned west and reached a point almost
within artillery range of Dagupan. Where was Wheaton?

Always cautious, Otis had given him oral orders which
could not be intercepted by the enemy. But they could be
misinterpreted more easily than written instructions, and
evidently Wheaton had failed to grasp the prime strategic
intent of the campaign. Nothing else can explain the inaction
of this once ultra-aggressive commander—this and decades of
narrow experience as a company-grade officer. The result of
his failure was to prolong the war for two additional years.

With twenty-five hundred men of the 33rd Volunteer
and 13th Regular Infantry regiments and a detachment
of the 6th Artillery, all convoyed by the navy, General
Lloyd Wheaton and his transports had set sail from Manila, rounded Bataan, cruised north through the China Sea
and then southeast into the Lingayen Gulf, and had reached
the port of San Fabian on November 7. After a heavy bombardment of insurgent trenches by the *Princeton, Helena,
Bennington, Manila,* and two captured Spanish gunboats, the

troops disembarked within two hours and brushed resistance aside. It is typical of Wheaton's unfathomable dilatoriness that Dagupan, the junction point for both him and Mac-Arthur, only twelve miles from San Fabian, was not occupied by Wheaton's men until nineteen days later. Meanwhile much aimless maneuvering went on. Wheaton seems to have been satisfied to guard the old Spanish coastal "King's High-way," to reconnoiter various towns without occupying them, to scout the general area, and to engage the insurgents in skirmishes of no consequence. But even the coast road was blocked only as far as San Fabian; north of there it was ignored. At no time during the ensuing all-important days did he manage to ascertain that Aguinaldo and his staff were in the immediate vicinity. Towns such as San Jacinto and Mangalden, through which the Filipinos later had to pass, were at most cursorily inspected. One battalion came within a mile of Rosario and turned back at the very moment when Aguinaldo's party was entering the place from the south.

On November 14 a few men from Young's 3rd Cavalry rode into San Fabian and finally told Wheaton what was happening to his east. Yet he continued to act halfheartedly. Ordinarily bold, almost rash, he wasted two entire days before dispatching elements of the 33rd Infantry toward Pozorrubio. But Aguinaldo, along with a thousand troops who had been driven north by MacArthur, had just left that town. The results of the sortie were therefore meager. Felipe Buencamino, once foreign secretary in the native government, was captured. Seventy-five thousand pesos in specie were located in a buried cache. As usual, the insurgent force was scattered. Aguinaldo's mother and his only remaining son were captured,* his youngest having died shortly after the flight began. His wife was suffering from fainting spells; being

---

* The news made headlines in the States. Thomas ("Czar") Reed is quoted as saying to his law partner, "What, are you working to-day? I should think you would be celebrating; I see by the papers that the American army has captured the infant son of Aguinaldo, and at last accounts was in hot pursuit of the mother."

hunted like a criminal had begun to tell upon her. Sick at heart, burning with hatred and despair, the Philippine *presidente* and his entourage finally reached the coast road and proceeded at a slightly faster pace.

With the cat practically out of the bag, General Young made one last effort to tighten the string. Leading a battalion of three hundred native Maccabebe traitors and one troop of the 3rd Cavalry, he prepared to push toward the settlement of Alava, about thirty miles north-northeast of Dagupan. Lying almost in the shadow of the majestic Benguet range, this was one of the last populated points on the north-central plain. Somewhat listless from lack of sleep, short of food, facing an expanse of harsh and unknown territory, Young and his men started off on November 18. Before doing so, he coolly wrote Otis, helpless and fuming back in Manila: "Aguinaldo is now a fugitive and an outlaw, seeking security in escape to the mountains or by sea. My cavalry has ridden down his forces wherever found, utterly routing them in every instance, capturing and liberating many prisoners . . . My men have had no supplies from the government for the past five days . . . Please inform Major General Lawton, as floods prevent my communicating with him by courier." He then communicated with Lawton by courier, requested that more light infantry follow, passed through Alava, turned west, and hurried up the coast highway. Some men from Wheaton's 33rd Infantry had also drifted into the chase. When Wheaton, still cooling his heels in San Fabian, heard of this, he recalled them; whereupon Young wrote him imploringly, "My forces are much depleted and worn out. Aguinaldo has been playing hide and seek. One day in the mountains, the next . . . on the coast road . . . Am sorry that you found it necessary to recall Faison . . . If you can assist me in this matter, I don't see how he can escape." Wheaton grudgingly released one battalion under Major Peyton C. March, who at first precipitated a quarrel by refusing to fight under anyone but Wheaton and then proceeded toward the Tirad Pass.

Having wasted time (perhaps necessarily) doubling back from the coast road, Aguinaldo was now only a few miles ahead of the Americans. A crucial moment in the history of the insurrection was at hand.

Throughout Aguinaldo's hegira, his rear guard had been under the command of Brigadier General Gregorio del Pilar, a former Manila college student who had become the president's inseparable companion ever since the death of Aguinaldo's brother, General Crispulo Aguinaldo. It was del Pilar (not to be confused with his infamous brother Pio) who recommended a delaying action at Tirad Pass while Aguinaldo's group continued toward safety. With sixty riflemen he fortified the place and awaited Major March and his nine hundred men. They arrived the morning of December 2. Among them was the war correspondent Richard Henry Little, whose description of what happened was published in the Chicago *Tribune*:

> We had seen him cheering his men in the fight. One of our companies crouched up close under the side of the cliff where he had built his first intrenchment, heard his voice continually during the fight, scolding them, praising them, cursing, appealing one moment to their love of their native land and the next instant threatening to kill them if they did not stand firm. Driven from the first intrenchment he fell slowly back to the second in full sight of our sharpshooters and under a heavy fire. Not until every man around him in the second intrenchment was down did he turn his white horse and ride slowly up the winding trail. Then we who were below saw an American squirm his way out to the top of a high flat rock, and take deliberate aim at the figure on the white horse. We held our breath, not knowing whether to pray that the sharpshooter would shoot straight or miss. Then came the spiteful crack of the Krag rifle and the man on horseback rolled to the ground, and when the troops charging up the mountain side reached him, the boy general of the Filipinos was dead.
>
> We went up the mountain side. After H company had driven the insurgents out of their second position and killed

Pilar, the other companies had rushed straight up the trail
. . . Just past this a few hundred yards we saw a solitary
figure lying on the road. The body was almost stripped of
clothing, and there were no marks of rank on the blood-
soaked coat . . . A soldier came running down the trail.

"That's old Pilar," he said, "we got the old rascal. I guess
he's sorry he ever went up against the Thirty-Third."

"There ain't no doubt its being Pilar," rattled on the young
soldier. "We got his diary and letters and all his papers, and
Sullivan of our company's got his pants, and Snider's got his
shoes, but he can't wear them because they're too small, and a
sergeant in G. Company got one of his silver spurs, and a
lieutenant got the other, and somebody swiped his cuff buttons before I got here or I would have swiped them, and all
I got was a stud button and his collar with blood on it."

So this was the end of Gregorio del Pilar . . . A private
sitting by the fire was exhibiting a handkerchief. "It's old
Pilar's. It's got 'Dolores Hoses' on the corner. I guess that was
his girl. Well, it's all over with Gregorio."

"Anyhow," said Private Sullivan, "I got his pants. He won't
need them any more."

The man who had the general's shoes strode proudly past
. . . A private sitting on a rock was examining a golden
locket containing a curl of woman's hair. "Got the locket off
his neck," said the soldier . . .

As the main column started on its march for the summit of
the mountain a turn in the trail brought us again in sight of
the insurgent general far down below us. There had been no
time to bury him. Not even a blanket or a poncho had been
thrown over him.

A crow sat on the dead man's feet. Another perched on his
head. The fog settled down upon us. We could see the body
no longer.

> "We carved not a line and we raised not a
> stone, but we left him alone in his glory."

And when Private Sullivan went by in his trousers, and
Snider with his shoes, and the other man who had the cuff

buttons, and the sergeant who had the spur, and the lieutenant who had the other spur, and the man who had the handkerchief, and another that had his shoulder straps, it suddenly occurred to me that his glory was about all we had left him.

The body lay naked for several days until an American lieutenant, Dennis Quinlan of the 11th Cavalry, arrived and buried it with military honors. On the headstone he inscribed:

GENERAL GREGORIO DEL PILAR
KILLED AT THE BATTLE OF TIRAD PASS
DECEMBER 2D, 1899
COMMANDING AGUINALDO'S REAR GUARD
AN OFFICER AND A GENTLEMAN

Aguinaldo scaled the Benguet Mountains and escaped. After crossing the High Sierras he found temporary refuge in the sleepy town of Palanan, Isabela Province, having first persuaded his ailing wife to give herself up to the Americans. His brother, mother, wife, two sons, and best friend were gone, but the Tagalog leader was still at large, and the war went on—a new and different and more baffling kind of war.

II

Before disappearing into northern Luzon, Aguinaldo abrogated open warfare and issued orders to conduct the war along guerilla lines. Henceforth his hideouts became secret even to his own commanders. The troops returned to their various home provinces. The archipelago was divided into guerilla districts, each under a general officer, and into subzones commanded by majors or colonels. Everything now depended upon whether the people at large would support and provision the resistance movement.

Upon learning of this development Otis inferred that the insurrection was definitely finished. In his rigid, conservative mind there was no longer a doubt, and he allowed himself to be quoted thus in *Leslie's Weekly*:

> You ask me to say when the war in the Philippines will be
> over and to set a limit to the men and treasure necessary to
> bring affairs to a satisfactory conclusion. That is impossible,
> for the war in the Philippines is already over . . . all we have
> to do now is protect the Filipinos against themselves . . .
> There will be no more real fighting . . . little skirmishes
> which amount to nothing . . .

Two years and six thousand U.S. casualties later these
words were to come true. Meanwhile the insurgents adopted
their new tactics with relief. They had known for some time
that they could not stand up to the invader in formal battle;
their ammunition was running alarmingly low; it was common knowledge that the American force was nearing its 1899
peak of 59,722, with many thousands more available if
needed. Head-on resistance to this trained, heavily equipped
army was sheer madness. Yet the *insurrectos* had no hope of
winning the war by guerilla tactics. With their eyes fixed on
the political future, when Bryan's victory would bring them
almost automatic deliverance, they played a waiting game.

Through an elaborate system of codes and couriers Aguinaldo continued to direct his scattered forces; and as the year
ended it was clear to all men in the field (if not to the moody
general poring over his huge Philippine map in "The Palace")
that the people of the islands stood behind the guerillas.
"Wherever throughout the Archipelago there is a group of the
insurgent army," commented General MacArthur, "it is a fact
beyond dispute that all the contiguous towns contribute to
the maintenance thereof . . . Intimidation has undoubtedly
accomplished much to this end; but fear as the only motive
is hardly sufficient to account for the united and apparently
spontaneous action of several millions of people." A single
Judas among them could have betrayed Aguinaldo's whereabouts, but none appeared, and continuing efforts by the
Americans to drag such information out of the natives failed.
Troops under Young, MacArthur, Bell, Wheaton, Lawton and
other generals roamed at will over all of central and northern

Luzon as far as Aparri, at the uppermost reaches of the island.
There were no more pitched battles of any magnitude, but
Don Emilio could not be found, and the statistics of killed,
wounded, and sick curved relentlessly onward and upward.
Dozens of provinces in Samar, Mindoro, Panay, Leyte, Mindanao, Negros, and Cebu remained to be pacified. Southern
Luzon still presented a problem. Most annoying, insurgent
activity was actually increasing even near the capital city,
where U.S. control was supposedly unchallenged. Restive under supply duties and anxious to fight, General Lawton asked
permission to stamp out the insurgents in the provinces south
of Manila.

Very likely boredom explained the request. Hitherto Mr.
McKinley's most ardent advocate of benevolent assimilation,
Lawton had recently begun to change his views and had just
spoken out in a manner which had aroused uneasiness in certain quarters:

> Taking into account the disadvantages they have to fight
> against in arms, equipment and military discipline,—without
> artillery, short of ammunition, powder inferior, shells re-
> loaded until they are defective . . . they are the bravest men
> I have ever seen . . . What we want is to stop this accursed
> war . . . These men are indomitable. At Bacoor bridge they
> waited until the Americans had brought their cannon to
> within thirty-five yards of their trenches. Such men have the
> right to be heard. All they want is a little justice.

But even Lawton, a captive of his professional class and
decades of military environment, proposed to dispense that
justice with a Krag. Otis toyed with him for two weeks,
disapproved his scheme for a major roundup of *amigos* in
Laguna, Tayabas, and Batangas provinces, and at length authorized him to mount an attack against a handful of enemy
troops at San Mateo. It was little more than a scout-in-force—
almost an insult to a man of Lawton's rank—but without comment he shoved off on the evening of December 18 with two
battalions of infantry and some cavalry. It was raining hard.

In "The Palace" Otis was dining with several officers and their wives when Lawton passed by with his troops. Like a specter out of the night—tall, forbidding, his yellow slicker streaming with water—he stopped and waited outside for the Governor-General to appear. An edged conversation took place. Lawton asked if there were any further instructions. There were not. When Lawton saluted and prepared to leave, Otis remarked that in view of the weather the expedition might be called off. Lawton responded that his troops were already on the move and suggested that the orders be allowed to stand. Otis acquiesced without interest, and Lawton mounted his horse and rode off.

The Americans reached San Mateo, eighteen miles northeast of Manila, at dawn and found the insurgents under General Licerio Geronimo awaiting them in trenches near the Mariquina River. All these natives were marksmen who had been trained by an English soldier of fortune, and they stood their ground when Lawton launched his attack—a meticulous, painstaking, flanking and fording maneuver of the type he had led time and again in the past. This time it failed. Conspicuous in his large white helmet, Lawton personally rallied his men for another charge. In so doing, he was spotted by the Filipino general, who directed his *Tiradores de la Muerte* ("Death Shooters") to concentrate on him. One of his aides at his side, Lieutenant Breckenridge, was hit. Lawton carried him to shelter and returned to the firing line. Suddenly he made an awkward motion in front of his face. "What's the matter, General?" asked his remaining aide, Captain E. L. King.

"I'm shot."

"Where?"

"Through the lungs."

With blood pouring from his mouth, he lay down on the wet ground. In a few minutes America's greatest army officer, the one man whom the Filipinos regarded with superstitious terror, was dead, his head resting upon the thigh of a staff officer. The nemesis of Geronimo the Apache, at the Yaqui River thirteen years before, had been struck down (as if revengefully) by another Geronimo on the banks of another river thousands of leagues away. After the funereal return of the expedition Otis approved Lawton's earlier grand plan for encircling the rebels south of Manila; but it was Major General John C. Bates, Lawton's successor, who later executed it.

III

So the first year of war approached its unhappy end, and although it rained that December as never before in Luzon the campaigning had to continue. More and more areas were occupied, if not pacified, by U.S. troops. The list of garrisoned towns, provinces, and islands grew steadily until it encompassed most of the archipelago; but still there was no peace, for guerilla operations showed signs of intensifying rather than dwindling as the weeks slipped by.

Handicapped in flight by his illness, Apolinario Mabini was captured and thrown into prison, from where he continued his stream of revolutionary writings which were widely reprinted both in the islands and in the States. Not wishing to make him a martyr, Otis turned him loose; but since Mabini had no money he continued to live mostly in prison ("at the expense of the public," Otis complained) issuing challenges to debate the whole issue in public. The American commander ignored the man. Debate what? The war was over, the insurgent government non-existent; nothing remained (he cabled Adjutant General Corbin) but roving bands of "banditti . . . playing the role of amigos with arms concealed."

But guerilla resistance had become the nightmare of American troops. Being incessantly boloed and fired upon from cover was, if anything, more nerve-racking than out-and-out fighting. As a rule the Filipinos allowed their foes to capture any town they wished. Later they would attack by surprise or lead them into ambush by moving columns. Then they would blandly walk around the outskirts, fully armed and sometimes even in uniform. It was infuriating, but there was little militarily that could be done about it. Everyone was an *amigo;* "everyone was against us," grumbled General R. P. Hughes; and since it was impractical to kill off the entire native male population the problem might go on indefinitely, or at least until Aguinaldo was captured.

Quite openly the people of the countryside held mass meetings in honor of national independence and (as one Tarlac poster stated) "Of Those Among The American People Who Sympathize With The Filipino Nation." After the national march, an address by the local *presidente*, the reading of telegrams, speeches, and poems, the two-step "La Independencia," and donations for the wounded, usually came the crowning insult—a hymn, "Aguinaldo-Bryan!" It was fortunate for his health that Mr. Bryan had decided not to visit the Philippines that winter.

Whenever the Americans captured a town they set up a local native government. Simultaneously the guerillas would create a hostile "shadow" government. In almost all cases the latter governed, while the former tried to resign or tacitly refused to exercise authority. The lives of collaborators hung by a thread. Passive quasi co-operation was tolerated, but anything resembling treason sooner or later meant sudden death. For example, after General Parker proclaimed in Vigan that the war was at an end and that the Americans were bringing order and prosperity to the province, the insurgent general (Tinio) replied with a counter-proclamation to the effect that Parker lied and that there would be a bullet for every Filipino who practised collusion with the *norte americanos*. In any event, the natives expected no liberty or decency from the foreigners. A statement once made by Rizal—"America is the land *par excellence* of freedom, but only for the whites"—was accepted as gospel, and Americans, despite their high-sound-ing promises, were assumed to be of the same breed as their Spanish predecessors. In fact, there had been certain ties of religion, intermarriage, language and psychology between Filipinos and Spaniards; but between Filipinos and Americans there was hardly anything at all in common.

By the end of 1899 American civil government had made no appreciable headway beyond Manila and its suburbs. Even here the attitude of the populace was mixed. Some tolerated the Americans, a few welcomed them, most detested them. The masses remained generally in a state of limbo, waiting to see which way the wind would blow after the 1900 U.S. elections. However, an undercurrent of discouragement and apathy also existed. With their central government extinct and their armies dispersed, many islanders were willing to accept any overlord, provided they could be left in peace to eke out a living and repair their ruined lives.

Yet unqualified American control, as Albert Robinson wrote for the New York *Evening Post,* even in Luzon extended only about as far as a Krag could throw a bullet. No U.S. civilian could leave Manila or any other town without a military escort—a fact which Otis tried ceaselessly to suppress. Newcomers from the States were astonished at the discrepancy between fact and fable. They had read and had been told that the fighting was over except for minor police actions. Instead they found that the "quiet countryside" meant constant scouting parties, petty engagements, ambushes, and tense garrison duties in hundreds of far-flung villages. Every supply column expected the worst and was armed to the teeth. No man could afford to be a straggler, and extreme measures were always taken to retrieve American wounded. The need for outposts everywhere had seriously thinned out Otis' sixty-thousand-man army. Sometimes squads of Americans were overpowered by sheer weight of numbers. In a derisive army song modeled after a stanza in *Pinafore* these lines, so to speak, were sung by Otis:

> Am I the boss, or am I a tool,
> Am I Governor-General or hobo?
> Now I'd like to know who's the boss of the show,
> Is it me or Emilio Aguinaldo?

In Panay civil government was thought to be working smoothly, but it was found necessary to send the 44th Regiment there—this in addition to the 6th, 18th, 19th, and 26th. Thus five regiments of infantry were engaged in subduing one small island. In allegedly peaceful Negros, too, conditions had become so bad that two thousand troops were dispatched in late December to reinforce the original holding force. This sort of thing meanwhile was being duplicated elsewhere throughout the archipelago. Thus, oddly enough, during the same month that Otis had flatly cabled four times that the war was over, it had become clear in Washington that his army was, in fact, insufficient to hold down the kettle lid. Unknown to Manila headquarters, a decision was reached to send him at least ten thousand more troops in 1900.

Great victories were attributed to General Schwan's expedition in the south, but scarcely had Manila and American newspapers published them when renewed heavy fighting broke out near Imus. Thousands of *insurrectos* were back in the area, scouts reported; and Mr. Robinson advised his readers that the new aggregation was said to occupy a stronger position than the previous one. It was like sweeping back waves, and, countering Professor Dean C. Worcester's speech to the effect that the United States was waging the most humane war in history, Robinson went on: "A war that kills five thousand men on both sides, maims, cripples and breaks down ten thousand and causes endless misery to countless thousands more, is a curious variety of humane war." Of course the *Post* was anti-administration; surely Robinson was not telling the whole truth. As the century waned, even the most zealous anti-imperialists reluctantly had to conclude that the insurrection had probably been beaten down.

IV

The forests and mountains of the Philippines, interlaced by blue streams and stunning expanses of lake country resembling that of Wisconsin and Minnesota, are unparalleled in their natural splendor. Amid such scenes U.S. regiments completed their occupation of the islands. Slowly and sinuously, like hundreds of caterpillars, columns of men moved into cool northern provinces, luxuriant Moro jungles, and placid little oriental ports never before seen or heard of by an American. . . .

Bivouac was made without shelter where darkness found the troops. In flat, muddy country the same stream often had to be crossed a dozen times, with the water chest-high. As they penetrated the interior, engineers built temporary bridges. For miles the men hiked along ancient highways and through flooded rice fields. In canyons and at the mouths of passes the insurgents had built barricades; here danger lay and fighting always flared. Dry creek beds were prized for their easy walking, until they led inevitably into foothills. Even narrow trails were welcome, until they too dwindled into swampland or steeply rising ground. Many Americans dropped from exhaustion; often it was necessary to descend hundreds of feet for water in the streams below.

Single-file the men knifed through the tall grasses, with only their heads and shoulders in view. Sometimes the retreating *amigos*, as they moved along these same faint trails, slashed the brush and interlaced the branches on both sides. This they did in two quick motions, greatly slowing down their enemy. In the mountains at night absolute quiet was enforced. No fires or cigarettes were allowed, while the Americans stared down in fascination at lights flickering in the valleys, where the insurgents were moving about. On their rocky beds they looked up at perfect, tropical, starlit skies. Often at dawn they found themselves high above the clouds and mists swirling in the canyons and river beds below.

Occasionally they encountered abandoned clothing, supplies, and Spanish prisoners, but never an American. In towns where they had been held in prison—invariably dark, odorous affairs—boys from the States had left their names on the walls, in the way of all prisoners since wars began.

Dirty, unshaven, haggard, the Americans stalked their prey. They walked atop ridges among groves of pine trees and could see guerilla officers (some still in their white or blue uniforms) watching them in turn. In the canyons, insurgent shots echoed like diminishing cracks of doom, but inexorably the white men came on—personifying Mr. Kipling's ideal, burning warehouses, barracks, and *barrios* in their path. Living on the country or under short rations, marching and fighting from sun-up until dusk, most of them were shoeless and dispirited. Only the luckiest columns could be accompanied by little Filipino pack ponies. After four-thirty supper, the December moon would break out. Then the Americans seemed like men on that moon, following the rocky bed of a lunar canyon, winding in and out of the milky moonglow and the shadows of the great walls. At last came a steep descent into the canebrake.

The 34th Infantry marched to the Apayao River down a freshly beaten track. Typical of many mountain streams, this was sixty yards across and seven feet deep of clear, fast-running water. Bamboo rafts ferried the troops to the opposite bank. An American prisoner had left a note in the sand: "Here we are, God knows where."

Sometimes the men found rice or bought it from the natives, or a little pork, or managed to kill a wild hog; and sometimes they discovered a supply of precious salt or parched Indian corn. Sugar cane in cultivated fields was another splendid prize. Tobacco—a fine, rich cigar leaf—was smoked by the men as soon as they cut it. Their worst problem was the rapids, which kept demolishing their jerry-built rafts. If the streams were impassable, wearisome detours by land became necessary; and after a hard day the Americans might find themselves only a mile or two from where they had started. Often the nearby natives planted sharp bamboo sticks on the paths leading to their villages and on adjacent sand bars. They could not be detected until stepped upon. Such resultant casualties—useless, painful, treacherous—were particularly distressing and put an added burden on fellow troops.

As each town of any size was reached and captured, it was garrisoned by a small detachment. This, plus losses en route, meant that only a fragment of each expedition reached its goal. Until reinforced, these detachments all along the line invariably received the attention of guerilla marauders. Sometimes as few as a dozen American soldiers had to be left occupying a village in an area teeming with rebels. Their lives depended upon ruthless, co-ordinated defensive actions, the speedy uncovering of all possible insurgent arms caches, and the emplacement of Maxim guns to sweep the area around their little command post. In itself each column was isolated and insignificant, but a network of hundreds of them over most of the archipelago, enveloping every city, port, and road juncture of importance, was quite another matter. Three months after the beginning of his autumn campaign, Otis could rightfully claim to have geographically conquered the Philippine Islands.

It is true that by the turn of the century this occupation was rather embryonic; but already it had evoked the usual by-products of war. Inter-island, inter-province trade was at rock bottom. The agricultural effort of each family was concerned with mere survival. The burning of countless nipa huts had aggravated the housing and refugee problem, so that untold additional thousands of natives were roaming the land in search of food and shelter. Under Otis, American military government was making little effort to alleviate matters.

The governor conceived of his duties as almost exclusively military in character. His attitude was underscored by General Shafter in the Boston *Transcript*, dated January 12, 1900: "My plan would be to disarm the natives of the Philippine Islands, even if we have to kill half of them to do it. Then I would treat the rest of them with perfect justice." A pamphlet of The Anti-Imperialist League published the following chart of conditions in the towns of Balayan, Tuy, and Calatagan in Batangas Province:

	1896	1900
Number of inhabitants	41,306	11,560
Cultivated land (hectares)	19,500	632

Only in Manila, where the sale of liquor, trinkets and other secondary commodities was flourishing, was there any longer much semblance of business activity. The world's most enormous licensed brothel—"guarded by United States soldiers, and under the supervision of United States army surgeons, over whom Wm. McKinley is Commander-in-Chief," as Mr. Atkinson acidly described it—also existed there; and far to the south the so-called hemp provinces had been reopened for trade upon urgent orders from Mr. McKinley. Otherwise it may be fairly said that the Philippine Islands were a wreck commercially and otherwise after eleven months of war, as the nineteenth century closed down upon them and their new owners across the Pacific.

12

. . . There's been many a good man murdered in the Philippines,
Lies sleeping in some lonesome grave . . .

EXIT
OTIS

MOST PEOPLE IN THE STATES KNEW LITTLE ABOUT THESE
melancholy happenings and cared less

("The papers 'id it 'andsome,
But you bet the army knows . . .")

as the twentieth century burst into being, flushed with confidence and prosperity. That Monday morning the daily
papers had much to say about the Philippines and Señor
Aguinaldo, but by now it was all getting a bit tiresome; in
any event, it no longer amounted to much militarily. In the
news columns there was also a good deal concerning the Boer
Insurrection. It was going badly for the British, to America's
intense satisfaction, for the sturdy Boers were fighting for
their independence just as we had once done. But, as *Life*
sadly pointed out, "a small boy with diamonds is no match
for a large burglar with experience"; in the long run the
Dutch had no chance against Kitchener's legions.

Mr. Roosevelt was still governor of New York as the centennium commenced—mathematically it would not do so until January 1, 1901, it was pointed out by some kill-joys, who were ignored—and Mr. Henry Cabot Lodge quite appropriately had been appointed chairman of the Senate Committee on the Philippines. He remained unbending in his attitude toward Philippine self-government. We had not robbed the natives of liberty, he observed in a senate speech, for they never had any; their natural form of government was a despotism. And only recently in his annual message to congress Mr. McKinley had voiced similar sentiments. After eleven months of fighting and the end not in sight, he still thought (though with a perceptible note of doubt), "I had reason to believe, and I still believe" that American rule "was in accordance with the wishes and aspirations of the great masses of the Filipino people."

No one could foresee that the next fifty years would be troubled by wars more ghastly than any in history, and Monday's editorials throbbed with hope and thrilling predictions. All over the land a thousand editors addressed themselves to a brave new world forevermore at peace, with new inventions (aeroplanes, washing-machines, wireless, horseless carriages, and the like) to enhance the glory of living. To Cecil Spring Rice, Mr. Roosevelt dictated an equally optimistic note: "In the Philippines, where we have blundered for a year in a way that would have cost us dearly had we been matched against Boers instead of Tagals, we at last seem to have things pretty well in hand." He had lost patience with the "ingrates," as he termed them. Altruism had waned; motives emerged more frankly than in the past. The Washington *Post*, a member of the no-nonsense school, advised people on Thursday of that week to face the fact that we had deliberately acquired the archipelago and intended to use it to our own profit. Aguinaldo had become a bogeyman, a legend, a name with which mothers frightened naughty children, as the Kaiser was to be some years later; and boys and girls sang this rhyme:

> Oh, Aguinaldo leads a sloppy life,
> He eats potatoes with his knife,
> And once a year he takes a scrub,
> And leaves the water in the tub.

"Czar" Reed had resigned his seat in congress, but from
retirement he continued to bait the administration. "Thanks
for the statistics," he wrote a friend in the House Committee
on Appropriations. "I have to hunt all over your figures even
to find out how much each yellow man cost us in the bush.
As I make it out he has cost $30 per Malay and he is still in
the bush." He suggested that the Spanish general, "Butcher"
Weyler, be reimbursed for teaching the American army how
to murder and reconcentrate brown-skinned natives. And on
or near that Monday morning further names and items were
in the news. . . .

The Visayans and other "tribes," reported Elihu Root in
another artless speech, were delighted to be freed by Uncle
Sam's army from the military domination of the Tagalogs.

Mr. Roosevelt, determined not to enter the lists as a candidate for the vice-presidency, was yearning instead for an
appointment as civil governor of the Philippines. But in answer to Mr. Lodge's personal request the president replied
evasively that such a move might be unwise while Aguinaldo
remained at large. In some Democratic papers a German
cartoon was reprinted showing Uncle Sam trying to encircle
the globe with his arms and saying, "I can't quite reach
around—but that may come later." Europeans were scoffing
at the thought that American intentions in Cuba, the Caribbean generally, the Pacific, and South America were less than
megalomaniac, and the English *Saturday Review* warned
its readers against "the honeyed expressions of American
Senators."

Before the Iroquois Club of Chicago, Judge Murray F.
Tuley spoke of the Philippines and looked to the political
future:

This President of the United States—of whom it has been said that he always keeps his ear to the ground to find out the popular will—if he keeps his ear to the ground in the Ides of November next, will hear the voice of an overwhelming majority of the electors saying to him in thunderous tones, "Get thee gone, thou unfaithful servant."

On January 8 Albert Beveridge—a thin, pale young man facing a senate jam-packed to the galleries—delivered the next in his famous series of ultra-imperialist addresses:

We will not renounce our part in the mission of our race, trustees under God, of the civilization of the world. And we will move forward to our work, not howling out regrets like slaves whipped to their burdens, but with gratitude for a task worthy of our strength and thanksgiving to Almighty God that He has marked us as his chosen people . . .

Trade with China, he noted less floridly, was paramount to America's future, while the Philippines themselves abounded in rice, coffee, sugar, hemp, tobacco, copper and gold. We must defeat the people of those islands by "overwhelming forces in ceaseless action"—but gently, for had he not seen with his own eyes "wounded Filipinos as carefully, tenderly cared for as our own"? And then America would govern and uplift them, for

God has not been preparing the English-speaking and Teutonic peoples for a thousand years for nothing but vain and idle self-admiration. No! He has made us the master organizers of the world to establish system where chaos reigns . . .

It was duty, destiny, dollars and divinity carried to a new high—so high, in fact, that smiles and catcalls mingled with applause as the flushed little man resumed his seat. As soon as Senator Hoar could get the presiding officer's eye, he rose to deliver a few cutting comments which ended: "The devil taketh him up into an exceeding high mountain, and showeth him all the kingdoms of the world, and the glory of them: and saith unto him: All these things will I give thee, if thou wilt fall down and worship me. Then saith Jesus unto him, Get thee behind me, Satan." And needless to say next week Mr. Dunne satirized Beveridge's speech (via Mr. Dooley) in one of his most devastating pieces.

Exploding in the Louisville *Courier-Journal*, Colonel "Marse" Watterson used language less than judicious in describing the people of our newly acquired possessions:

> But the riff-raff; Lord, the riff-raff; injun,
> nigger, beggar-man, thief—
> > "Both mongrel, puppy, whelp and hound,
> > and cur of low degree."

It put the case rather too strongly, some readers thought. The Filipinos were uncivilized, of course, and they were shooting down fine young Americans; but surely they were not as low as the good colonel claimed. . . .

So ended the Gay or Mauve or Naughty Nineties. Winter departed and spring arrived, with baseball, sunny skies, increasing excitement over the impending political conventions, the first abortive Hay-Pauncefote Treaty concerning the construction of a Nicaraguan Canal, more speeches by Bryan, more speeches by Hoar, Beveridge, Lodge ("I believe that to abandon the islands . . . would be a wrong to humanity . . . Manila, with its magnificent bay, is the prize and the pearl of the East . . . it will keep open to us the markets of China . . . Shall we hesitate and make, in coward fashion, what Dante calls 'the great refusal'? . . ."), more speeches by Roosevelt, Schurz, Root, and Carnegie—and another scandal.

II

Mr. Atkinson and his Anti-Imperialist League had described something of the nature of the war in the Philippines, but it was not until early 1900 that it was exposed in detail by the general press. For one thing, some American soldiers were discovered to be using dumdum (expanding) bullets; in this connection it was noted that the United States had neglected to ratify the 1899 Hague Convention clauses concerning humane warfare. Next came a torrent of other revelations, some reported dispassionately and regretfully by Republic periodicals, all gleefully disseminated by Democrats and other anti-annexationists.

Generations later it is difficult to recapture the mood of a nation, if such a mood can be said to exist, or if it is truly echoed by the newspapers and magazines of the day. One feels, however, that the American people had not yet fully grasped the magnitude of the Philippine war effort or the ruthlessness with which it was being waged. Largely this was caused by the administration's efforts to play the struggle down, to insist that the revolt was strictly Tagalog in nature, and that almost all of the natives welcomed U.S. sovereignty. As in every war, salient facts and figures were suppressed and did not emerge until later. For example, that spring it was not publicly known that seventy thousand soldiers and sailors were being employed to crush the insurrection, nor that four hundred army posts had been set up throughout the islands to hold it in check. Severities committed by U.S. personnel seldom saw the light of day. Those that did were systematically denied or minimized. Nevertheless, some were highly publicized—perhaps luridly so—along with opposite tales of Filipino barbarisms against Americans and native traitors—for example, the burying alive of U.S. soldiers, the boloing of prisoners, and so on.

To the Fairfield, Maine, *Journal*, Sergeant Howard McFarlane of the 43rd Infantry wrote: "On Thursday, March 29, eighteen of my company killed seventy-five nigger bolomen and ten of the nigger gunners . . . . When we find one that is not dead, we have bayonets . . ." On January 9 Lieutenant John F. Hall of the Kansans brought formal charges against his own major:

. . . the said Wilder S. Metcalf did maliciously, wilfully, and
without just cause, shoot and kill an unarmed prisoner of war
on his knees before him, begging for life . . .

The water cure has been described. It came in for detailed
publicity in 1900 by a host of U.S. newspapermen. One native
in his agony was said to have flattened out with his teeth a
brass cartridge case being used to prop open his mouth while
water was being poured in. The "rope cure" was less common.
It consisted of tying the victim's neck and torso together and
then twisting the rope with a stick. The result was a combination of garrotting and smothering. Ordinary beating up
was simple and routine, but seldom accomplished its purpose
of forcing the *amigo* to tell where his comrades or rifles were
hidden.

In 1900 a War Department official reported that to date
14,643 Filipinos had been killed and 3,297 wounded. The
strange ratio of nearly five to one—reversing the figures of the
Civil War and the current Boer War—was remarked upon by
Mr. Atkinson and drew a deadpan rejoinder from General
MacArthur: "It arises from the fact that our soldiers are
trained in what we call 'fire discipline'; that is, target practice.
In other words, they know how to shoot."

Lieutenant Bissell Thomas of the 35th Infantry was convicted of striking prisoners, one of whom was lying on the
ground and bleeding from the mouth. The officer was reprimanded and fined three hundred dollars. Just before Mr.
Root took office, Robert Collins of the Associated Press was
permitted to cable: "There has been, according to Otis himself and the personal knowledge of everyone here, a perfect
orgy of looting and wanton destruction of property." Private
Jones of the 11th Cavalry wrote that his troop, upon en-
countering a wedding party, fired into the throng, killing the
bride and two men, and wounding another woman and
two children. A captain and lieutenant of the 27th Regiment
were tried for hanging six Filipinos by their necks for ten

seconds, "causing them to suffer great bodily pain." After the
words were changed to "mental anguish," the officers were
found guilty and sentenced to reprimands.

In April the mayors of San Miguel and San Nicolas were
beaten to death by rattan rods. The episode leaked out when
two officers of the American regiment reported it to the governor and to General Young. And in its July 26 issue the New
York *World* carried this story:

> . . . our soldiers here and there resort to horrible measures
> with the natives. Captains and lieutenants are sometimes
> judges, sheriffs and executioners ... . "I don't want any more
> prisoners sent into Manila," was the verbal order from the
> Governor-General three months ago . . . It is now the cus-
> tom to avenge the death of an American soldier by burning
> to the ground all the houses, and killing right and left the
> natives who are only "suspects."

A myriad of such cases were subsequently investigated by
Mr. Lodge's committee, the testimony coming to three thousand printed pages. Only a relatively small number of them,
such as those summarized above, had come under public
scrutiny in 1900, but in themselves they were sufficiently distressing, especially since they tended to dilute official propaganda that the Filipinos were our friends and that the American soldier was on a mission of mercy. Akin to Spanish
methods in Cuba, they caused the Baltimore *News* to groan,
"And now we have come to it."

That American boys could harbor such impulses, even
under the exigencies of conflict, seemed hard to believe; yet,
if only half the accusations were true, something had gone
amiss. Caught in the storm-center, under renewed vilifica-
tion, his conscience stirring, Mr. McKinley turned to Judge
William Howard Taft. Here was the man—huge, wise, and
benign—to wrest civil control from the horny hands of the
generals and to restore mercy and enlightenment to the great
crusade. When McKinley offered him the job in April, a dia-

logue followed almost identical with the McKinley-Schurman
and McKinley-Root exchanges. Taft said he didn't want the
islands. "Neither do I," the president is said to have replied,
"but that isn't the question. We've got them."

A stubborn, conservative, middle-class Ohioan well known
as a Federal Circuit Judge, Taft accepted the chairmanship
of the commission, and that month he and four other civilian
aides sailed for Manila. His biographer (Henry F. Pringle)
has demonstrated that he knew next to nothing about Philippine geography or sociology, nor even about the recent
Filipino revolutions against Spain and America. From start
to finish, the history of the insurrection follows this remarkable pattern. Anderson, Otis, Dewey, Merritt, Schurman,
Root, McKinley, Greene, Lawton, MacArthur, and Taft drift
across the scene like ghosts, as unfamiliar with the Philippines
as with the differential calculus. Their education began on the
day they reached Manila, and some of them never did learn.

Up to June 4 over fourteen thousand Filipino soldiers had
been killed by the U.S. army. This figure represents corpses
counted and does not include other military dead, military
wounded, civilian dead, and civilian wounded. Of these totals
Taft was unaware. He had heard something of Filipino independence ambitions, but like other Americans he assumed
that the reference was to "dissatisfied Tagals," and he expected to solve everything by treating the islanders with kind-
ness. Since this was like trying to placate a wildcat by patting
its head, it was not surprising that the insurrection steadily
gained in violence after he arrived.

Yet he sailed with as humanitarian a set of instructions as
ever were handed to a colonial potentate. Unlike Schurman's
investigative commission, his was a legislative and executive
organ with orders to take over civil control of the islands no
later than September 1, 1900. It came with the law in its
hands, and this law was progressive. Composed by Mr. Elihu
Root, its fundamental principle was that the Filipinos should
control their own affairs insofar as possible. They were given

all the guarantees of the American Bill of Rights except trial by jury and the right to bear arms. There would be a civil service system staffed by natives. Elementary education would be free and compulsory, with English the official language. All local government officers were to be elected by the people, and natives would be preferred for higher positions. The land problem—especially in reference to tracts formerly owned by Spain and the Roman church—would be equitably resolved by redistribution. Local customs were to be left inviolate. Only certain unpleasant habits of the lower tribes, such as head-hunting, were to be abolished. In all these matters the United States would intervene only when its superior civilization made such intervention advisable, as well as at the highest level of policy, law, commercial regulation, and taxation.

But the Philippine people viewed this matriarchal code without enthusiasm. Its rolling phrases could not feed the hungry, house the homeless, or restore the dead; and—above all—the independence they craved was denied them. To some Japanese interviewers who had once asked President Ulysses S. Grant how to learn the art of self-government, he had simply replied, "Govern yourselves." This was the Filipino philosophy, and no amount of enlightened suzerainty could nullify it. In addition, the commission said nothing to allay Filipino fears of economic exploitation. Finally, almost every native thought that Mr. Taft was lying, just as all Spaniards down to Primo de Rivera had lied, and just as they thought Dewey had lied. During his balmy cruise from San Francisco to Hawaii to Manila, Mr. Taft envisioned no such ungrateful reactions from those whom he was coming to civilize, although he did confess to qualms that General Otis might not take kindly to him and his mission. He need not have worried. The judge and the general passed each other in midocean, for the general had resigned.

The scope and success of guerilla resistance had shaken "Grandma" Otis. Unlike the old war he thought he had won,

the new one had gotten quite out of control. American soldiers were daily being placed *hors de combat* in disconcerting numbers, rifles were constantly and incomprehensibly
being stolen, telegraph lines were being cut (this happened
twenty-three times within six weeks in Illocos Norte Province), some detachments had almost been wiped out (in
Catubig, Samar, for example, eighteen of the thirty-one men
garrisoned there were killed on April 15), and it had finally
dawned upon him that the *insurrectos* were being aided and
abetted by the population at large. His prim mind was unable
to cope with a situation so bizarre. This was not war as he
knew it—no tactics, no battles, no charges, no victories, no
glory. It was a kind of nightmare of which he wanted no part;
and perhaps he sensed that it would get worse before it got
better. The newspapermen were still driving him frantic with
innuendoes and direct accusations of ineptitude. News of
Taft's appointment capped the climax. Otis wired for relief
on the grounds that personal affairs, neglected for twenty
months, required his urgent attention back home. It may be
that neither the White House nor the War Department were
unhappy to receive the request. It was granted immediately
(May 5), upon which date his command was turned over to
General MacArthur.

III

For the first time, VIII Corps was now headed by a man who
had seen intensive field service in the Philippines and who
entertained no military illusions. MacArthur was also intel-
lectually honest, and he was not interested in being McKinley's political henchman. He had always freely admitted that
most Filipinos hated the Americans, that they were united in
their demand for freedom, and that the insurrection was a
nasty and perplexing affair. It made no difference that he himself was a thoroughgoing expansionist; he faced facts, and

was not afraid to state them for publication. As early as March, 1899, just after his capture of Malolos, he had told a war correspondent, "When I first started against these rebels, I believed that Aguinaldo's troops represented only a faction. I did not believe that the whole population of Luzon was opposed to us; but I have been reluctantly compelled to believe that the Filipinos are loyal to Aguinaldo and the government which he represents."

Fourteen months later we still find him pointing to the loyalty of the populace as fundamental to the success of guerilla warfare. It is probable (he wrote the War Department)

> that the adhesive principle comes from ethnological homogeneity which induces men to respond for a time to the appeals of consanguinous leadership, even when such action is opposed to their own interests . . .

In other words, the poor but proud family wanted the social worker to go away. MacArthur neither liked nor disliked the Filipino people. They and their land had to be assimilated. He estimated to one reporter that doing so would require ten years of bayonet treatment. When he moved into the stately white mansion in Malacanana Park it was, therefore, with the air of a man who had come to stay. Letters and documents left by Otis atop his desk, bulging from a dozen drawers and streaming over other desks and chairs, presented the first problem. Which to answer, what to file? MacArthur solved the mess by direct assault. He had every scrap of unfiled paper removed from the room. Next he assigned three officers under his adjutant to sort them out, to answer them (over his signature), to get rid of them, to bring to his attention only those requiring his inescapable personal attention. Within a week he had disposed of all correspondence and details at hand, including the requisition of two thousand shotguns for concentration-camp guards; and then, unsmiling behind his little glasses, he sat back to await Mr. Taft.

That equally formidable gentleman steamed into Manila

Bay early in June. (The average weight of his five-man commission was 228 pounds, and one Manila newspaper referred
to its disembarkment as an imposing spectacle.) In other respects, its arrival was not imposing. There was no ceremony,
and no U.S. officer above the rank of major was at the dock.
Taft later commented: "The populace that we had expected
to welcome us was not there and I cannot describe the coldness of the army officers and the army men who received us
better than by saying that it somewhat exceeded the coldness
of the populace." They were driven to MacArthur's office,
where they found the general grim; their presence, he stated,
was "an injection into an otherwise normal situation." Taft
replied that MacArthur would continue to possess full military powers. "That would be all right," said the general, "if
I had not been exercising so much more power before you
came." The meeting broke up within a half-hour.

It was plain that quashing military government would be
easier said than done; but Taft held a trump card in the form
of control over expenditures. Every dollar for the Philippines,
even from the War Department, was to be allocated by his
commission. Holding this lever, the civilians could not lose.
The situation facing Taft was nonetheless onerous. Throngs
of American merchants and speculators had preceded him,
were already edging out Filipino farmers and manufacturers,
and had taken title to a good deal of real estate which he had
intended to sell cheaply to the natives. U.S. army officers were
encouraging and protecting the land-grabbers, and all concerned were treating the masses of Filipinos much like plan-
tation darkies. When Taft announced that we were holding
the islands for the primary benefit of the Filipinos, Americans
who had come there for fast profits turned on him viciously.
The English-language press in Manila began to attack him
the day after he landed and publicly stated his policy. One
American firm bought large newspaper space to show his picture above the caption: "This is the cause of our leaving the
Philippines." (The establishment remained and flourished, al-

though in a speech at Iloilo Taft referred to such Americans as neurotics who should take the first ship home.)

"We have in these islands possibly eight thousand Americans and we have about eight millions of Christian Filipinos," he declared. "If business is to succeed here, it must be in the sale of American goods to the eight millions of Filipinos. One would think that a child in business might understand that the worst possible policy in attempting to sell goods is to abuse, berate and vilify your only possible customers." He referred to the native as "our little brown brother." The phrase drew sneers from businessmen and soldiers alike, for it was unhappily true that these alleged kinfolk were capturing Americans in fetid jungles, ambushing them, killing them, mutilating them, even burying them alive; and to the tune of "Son of a Gamboleer" the men in uniform sang:

> I'm only a common soldier in the blasted
>   Philippines.
> They say I've got brown brothers here, but
>   I dunno know what it means.
> I like the word fraternity, but still I
>   draw the line.
> He may be a brother of Big Bill Taft,
> But he ain't no brother of mine!

Like an albatross, the friar problem had come back to roost. "If the friars occupy the parishes they will be considered as elements of order and therefore as American agents," wrote papal delegate Mgr. P. O. Chapelle in the Walled City; and once more the whole issue was up in the air. Delegates of monks descended upon Taft, as they had descended upon Merritt and Otis, for the restoration of their property and authority. The Filipinos reacted as in the past. Open demonstrations were held, the cry *"Muerte a los frailes!"* was heard again, and guerilla commanders issued proclamations breathing fire and thunder. And while America (in the person of Judge Taft) had no intention of putting the Spanish clergy back in civil power, what of their lands? Private property had to be respected. On the other hand, we had promised to redistribute the church's estates. In what McKinley's official biographer refers to as a possibly needless act of abnegation, Washington decided to buy them from the Vatican. Accordingly Taft took title to all 410,000 acres for $7,239,000* in gold and sold them to natives on installment payments mortgaged over several years.

As scheduled, Mr. Taft and his aides assumed administrative control over the archipelago on September 1 and with celerity began to prove that benevolent assimilation was no smoke screen. The power of the military was undermined, except for its conduct of the war. Highways and harbors were improved, schools were built and amply staffed, sanitation measures were instituted, eminently fair modes of taxation came into being, civil graft was almost extinguished, Filipinos were brought into the Philippine Commission, and a Filipino assembly was authorized as the lower house of the legislature relative to the upper house, which was the commission itself. It is true that Mabini's constitution had made provision for most of this and more, in addition to self-government; nevertheless, here it was in operation.

It was and remains a novelty in the colonial history of the western world. Could it be that the United States had been sincere all along? Had Mr. Lodge, Mr. Beveridge, and others meant what they said about the American responsibility for uplifting an oppressed people? Many Americans and Europeans watched and pondered. Of course the islands were being intensively utilized for commercial advantage, but that was to be taken for granted, and meanwhile most legal and social rights common to French, German, English, and American citizens were being thrust upon the Filipinos, whether they liked it or not. Such a process had never occurred in the course of empire. In the Congo, India, Somaliland, and Indo-China—to name four instances out of forty—the acquired na-

* In 1893 the acreage had been evaluated at $1,500,000.

tives had been treated (quite unthinkingly and as a matter of course) with routine callousness. They had been exploited in the most repulsive sense of the term. What devious game was America playing? To make matters more suspicious, she had not even annexed Cuba.

It was unfathomable because it was indeed altruism, if in a somewhat limited sense. Yet during the summer of 1900 it was only a set of promises. Behind them flamed the Insurrection. And every account thereof—all histories, all dispatches emanating from Manila headquarters, all newspaper reports and magazine articles, whatever their respective biases— agree that guerilla warfare reached its bloodiest pitch late that year.

IV

During 1900 the United States Army completed its embrace of the islands while the navy blockaded all major ports. "I have sworn that as long as life lasts," Aguinaldo wrote to a friend in the capital, "I shall labor until I gain the independence of the Philippines"; but little attempt was made to ensnare him, although it was conceded that the insurrection would continue so long as he remained in the picture. He could be disposed of later; the military domination of all provinces was a more immediate necessity.

General Kobbe invaded Leyte and Samar, and almost had to annihilate the revolutionary element before he could contrive peace and military law. *Amigos* who possessed no rifles fought on with bolos, even with bows and arrows. "We began to understand why the Spanish would never permit these people to even possess a table knife," recounted one newsman. Enemy troops who were shot down included a number of workmen armed with hemp-beaters. After this "mad, exultant carnage," in the words of a New York *Herald* reporter, all natives who otherwise might have been passive turned extremely hostile. General Kobbe—a silent, ironical ex-Austrian, never armed with more than a cane—was forced to remain in charge of the military detachments there, after the initial fighting ended.

In Cavite and other Luzon provinces south of Manila, General Bates finally consummated the plan originally conceived by Lawton.

General R. P. Hughes—who may be recalled as the brigadier who had negotiated tongue-in-cheek with Aguinaldo's emissaries before war started—now inaugurated stern offensives in Panay, Negros, and Cebu, the details of which need not be elaborated upon.

Treaty payments after the Spanish-American War had included fifteen gunboats used by the Spaniards for offshore patrol. Taken over by the U.S. navy under their original names—*U.S.S. Villalobos, U.S.S. Pampanga, U.S.S. Callao,* and so on—these little two-hundred-ton, twin-screw, nine-knot iron ships concentrated all summer on insurgent headquarter towns along the coast. Their lieutenant and midshipman skippers banded together in what they called "The Ancient and Honorable Sons of Gunboats" and performed invaluable blockade duties; however, five thousand English rifles slipped through and helped prolong resistance in Samar.

Earlier General Bell had sailed south and seized the provinces of North and South Camarines, and West Albay. Similar expeditions were also dispatched to the Visayan group. The conditions encountered here were disturbing, for while the natives were not Tagalogs there was no perceptible difference in the scale of fighting. American field commanders, it was noted, "had expected to find little opposition on the part of the Kagayans, Ilokans, Pangasinans, and Sambals; yet had speedily discovered that this 'official view' of the situation was . . . of no value as a working hypothesis in dealing with the people." By autumn no U.S. soldier any longer accepted his government's assertion that he was dealing with a mere

Tagal rebellion—a delusion which General MacArthur had discounted all along.

With another expedition General Bates, a veteran of the Civil War and the Cuban campaign, proceeded to Mindanao. In that fabulous Mohammedan island, nearly as large as Luzon, all males were religious fanatics who believed that they would go to heaven by killing seven white Christians, and that the more they killed the more houris they would possess there. These were powerful incentives, and the Spaniards had never been able to impose their rule here. No Moro was ever without his bolo, and it was worth one's life to try to borrow it or even to look at it. They struck their victim only twice: once on each side. If this failed to kill or disable, they departed respectfully. They knew little of guns, and those they possessed were rust-eaten relics. "I would have considered it safer to be shot at by one of them than to shoot the gun," wrote an American trooper. After stupefying the Sultan of Jolo (spiritual leader of all Philippine Moros) by demonstrating the *Charleston*'s eight-inch guns, mild electric shocks, Colt automatics, masthead lights, and other marvels, Bates managed to extract a treaty which obviated the need for heavy fighting. It included a monthly payment of $250 in gold for the Sultan himself and $15 per month for his counsellors. Swiftly the ports of Dapitan, Misamis, Iligan, Cagayan, Surigao, Parang, Davao, Pollack, Cottabatto, and Zamboanga were occupied by U.S. detachments. But troubles with the Moros had not yet begun; oddly enough, they were to be the last and most ferocious holdouts against American authority.

During these actions a long series of minor disasters had been taking place, and it was becoming increasingly clear that occupation in itself was anything but a panacea for what ailed the campaign. In thirteen months roughly covering the period under discussion, the following figures were officially tabulated: there were 1,026 engagements, 245 Americans killed, 490 wounded, 118 captured; while 3,854 rebels had been killed, 1,193 wounded, and 6,572 captured. Late in September, near Laguna de Bay, after an insolent message from Juan Cailles, elements of the 15th and 37th Infantry regiments were sent to make that ostentatious young man (now a brigadier general) "eat his words." In the event, they suffered forty-four casualties and were forced to withdraw. Cailles next day, in a characteristic gesture, returned the bodies of eight of the twenty dead Americans. One week later an entire company of the 29th Volunteers was ambushed on the island of Marinduque, east of Luzon, and forced to surrender.

Occasional successes like these electrified guerillas and civilians throughout the islands. Simultaneously and spontaneously, a desire for revenge spread through the American army. The men were fed up with the methods of the guerillas, their constant attacks against weak detachments, and the atrocities they committed. John T. McCutcheon, a conservative reporter, told of what usually happened when the body of a mutilated American was found: ". . . a scouting party goes out to the scene of the killing. It can be imagined that the comrades of the murdered man do not feel in a merciful mood, and they proceed to burn the village and kill every native who looks as if he had a bolo or a rifle." General Funston reported the hanging of two Filipinos ten minutes after their capture. In Leyte a colonel protested the "indiscriminate shooting" of women, children, and wounded prisoners. In this fashion the war moved to its climax even as Judge Taft was unfolding his program of law and compassion.

Another rainy season had arrived—the third since American fighting men had come to the islands—and it seemed to emphasize that essentially little had changed since Otis began floundering the previous June. As the saturated summer wore on, it may well be that MacArthur fretted behind his dispassionate exterior. He had been warned to get matters "well in hand" by June 30, 1901, on which date the enlistments of the twenty-five volunteer regiments organized under the act of March 2, 1899, would expire. It would be embarrassing, therefore, if he were unable to win the war within nine or ten months. Almost a tenth of his command was sick. For every man who died in battle three were dying of disease. The moral caliber of his army—aside from its morale and fighting ability—was not impressive. Few volunteers who had turned their backs on booming prosperity to join the service had done so out of avid patriotism. The ranks were sprinkled with undesirables, and the average age of privates was almost two years younger than those who were to enlist in 1917. Some were unfit for war, did anything possible to avoid outright battle, and told lurid tales of close shaves, attacks by hordes of insurgents, sharpshooters in trees, dangers everywhere. They were usually found in small groups under the shade of a tree, unable to advance because of an imaginary hail of bullets at some bridge or crossroads. While there is a percentage of such troops in any army, this one possibly had more than its share. It also had its humorists. In San Fabian headquarters personnel of the 13th Regiment posted the following notice for the enlightenment of all concerned:

WE ARE MIND-READERS—THEREFORE WE KNOW:

1. That you have had the hardest time, the muddiest roads, brought through the biggest train in the quickest time, and we sympathize with you.
2. That the road between Arayat and Copias is h——l.
3. That you have had hair-breadth escapes in ferrying at Arayat, San Isidro and Cabanatuan, and that you have forded unfordable streams, penetrated impenetrable forests, passed over impassable roads and we MARVEL at it.
4. That from Cabanatuan to Talavera the roads could not be worse.
5. That from Talavera to Balic they are very much worse.
6. That from San Jose for two miles they are a d——n sight worse than (5) . . .

Men stationed in Manila were more lucky. Unfortunately, due to the nature of the war and the difficulties of movement,

"rotation" (to use the term of a later conflict) to the metropolis was rare. It was a soldier's paradise of theatres, brothels,
shops, joy-rides, and cafés. Many *mestizo* girls were attractive by *norte americano* standards, with trim figures, clear
complexions, and hair cascading down to their waists. In
making purchases, the Americans preferred to be swindled
by them rather than by the Chinese. Each "shop"—not much
more than a wooden-box affair five feet by ten—sold garishly
retouched colored prints, fruits and vegetables, cheap handkerchiefs, undershirts, and other trivia, amid a family welter
of three or more clerks.

The Escolta runs parallel with the river about a block away.
Only thirty feet wide, roughly paved, with narrow sidewalks,
by late 1900 it had become a pandemonium of natives,
Chinamen, and U.S. troops. Two-wheeled carts were drawn
through the tangle by ponies not much larger than New-
foundland dogs, half-starved and cruelly whipped. Drays
hauled by carabaos were so slow that they stopped traffic.
Betwixt all this trudged the Chinamen, balancing shoulder
poles tied to baskets at both ends. As the street approached
the Bridge of Spain there was a feeble grade where carriages
kept stalling and slipping backward, to the accompaniment
of confusion and Filipino profanity. One wretched tram also
helped to block traffic. Despite its meager size, four ponies,
and a clamor fit to raise the dead, it was always touch and
go whether it would get up the rise and onto the bridge.
Daily the U.S. band still played on the Luneta bandstand,
and nightly there were parades and reviews. The Americans
acquired native sweethearts; the storekeepers got rich. Some
innocent Chinamen who extended credit until payday found
themselves holding I.O.U.s signed by such notables as
George Washington, Thomas Jefferson and Andrew Jackson.

When it rained it poured, and then the streets were deserted, the shops locked, the Luneta a portrait in puddles and
gloom. Naval and merchant shipping dozed nearby at anchor,
hardly visible through the downpour. In barracks and "tent

cities" the troops played cards, wrote letters, shot craps, and
waited for the sun to emerge. The bark and grumble of war
could no longer be heard from the Old City or its suburbs.
In a formal sense the back of the insurrection had been
broken. Was it time to make peace?

V

Unfortunately, few of the prerequisites for peace existed as
yet. The guerilla organization was fairly intact and numbered
at least twenty thousand rifles. William Jennings Bryan had
not yet moved into the White House; when he did he would
set the Filipinos free. Don Emilio Aguinaldo was still holding
court somewhere in Luzon, still the legal president of the islands, still instructing his people to fight on. By and large
they were loyal to him and to the insurgents. From a rebel
point of view, in fact, affairs were not going too badly, in that
guerilla warfare had proved effective as a delaying action.

On the debit side, however, there existed certain fallacies
in reasoning: 1) The guerillas could not win the war. 2) If
Bryan became president he would free the Philippines anyway. 3) Occasional guerilla triumphs could not force Taft to
liberalize his program further. Therefore some natives felt
that armed resistance no longer made sense. Apart from this
logic the insurgent cause was in material difficulties. The
naval blockade had stopped almost all imports of arms,
ammunition, supplies and food. Cartridges were especially
needed. They had been filled as many as fifteen times each
and the majority were almost worthless. During constant
raiding and retreating actions, many wounded men had been
necessarily abandoned. Such losses were as permanent as battle deaths. In other words, only the walking wounded could
be expected to fight again another day.

Even a guerilla army needs cash, and precious little remained by late 1900. In its place Aguinaldo caused one-peso

paper money to be issued. Crudely printed on common stock, pathetically ornamented by brackets and asterisks, it informed the bearer that counterfeiting would be *castigado con todo el rigor de la ley*. Since these *billetes* were held in low esteem, the warning was perhaps needless. In their dire need, the Filipinos had also taken up the dangerous game of stealing American horses out of convoy. Many losses were sustained in the process, although (it was said) in one province fifty-four of Aguinaldo's officers sat upon U.S. steeds.

From his hideout Aguinaldo issued General Order to the Philippine Army No. 202, to the effect that during the summer months it must "give such hard knocks to the Americans that they will . . . set in motion the fall of the Imperialist party, which is trying to enslave us." Scarcely had the ink dried on General Bates' treaty with the Sultan of Jolo when heaven-seeking Moros fell happily upon several American contingents. Around Cottabatto they entrenched themselves in old Spanish forts and could not be dislodged. From all over Mindanao came sudden calls for reinforcements. This was the last straw, because it was so unexpected, and not even the Sultan could (or would) put a stop to it.

Nor could the newly formed Federalist Party end the war. Its wealthy, conservative, professional nucleus sought military surrender, eventual U.S. statehood, and immediate Philippine representation in the Washington congress. Though Mr. Taft backed it enthusiastically, the party was joined by few natives. The idea of statehood seemed unrealistic to the point of whimsy, and in any event the great majority of people wanted independence. Revolutionary leaders suggested that it might be unhealthy for a Filipino to become a *federalista*. The party attained its peak the day it was organized; from then on it went downhill.*

More as an experiment than a serious peace bid, MacArthur offered immunity to Filipinos who would take an oath

---

* In time it was forced to call for total independence, a move which came too late to stave off its demise.

of allegiance to America, plus the usual thirty pesos for each rifle surrendered. Again the sequel was disillusioning. Only 5,022 people, mainly civilians, took the oath, along with a smattering of officers and men, most of whom were already prisoners. They included three generals (Garcia, Concepcion, and Soliman) and the inevitable Pedro Paterno. One hundred and forty rifles were turned in, all but ten from a small area near Tarlac.

Despite the feeble results, Taft and MacArthur decided to proceed with an amnesty banquet scheduled for July 28. That afternoon the U.S. provost marshal inspected the dining hall and discovered that all the flags were Philippine, all the pictures were of Aguinaldo. They were hurriedly replaced by more appropriate decorations. Next Taft learned that the speeches would concern Philippine independence. Since he had warned Paterno to steer clear of such references, he sent word that no Americans would attend. Paterno was handed the message while his famished banqueteers were seated and awaiting their guests. He scribbled back that there would be no inflammatory utterances. The Americans arrived just before midnight and dinner was finally served—a doleful affair with everything cold including the speeches, which avoided any reference to the amnesty disaster.

The ninety-day trial period expired late in September and was not renewed by General MacArthur. In the meantime, dispatches from sundry field commanders—all to the same effect—had been reaching his desk. From southern Luzon:

> I regret that I cannot recommend the reduction of the forces in this Department by so much as a single soldier. The duty of occupation, in fact, renders necessary a larger number of troops than would be needed in conducting a campaign against armed forces . . .

From Abra Province:

> The insurrection has assumed such proportions in Abra that I do not consider it advisable to send a detachment out with

less than 100 rifles . . . I request that two [additional] regiments be sent here to relieve the strain on the troops . . .

From Nueva Ecija Province:

Everything possible is being done to locate the Insurgent bands in this vicinity, but so far without success . . . they will no doubt concentrate somewhere again before long.

From Donsol:

This seems a critical time . . . I therefore request that the question of more troops to garrison Pilar and Banaguran be considered . . .

On the eve of the U.S. elections conditions had become so bad that General Young in northern Luzon suggested that "European methods with rebellious Asiatics" be employed. Specifically he recommended death for each native captured with a firearm after taking the allegiance oath, the replacing of all native officials by U.S. soldiers, the confiscation of property held by insurgent officers, the deportation of any Filipino deemed excessively obnoxious, the razing and burning of areas used by *amigos* as hiding places, total press censorship, and more stringent reconcentration of natives living in particularly hostile zones. General MacArthur temporarily vetoed the plan as too severe, however, especially from the standpoint of U.S. public opinion.

VI

Any possibility that Admiral Dewey might have become one party or the other's presidential nominee had been dispelled by the admiral himself when, on April 4, he called in a New York *World* correspondent and revealed that he had decided to become a candidate. "If the American people want me for this high office, I shall be only too willing to serve them," he said. "Since studying this subject, I am convinced that the

office of the President is not such a very difficult one to fill,
his duties being mainly to execute the laws of Congress."

"On what platform will you stand?" asked the startled reporter.

"I think I have said enough at this time, and possibly too
much."

In a nationwide wave of laughter Dewey was brushed from
the scene. There was now no question about the two major
candidates. During conventions held in hot weather unprecedented even for July conventions (the Republican in Philadelphia, the Democratic in Kansas City), Mr. McKinley and
Mr. Bryan were both chosen unanimously. It is true that behind the landslides there was a difference in party attitude.
McKinley was nominated jubilantly, for he had delivered
riches and glory for three years and was certain to win again.
Bryan was put forth with reluctance. The Boy Orator's glamor
was wearing thin; his silver issue was unsound and becoming
a positive bore; yet no other Democrat had even an outside
chance to unseat the incumbent.

Without much debate the Democrats nominated Adlai E.
Stevenson of Illinois for the vice-presidency. In Philadelphia the maneuvering was more interesting. Long had
Theodore Roosevelt resisted being dragged into the vice-
presidential graveyard, and up to the fateful morning it was
not known if he would run. Certainly the president did not
want him; on the other hand he had refused to name anyone
else. He threw the issue back into the hands of his campaign
managers, most of whom were equally opposed to Roosevelt.
It was rumored that Mr. McKinley was suffering from an advanced stage of Bright's disease, and Mark Hanna exclaimed,
"Don't you understand that there is just one life between this
crazy man and the Presidency?" But when "Teddy" strode
into the convention hall, wearing his famous cowboy som-
brero to a storm of applause, it was plain that he had been
won over by Henry Lodge, Senator Platt, and a host of fervid
delegates. Gone were his dreams of becoming secretary of war

or governor of the Philippines, or of continuing to reign at
Albany in local splendor. The future of the party came first.
It was essential that his immense popularity strengthen the
Republican ticket against any possibility that the unspeaka-
ble Bryan might win. Amid wild acclaim the Rough Rider
was chosen with only one dissenting vote. He walked out as
grimly as he had walked in, convinced that his political future was at an end and that he would prepare for a private
law practice in 1904.

13

*"For they have healed the hurt of the
daughter of my people slightly, saying—
Peace, peace; when there is no peace."*

Jeremiah 8:11

FUNSTON
AND
AGUINALDO

DESPITE MASTERFUL ORATORY AND AN ENDURING REPUTA-
tion as an American titan, Bryan was by today's
standards a poor and irrational politician, who in 1900
managed to lose the votes of all Populists, stray anti-
imperialist Republicans, and eastern Democrats who feared
abandoning the gold standard more than they hated the Philippine adventure. Some party leaders contended that their
one chance was to concentrate dramatically upon the evils
of imperialism to the exclusion of all other issues, but their
only effect was to drag a promise out of him that the Philippine question would be stressed primarily. At the convention,
therefore, imperialism was labeled the "burning" and "paramount" issue, Republican foreign policy was duly castigated,
and it was stated that the Filipinos should be given independence—plus "protection from outside interference." In
other words, they would be placed under a kind of protectorate. So as to those islands there was, after all, little difference
between Tweedledum and Tweedledee. For good measure
the Democrats also declared (speciously, perhaps) that the

tariff problem was crucial. They now had for sale a slovenly grab bag of silver, diluted anti-imperialism, anti-monopoly, the tariff, and the Nicaraguan Canal, plus the Great Commoner's own waning popularity.

The Republicans ran on the full dinner-pail, made much of Bryan's free-silver heresies, and defended their foreign policy in phrases too familiar to bear excessive repetition here. In his letter accepting the nomination Mr. McKinley observed blandly that there was no Philippine issue at all; out of eighty Filipino tribes (one thinks of U.S. tribes such as Massachusetts-ites and Wyoming-ites) only one—the Tagalogs—was opposed to American rule. He also expressed horror at being asked by his opponents "to abandon the largest portion of the population, which has been loyal to us, to the cruelties of the guerilla insurgent bands." As to whether the islands would ever be set free, party policy was evasive: "The largest measure of self-government consistent with their welfare and our duties shall be secured by law." The specific words "Filipino" and "Philippines" were not mentioned once in the platform proper.

The campaign was quite dull. From New York Roosevelt wrote Lodge, "There is not the slightest enthusiasm for Bryan and there is no enthusiasm for us . . ." The people were not overconcerned about the Filipinos. They thought the Krag-and-bayonet phase was pretty well over and that the natives were now about to receive the dividends and decencies of civilization. Farm prices, production, and employment were high. When during the course of a western speaking tour Marcus Hanna suggested that the only issue in the campaign was to let well enough alone, voters were inclined to agree, nor could there be much argument with his *Realpolitik:* "If it is commercialism to want . . . a foothold in the markets of that great Eastern country [China], for God's sake let us have commercialism." It was crude, but it was at least frank and it meant votes.

During the past two years the Democrats had said everything they had to say concerning imperialism, and could do nothing but repeat themselves. Bryan seemed to speak, as usual, only for minorities who had no use for each other. As fast as he soothed one group he piqued another. The discovery of new gold deposits and the introduction of cyanide extraction had increased gold production and raised the price level, and had demolished whatever was left of the silver temple, except in the eyes of yokels who still believed that salvation lay therein. By October the Democrats realized they were in trouble. Bryan had practically stopped talking about his Philippine protectorate plan, which was neither fish nor fowl and satisfied no one. His attitude and remarks took on a bitter and eccentric tone. He accused the Republicans of coercion, vote-buying, bribery and intimidation. In New York he openly allied himself with the devil: "Great is Tammany! and its prophet is Croker," he intoned, to the sorrow of eastern reformers.

McKinley wisely took no active part in the campaign. He rocked on his front porch, addressed visiting delegations, and watched Bryan dig his political grave. Masses of apathetic voters probably felt much like a friend of Grover Cleveland who wrote the former president, "It is a choice between evils, and I am going to shut my eyes, hold my nose, vote, go home and disinfect myself." The Cleveland *Plain Dealer* published a cartoon showing McKinley patting the head of a disenfranchised Negro voter, Bryan patting the head of a Filipino, both pointing to each other and saying in unison, "Beware of that man!"

From afar Filipino leaders and intellectuals anxiously watched and waited. In Manila a pro-independence newspaper published a curious prayer just before the election: "On this day there is a struggle indeed in America: On this day is decided our life . . . Glory to Bryan . . . Grief to Imperialism, Grief to McKinley . . . Mother Philippines— Blessed be Thou. Mr. Bryan—Triumphant be Thou . . ." Upon instructions from Mr. Root, General MacArthur had been censoring dispatches even more ruthlessly than Otis. Resentful correspondents were informed that the process would continue until after the election. Among other restrictions, the word "ambush" was deleted from all cablegrams.

Weeks passed. In its closing phase the campaign was somewhat rejuvenated by America's pre-eminent literary figure. Mark Twain had been abroad for years and had commented only once or twice upon the Spanish-American War. It was, he thought, a worthy crusade—the only one in history he had ever heard of. With the advent of the Philippine Insurrection he had begun to feel uneasy, and by 1900 he was definitely alarmed. Interviewed by the London correspondent of the *World* on October 6, just before sailing for home, he said, "There is the case of the Philippines. I have tried hard, and yet I cannot for the life of me comprehend how we got into that mess. Perhaps we could have avoided it—perhaps it was inevitable that we should come to be fighting the natives of those islands—but I cannot understand it, and have never been able to get to the bottom of the origin of our antagonism to the natives. I thought we should act as their protector—not try to get them under our heel." He disembarked at New York harbor and was swarmed upon by reporters. After he had repeated his previous views in words somewhat more irascible, a Chicago *Tribune* man observed, "You've been quoted here as an anti-imperialist." "Well, I am," Twain replied.

On the other side of the hill Mr. Roosevelt had also been enlivening matters in his fashion. Unlike other Republican spokesmen, he made no attempt to shove the insurrection under the rug, and it turned out, astonishingly, that he was an anti-imperialist. His letter accepting the vice-presidential nomination reads in part:

> We made a great anti-imperialist stride when we drove the Spaniards from Porto Rico and the Philippines . . . of course the presence of troops in the Philippines during the Tagal insurrection has no more to do with militarism or imperialism

than had their presence in the Dakotas, Minnesota and Wyoming during the many years which elapsed before the final outbreaks of the Sioux were definitely put down.

He confessed that, while the inhabitants did not seem to enjoy the process, to proffer self-government to "Luzon"

> under Aguinaldo would be like granting self-government to an Apache reservation under some local chief . . . They would simply be put at the mercy of a syndicate of Chinese half-breeds.

He visited twenty-four states, travelled over twenty thousand miles, made almost seven hundred speeches, and carried the burden of the campaign by constantly defending the administration against the worrisome charge of militarism—"the most shadowy ghost that was ever raised to frighten political children." There was nothing warlike, he said, about America's historic policy of expanding; for was it not indeed true that the nation had been doing just that from the time when it consisted of thirteen small colonies? In Utah he declared that he had never met an American imperialist. Why were we killing Filipinos? he was asked. The answer—because they were killing Americans—could scarcely have been simplified further.

Who were our opponents? He defined them as "Tagal bandits," "Chinese halfbreeds," "Malay bandits." Over and over he compared the *insurrectos* to Apache and Comanche Indian tribes. Nonetheless we would grant them liberty—but in due time, under U.S. tutelage, when they were civilized enough to appreciate it, when they knew how to handle it. The insurgents were traitors; those who collaborated with America were faithful. He compared Aguinaldo to Benedict Arnold, and at no time during his swing through the west and midwest showed much understanding of Philippine independence aspirations. Yet he was no demagogue. When he referred to the islanders as savages scarcely out of their Stone

Age, he believed it. He lumped Tagalogs and Negritos together. And if what he said about the rebellion was at least
debatable, America's future was the proof of the pudding; all
else was of no consequence. "We are for expansion and anything else that will tend to benefit the American laborer and
manufacturer." While McKinley pondered on his White
House porch, Roosevelt aggressively grappled with the realities of war and conquest, and convinced thousands that these
issues were as dead as free silver. He had accepted the run-
ning-mate post with regret. Now that he was saddled with it,
he did his duty to the party with determination; and if any
one man can be said to have clinched a Republican victory in
1900 it was Mr. Roosevelt.

From all that has been noted here, a G.O.P. landslide
would appear inevitable; but as it transpired the winning
margin was not inordinate. McKinley received 7,219,525
votes, Bryan 6,358,727. The voters stayed away in considerable numbers. Although the national population had increased
by five millions since 1896, only 65,000 more votes were cast.
Was it, as Mr. Hanna declared, "a clear mandate to govern
the country in the interests of business expansion"—that is, a
mandate for imperialism in the Philippines? As he pondered
the returns, Mr. McKinley surely reckoned that his policies
since 1898 had been marvelously vindicated; his cohorts must
have been convinced beyond doubt that in the minds and
emotions of their countrymen expansion had been granted
clamorous approbation. But as in all presidential elections it
was anything but clear what the voting meant. This was especially true in terms of the Philippines. Certainly the gold
standard had been reaffirmed and prosperity had been ac-
claimed; Bryan as an individual had been defeated—perhaps
not so much by McKinley as by Roosevelt. As to the war
between America and her stubborn brown opponents, now it
would definitely have to continue; and when it would end no
man knew.

II

Like a boxer who receives a crushing blow over the heart, the people of the Philippine Islands faltered at the news of Bryan's defeat. From this point on the insurrection lost strength, but gradually. "Expectations, based on results of election, have not been realized," MacArthur cabled Corbin; "Process of pacification . . . still very slow . . . likely to become chronic." Yet there were small but cheering developments. In Luzon two thousand more natives took the oath of allegiance to the United States. Martin Delgado, the insurgent general who had defied General Miller at Iloilo, surrendered with 30 officers and 140 men—not many, but straws in the wind which signalled the eventual collapse of resistance in Panay. There had been 241 engagements between the two sides in September and October. The figure dropped to 198 in November and December. In the first-mentioned two months, eighteen rifles had been turned over to the Americans. During November and December, however, only forty-seven were surrendered. Thus it appears that the capitulators were almost all bolomen of slight military significance.

Taft and MacArthur had expected so much from McKinley's victory that they viewed these paltry gains with disappointment. An even worse contretemps was taking place at the local government level. Those districts which were under the thumbs of U.S. officers of integrity and intelligence operated at least adequately, but many were dominated by harsh or indifferent men whose actions invited trouble. In Cebu, for example, the provisional assembly simply fell apart. Only a few municipal *presidentes* bothered to show up. Those who did announced that they had not been elected by their people and had no idea why they had been summoned. In other cases not a single assemblyman appeared. A few sent polite written thanks. In Pampanga the electors convened but refused to vote. The situation was absurd and irritating, and General Chaffee later summed it up in phrases requiring no elaboration.

> Throughout these islands, wherever a *presidente* of a *pueblo* or *cabeza* of a *barrio* was appointed or elected under American authority, he, with few exceptions, either acted in the same capacity for the insurgents, or maintained silence . . . This dual form of government existed everywhere, in strongly garrisoned towns like Manila and in the smallest *barrio* alike . . . [They] now commenced the difficult task of serving two masters. In all lawful matters they served with due appearance of loyalty the American government, while at the same time . . . in gross violation of the laws of war, they secretly levied and collected taxes . . . from the people, who, with universal accord, submitted silently thereto. They held communications with the enemy, and in all ways open to them gave the guerilla bands aid and comfort.

In consequence, MacArthur requested and received permission to arm the municipal police. Emboldened by the Republican triumph, bolstered by an army lately reinforced to seventy-five thousand men (it was to be VIII Corps' peak strength), no longer hampered by moderations which had necessarily prevailed during the election campaign, he issued a proclamation on December 20, 1900, placing the islands under martial law. The assassination of collaborators had to stop. Sending money, supplies, and information concerning U.S. troop movements to the *insurrectos* had to stop. The practise of refusing to co-operate because of the alleged fear of reprisal had to stop. The war, in other words, absolutely had to stop. Mabini and thirty-one others were deported to Guam, seventy-nine captives were convicted of war crimes and all executed, hundreds were imprisoned, MacArthur stated modestly that "as an educational document, the effect was immediate and far reaching"; but the war did not by any means stop.

The press was muzzled. All Philippine newspapers were

forced to publish U.S. handouts and to fill their remaining columns with trivia. A few overstepped the line and were instantly suppressed. These were *La Patria, La Democracia,* and *La Alborado* in Manila, and *La Opinion* in Iloilo. In Cebu the *Nuevo Dia* was so manhandled by enthusiastic military officers that it frequently appeared with entire pages blank.

The fact that McKinley's re-election had not ended the fighting seemed to startle America, where it had been assumed that the war would automatically cease on the morning of November 5. Arguments raged as to whether the permanent regular army should be increased to a hundred thousand men who would settle the Philippine "question" once and for all. Senator Sewell of New Jersey, who had once predicted that sixty thousand men and several years of battle would be required to subdue the natives, now called triumphant attention to his forecast and was quoted in the New York *Times* (January 5) saying, "Nobody believed it at the time." The *Times* writer added somewhat gloomily, "There is considerable reason to believe that it is now the administration's view." But in that same issue appeared a more hopeful note:

THINKS AGUINALDO IS DEAD

Benjamin Ide Wheeler Says He Has Information From The Philippines

From Washington Henry Adams was prophetically writing his brother Brooks in Europe that the world would "break its damn neck within five and twenty years." In his opinion it would be wise to "abandon China, Philippines, and everything else . . . to stand on our own internal resources alone." And he continued, "I incline strongly now to anti-imperialism and very strongly to anti-militarism."

Even "Teddy," the most avid annexationist of all, was not his usual self early in 1901. He despised his new job, its dusty obscurity, its technical difficulties (about which he knew lit-

tle and cared less) as a sort of sergeant-at-arms over the august body of senators; and he was not happy over the course
of events in the Philippines. True, he wrote Frederic Coudert,
it was our duty to sustain law and righteousness there; yet
were we "fortunate or unfortunate in having to hold them"?
For him it was an amazing thought, and his letter pursued
even more singular lines of reasoning. The nation should
never again assimilate a land, he warned, the people of which
were capable of self-government, unless they wanted to be
assimilated by us—"and not necessarily even then." It had begun to dawn upon him, he inferred, that the possession of a
colony entailed more obligations than glories and profits, and
that even the profits were restricted to a handful of large
corporations and entrepreneurs.

And if Mr. Roosevelt had begun to entertain qualms, Mark
Twain had finally freed himself of any lingering doubts and
hesitations. The most famous of all anti-imperialist screeds,
"To the Person Sitting in Darkness," appeared in *The North
American Review* in February, 1901:

> Would it not be prudent to get our Civilization tools together
> and see how much stock is left on hand in the way of Glass
> Beads and Theology, and Maxim Guns and Hymn Books, and
> Trade Gin and Torches of Progress and Enlightenment . . .
> and balance the books and arrive at the profit and loss . . . ?

There was, of course, money in the Blessings of Civilization if
carefully administered. Unfortunately the people sitting in
darkness had become suspicious of "Love, Justice, Gentleness,
Christianity, Protection to the Weak, Temperance, Law and
Order, Liberty, Equality, Honorable Dealing, Mercy, Education," and the like. They had begun to understand that there
are two American ideologies, one for home consumption and
one for export:

> One that sets the captive free, and one that takes a once-
> captive's new freedom away from him, and picks a quarrel

Oregon Volunteers firing by volley southeast of Manila

An insurgent outpost

A commissary train

22nd Infantry crossing the Tuliahan, March 26, 1899

General Frederick Funston

A pause in the advance on Santa Cruz

Wounded insurgents

(credit: U.S. Army Photograph)

Major General Arthur MacArthur

A line of skirmishers advancing under fire

Fighting (right background) near the Pasig River

Dead insurgents

Judge William H. Taft

with him, with nothing to found it on, then kills him to get
his land.

This is not Good for Business, he wrote. We must persuade
the Filipinos that it is all for the best:

> There have been lies, yes, but they were told in a good cause.
> We have been treacherous, but that was only in order that
> real good might come out of apparent evil. True, we have
> crushed a deceived and confiding people; we have turned
> against the weak and the friendless who trusted us . . . We
> have debauched America's honor and blackened her face be-
> fore the world; but each detail was for the best . . . Give
> yourself no uneasiness; it is all right.

Now, having explained to the natives why we are there and
the reasonableness of our intentions, they will understand the
fundamental graciousness of our occupation army and will
submit to its persuasions. We will also give them a bit of
bunting with which to flaunt their patriotism:

> And as for a flag for the Philippine Province, it is easily man-
> aged . . . we can just have our usual flag, with the white
> stripes painted black and the stars replaced by the skull and
> crossbones.

Thus, Twain concluded, by our simply employing a little ingenuity and a measure of psychology "Progress and Civilization in that country can have a boom, and it will take in the
Persons who are Sitting in Darkness, and we can resume
Business at the old stand."

Despite its length the piece was fully reprinted in scores
of newspapers and magazines; hundreds of others printed
excerpts; the Anti-Imperialist League, of course, published
and distributed it as a pamphlet. Satire clarifies statistics and
sharpens logic, and it had been long indeed since simple citizens had been faced by a light this blinding. They blinked,
but too late; for it was too late for mockery, too late to turn
back. "Conditions rapidly improving," cabled Judge Taft as

the rainy season approached. "Rifles, officers, privates are being captured or surrendered daily in considerable numbers . . ." The leaders of the guerilla movement remained refractory, but that was to be expected. They could not suddenly admit that the fight was (and by implication always had been) ill-advised. Perceptive though many of them were, they could not confess to their people that U.S. administration might be more efficient than their own. So they minimized and derided those benefits; and if in their hearts they feared the dangers of independence, they gave no voice to them.

Months after the election U.S. possession of the Philippines seemed virtually complete. What was that archipelago now? "Is it a nation, a State, a Territory, a republic, a colony, an annex, an ally, or a dependency?" wondered the Philadelphia *Public Ledger*. Were its people citizens? Our flag was there; did the constitution accompany it? If so, tariff barriers were impermissible and American sugar and tobacco producers, among others, would suffer accordingly. In the Dred Scott case (1857) Chief Justice Taney had stated in unmistakable terms that the federal government was not empowered "to enlarge its territorial limits in any way, except by the admission of new states . . ." On the other hand, Mr. Justice Bradley (*Mormon Church v. United States, 1890*) had spoken of "fundamental limitations" as to the rights of people in acquired territories. Which interpretation applied? After a long pause the Supreme Court settled the matter by the so-called Insular Decisions of May 1901.

To this day they remain confusing. The problem was a practical one. We had the islands and assuredly we were going to keep them, but statehood was out of the question and the tariff knot had to be cut—all this in the face of a constitution which did not exactly fit the exigencies of the case. It was accomplished by a narrow squeeze. The voting was five to four, with Mr. Justice Brown handing down the majority decision. The four others who concurred did so by means of different interpretations. Thus, it was observed at the time, the verdict was "by Brown, eight dissenting."

The process by which the Supreme Court sought its conclusions was involved. At the outset it decided that there were two kinds of acquired territories: incorporated and unincorporated. The Philippines were defined as unincorporated. Their natives were entitled to life, liberty, and property rights, but not necessarily anything more. Following this mystic distinction everything fell into place. Unlike (say) Alaska, the archipelago was a foreign country in the sense that American customs duties might be imposed by special act of congress. Here Justice Bradley's reference to "fundamental limitations" was utilized. The Filipinos had fundamental rights but not "formal" or "procedural" rights; only incorporated territories possessed all three. Trial by jury and customs uniformity were procedural rights which did not have to be granted. But neither congress nor the court possessed a neat list separating procedural from fundamental rights. In fact, they had never heard of the distinction until now. Was a given island a territory or (even more esoterically) "a territory appurtenant?" Was it incorporated or not? Did it deserve fundamental or procedural or formal rights? The answer followed automatically. It depended upon what had already happened in the course of historic events, or upon the intent of congress as revealed by the laws it chose to pass. It certainly depended no longer upon the Supreme Court, and Mr. Dooley said that there was at least one thing he was sure about.

"What's that?" asked Mr. Hennessy.

"That is," said Mr. Dooley, "no matter whither th' constitution follows th' flag or not, th' Supreme Court follows th' illiction returns."

In retrospect the three years' events possess a majestic fatefulness. Dewey sinks the Spanish fleet. Merritt occupies Manila. Otis occupies the provinces. The senate ratifies the Paris treaty. The electorate ratifies Mr. McKinley. Taft and Mac-

Arthur consolidate the conquest. The Supreme Court legal-
izes it. Nothing now remained on the agenda but to blot out
the diminishing insurrection. Until two months earlier this
had involved a small dilemma in the form of Señor Emilio
Aguinaldo.

III

Aimless attempts to learn his whereabouts had been unsuccessful in the past, but it was not until the capture of one of
his couriers, Cecilio Segismundo, early in 1901 that definite
information came to light. Twenty dispatches carried on his
person were brought to General Funston. When deciphered
they turned out to be from Aguinaldo to various guerilla commanders. One consisted of instructions to his cousin, General
Baldomero Aguinaldo, to replace General José Alexandrino
as head of operations in central Luzon and to send the president four hundred picked troops for deployment in the
Cagayan Valley. None of the documents mentioned Aguinaldo's hideout by name, but this one showed that it was known
to Segismundo, for he was to lead the reinforcements there.
  That luckless youth was therefore interrogated—"by exactly what means, history does not reveal," Edwin Wildman
wrote at the time, although Funston claims he talked voluntarily, while Aguinaldo says he was given the water cure
twice. In any event, Segismundo disclosed that Aguinaldo
was at Palanan, in the mountains of Isabela Province in northeast Luzon, a few miles from the coast. A scheme dawned
in Frederick Funston's mind. Thirty-six years of age, he was
one of the more curious individuals thrown up by the war—
five feet five inches tall, red-haired and muscle-bound, with
inclinations incurably romantic, adventurous, and adulative
of the Anglo-Saxon legend, a mild intellectual. He had joined
a botanical expedition to California's Death Valley ten years
previously. From there he drifted into Alaska. Before the

Spanish-American War broke out, he was to be found fighting Spaniards on the rebel side in Cuba, where he was wounded and contracted malaria. He returned to Kansas. After the *Maine* explosion he was given a colonelcy in his state's regiment, posted to the Philippines, and soon promoted brigadier general of volunteers. The opportunity he now faced was tailor-made for his quixotic talents.

Everything hinged upon the fact that Aguinaldo had called for guerilla replacements in his headquarters area and that they were expected in driblets. It occurred to Funston that the role could be played by his Maccabebe Scouts from Pampanga Province. They had always been mercenaries; after fighting against the Tagalogs for Spain they had switched allegiance to the United States. Indistinguishable in appearance and language from other Filipino Malays, they possessed such notorious proclivities for the rape, torture and robbery of their countrymen that the Americans had always had their hands full trying to restrain them. The root cause of the mutual detestation between them and other natives of the islands is not clear, but plainly they were ideal for Funston's purpose. He assigned eighty-one of them to his task force and disguised them in the nondescript garb of *insurrectos*.

U.S. officers would have to lead the expedition. Funston and four others would therefore accompany the Maccabebes in the guise of prisoners. The story would be that they had been captured during the march northward. Finally, it was essential to include some bona fide Tagalogs to act as rebel officers. Segismundo would be one, of course, and Funston also rounded up three renegades of certain loyalty to the United States, including one Hilario Tal Placido. He also brought along a shrewd Spanish secret-service officer named Lazaro Segovia. Masquerading under false colors, their lives would not be worth a *peso* if they were caught. This was especially true of the Maccabebes. To complete their disguise they carried Remington and Mauser rifles instead of the usual Krags.

MacArthur approved the plan—a desperate one, he called it. It was decided that the expedition would sail around the southern tip of Luzon on the gunboat *Vicksburg*, secretly land at Casiguran, and then proceed overland about a hundred miles to Palanan. By February 6 everything was ready. Funston kissed his bride goodbye, was advised pleasantly by MacArthur, "I fear that I shall never see you again," and in squally weather boarded ship with his ninety men. When under way, the skipper of the *Vicksburg*, Commander E. B. Barry, was told where they were going. The Maccabebes were carefully rehearsed. Stationery belonging to the insurgent general Urbano Lacuna had previously been captured during a raid. His signature had been forged at the bottom of two sheets, and now appropriate messages were written on them to the effect that the reinforcements were coming, along with five U.S. captives, plus (as Funston put it) "some mere rubbish, just to fill space down to the bogus signature." Just after midnight, February 14, the bedraggled group was landed by ship's boats inside the empty, desolate entrance of Casiguran Bay. It had been arranged that the *Vicksburg* would return there on March 25. Until then Funston and his men were on their own. They had about five weeks to traverse a hundred miles through wild, unknown country, snatch Aguinaldo, and return.

In Casiguran the Filipinos were welcomed as heroes, while the Americans were gazed upon with cold curiosity. "The village band was pressed into service," Funston recalled, "and we entered the town in great style." Both forged letters were sent ahead to Aguinaldo by courier. Two days passed here, while the Maccabebes became fidgety. After being provisioned with cracked corn, dried carabao meat and six live chickens, the little group started off for Palanan amid showers of rain. The solicitous village *vice-presidente* waved them *adios*. "Of the numerous ones that we made fools of, he was

the only one that I ever had the slightest qualms about,"
wrote Funston. Even on half rations the expedition, following
the beach northward, ran out of food within a week. The rain
continued without letup, and by the 22nd the men were
quite dazed. "It seemed impossible that the madcap enterprise could succeed, and I began to have regrets that I had
led all these men to such a finish." They were now at Dinu-
dungan, eight miles from Palanan.

So near and yet so far; but there was no proceeding further without food, and again Funston called upon the enemy
for aid. After a note had been sent ahead to Aguinaldo, more
cracked corn arrived in the morning. They started off on the
last leg of their journey, with the Maccabebes about an hour
in the van. "The trail led in a northwesterly direction and was
very muddy, as the sunlight seldom reached the ground in
these dense and gloomy woods. Despite our breakfast, we
were very weak . . . Of the Americans, Mitchell and I were
in the worst shape, the Hazzards and Newton standing it better. I had to lie down flat on the ground every few hundred
yards to get a rest of a minute or two." Then came a crisis.
Fearing to allow even U.S. prisoners to know his exact loca-
tion, Aguinaldo had dispatched some insurgent troops to take
them over. Two Maccabebes came running back along the
trail and hustled the Americans into the woods. When the
loyalists arrived, and were told that the captives were still
in Casiguran, they kept going. Meanwhile the other Maccabebes had entered Palanan.

Next Segovia, Placido and Segismundo showed up. They
walked straight into Aguinaldo's headquarters on the second
floor of a little house overlooking the village square. After a
few moments Segismundo departed. A group of natives,
wearing blue drill uniforms and white hats and armed with
Mausers, had been drawn up to greet the newcomers, who
faced them with their rifles at order-arms. "The poor little
'Macs' were in such a nervous state from their nervous excite-

ment over the strange drama . . . that they were pretty badly rattled."

From the window, while Placido bragged and joked, Segovia watched these little formalities with interest, waiting for the mercenaries to maneuver themselves into a shallow arc around their foes. Who else was upstairs? Funston says that Aguinaldo was accompanied by seven armed guards. In view of what transpired this seems unlikely. Aguinaldo, the only participant who ever described the incident in writing, refers to Funston as a fictionizer. There were, he says, only two rebel officers left in the room. The others had left, bored by Placido's yarns, or to watch the incoming troops, or to answer nature's call, or to get a drink. Segovia at last nodded to the ranking Maccabebe officer watching him from below. He, Gregorio Cadhit, turned to his men and called out, "Now is the time, Maccabebes. Give it to them." They fired wildly, killing two men and badly wounding the leader of the band, who had gotten in the way.

When Aguinaldo heard the shots, he believed that his men were celebrating the arrival of the reinforcements. In exasperation he leaned out the window and shouted, "Stop that foolishness. Don't waste your ammunition." At that moment Placido, a burly man, grabbed him from behind and Segovia began shooting. One of Aguinaldo's bodyguards was hit three times and fell. The other fled. Struggling to draw his revolver, Aguinaldo was thrown to the floor and held down by Placido. "You are a prisoner of the Americans," he explained, while sitting on him.

Meanwhile the Maccabebes, who outnumbered the entire rebel force in Palanan, had taken over the town and the Americans had entered it. When Funston trotted up he was met by Segovia, spattered with the blood of his victim and almost hysterical. "It is all right," he said. "We have him." Funston hurried up the stairs and found the little Filipino almost in a state of shock. "Is this not some joke?" Aguinaldo mumbled in Spanish. Funston introduced himself and Aguinaldo seemed to relax. It was all over.

After a day of rest, the expedition returned to the coast without incident and was met on schedule by the *Vicksburg*. She cruised around the island, steamed up the Pasig, and docked near "The Palace" in Malacanana Park on the morning of March 28. Funston, Aguinaldo and the others came ashore. The Filipino was put into a private room under heavy guard. General MacArthur, who had just awakened for breakfast, descended in a dressing gown to greet Funston—another, he thought, in the long list of men who had set out on wild-goose chases after the Philippine president. "Where is Aguinaldo?" he asked dryly.

"Right in this house," Funston replied.

For some time the insurgent leader remained almost psychopathically sullen. He had sworn never to be taken alive, and the humiliation, the loss of face, must have been overpowering. Guarded day and night by commissioned officers, he was made comfortable at American headquarters and supplied with a secretary. His family was sent for. MacArthur and others, American and Filipino alike, visited him often and tried to explain the U.S. point of view, the glories and prosperity which would follow as soon as the fighting ended, the hopelessness of allowing the struggle to continue. Aguinaldo said little. He had been captured alive because it was essential for him to tell his people to lay down their arms; but for three tense weeks he refused to do so. He understood the program somewhat too clearly. It was, as an Englishwoman in Manila remarked, "to have lots of American school teachers at once set to work to teach the Filipino English, and at the same time to keep plenty of American soldiers around to knock him on the head should he get a notion that he is ready for self-government before the Americans think he is." On April 19 he finally took the oath of allegiance to the American government and followed it by a proclamation which MacArthur published in all dialects throughout the islands:

> . . . There has been enough blood, enough tears, enough desolation . . . I cannot refuse to heed the voice of a people longing for peace . . . By acknowledging and accepting the sovereignty of the United States throughout the Philippine Archipelago . . . I believe that I am serving thee, my beloved country . . .

His capture startled the world. Manila went wild with excitement, and America awoke next morning to find the newspaper on the doorstep a shocker in 144-point banner headlines:

AGUINALDO CAPTURED!

Funston, who had no permanent rank whatsoever, was handed a commission as brigadier general in the regular army and, of course, the Congressional Medal of Honor. It was all due to him that now, finally, unquestionably, the insurrection was over. There was talk of running him for the presidency of the United States in 1904. Roosevelt wrote him (a man after his own heart): "I take pride in this crowning exploit of a career filled with cool courage, iron endurance . . ." and so on.

The only sour note was supplied by naïve souls in women's clubs who considered his methods beneath contempt. He had used disguises, mercenaries, forgeries, and deceptions, and he had begged food from the very people he was hoodwinking. These criticisms ignored the fact that the capture of Funston and his men would mean their execution as spies. Yet *Life* magazine jeered at his "treachery" and most British agreed that the incident was not cricket. In London the *Saturday Review* used it as a peg upon which to hang an over-all judgment:

> There have been more wicked wars than this . . . but never a more shabby war. It is nearly three years since the Ameri-

cans, having gone to war with Spain for the liberties of Cuba,
decided that it was their manifest destiny to deprive the
Filipinos of their liberty. This was called "taking up the white
man's burden." For some time the Americans quite honestly
believed that they were doing rather a noble, self-denying
thing; but the cant phrases of three years ago are worn thread-
bare . . . [The capture of Aguinaldo] was effected by a piece
of sharp practice thoroughly in keeping with the rest of the
war. Of all that curious mixture of sentiments, noble and
ignoble, out of which the war with the Filipinos sprang, only
the element of hypocrisy seems to have retained its original
vigor.

But who were the English, of all people, to talk? Meanwhile
at one stroke Funston had ended a costly, bloody war. So
it seemed for a day, a week; but when the cheers had died
down people noticed that fighting was in progress as though
nothing had happened—"with increased ferocity," some observers stated.

The incident proved that those impulses which had provoked and sustained the insurrection essentially had little to
do with its hero, or figurehead. Aguinaldo's capture shocked
the islanders and drove another nail into the coffin of the
rebellion; his proclamation also had its effect; but the two
factors were not decisive. Ambushes, raids, captures, local
shadow governments, night attacks in force, and covert non-
co-operation with American authority persisted. Luzon became somewhat more quiet, but the rebellion's center of
gravity moved southward, especially toward the Moro islands. In past centuries the Spaniards had been forced to
leave those feral heathen more or less alone, but the United
States was intent upon assimilating them no less than the
Tagalogs and Visayans and the rest. When the Mohammedans found their provinces suddenly teeming with white
Christians, they took to the warpath in earnest.

Between May and December they made twelve direct attacks against American garrisons. In one melee near Lake

Lanao, north Mindanao, the 27th Infantry suffered ten killed and forty wounded. In addition to these relatively major engagements, over two hundred smaller ones took place in 1901. Politically the situation here was vexatious too, for Moro co-operation with their new Christian masters was understandably fitful. In May Colonel O. J. Sweet, commanding the district of Mindanao and Jolo, reported in disgust: "Our relations with the Sultans and Chiefs remain friendly. They will promise anything in the way of reforms but these are never carried out . . . The Sultan stands on his dignity and quotes erroneously from the Koran as to his duties as Sultan toward his people." In addition to boloing stray soldiers, the people stole American horses, rifles and other equipment. They even made off with the cemetery gates of one American detachment, whereupon a sprightly exchange of notes took place:

> To His Highness the Sultan of Jolo, from his brother the Governor of Tiange, Greetings:
>
> Three nights ago the iron gates of the cemetery were stolen. Indications point to the Moros living in your territory as the thieves. I desire you to make a thorough search for said gates and have them returned and the thieves punished . . .

The Sultan replied:

> This letter comes from your son the Sultan Hadji Mohammed Jamalul, Kiram to my father the Governor of Tiange:
>
> Your letter of the 23rd instant received and I understand its contents. I am very sorry indeed that the gates to the cemetery were stolen. It would have been better if the thief had robbed the property belonging to the living, because they have a chance to earn more but the dead have not. Therefore aid me to think how to get rid of stealing in this country. Let us inquire at all places where there are blacksmiths. There are no blacksmiths in Maibun. Above all you must closely examine the blacksmiths in the Buz Buz and Moubu as these gates were too heavy to be carried a long distance.

> Very likely they are in these two places . . . If we find the
> thief let us bury him alive . . . You are an old man . . . per-
> haps you have pity on me. As for me I detest thieves . . .

Each time the Americans mounted an expedition—peaceful or otherwise—into the interior, various degrees of trouble
or annoyances were anticipated. By mid-1901 the question
was when and how, if ever, these ceaseless incidents could
be terminated. Further north, conditions had definitely improved. Near Manila, over fifteen hundred more *insurrectos*
gave themselves up, and so did General Manuel Tinio with
thirty-six of his officers in the Illocano provinces, and Generals Lacuna and Mascardo Alexandrino. Even the hot-headed
Juan Cailles surrendered. Only in Batangas, Luzon, did General Miguel Malvar hold out. With the fall of Aguinaldo, this
man became titular head of the revolutionary movement. All
in all, four thousand insurgents surrendered during June and
September, bringing with them 1,363 rifles.

Thirty thousand American troops were shipped back to the
States. To the War Department MacArthur cabled that except for Samar and southern Luzon the insurrection could
be considered at an end. He also reported (incorrectly) that
all Moros had submitted to U.S. authority and had been disarmed. General "Hell Roaring" Jake Smith was put in charge
of Samar, General J. Franklin Bell of Batangas. They both
had their hands full. Bell unceremoniously dumped the civil
regime overboard in Batangas, Cebu, and Bohol, replaced it
by military law, and suspended *habeas corpus.* "To combat
such a population," he wrote, "it is necessary to make the
state of war as insupportable as possible . . . by keeping the
minds of the people in such a state of anxiety and apprehension that living under such conditions will soon become un-
bearable. Little should be said. The less said the better. Let
acts, not words, convey the intention." Nothing but more
ruthlessness could bring these people to their senses, he continued; and General Wheaton wholeheartedly agreed:

The nearer we approach the methods found necessary by the other nations through centuries of experience in dealing with Asiatics, the less the National Treasury will be expended and the fewer graves will be made.

Practically speaking there was no denying it, although the methods may not have coincided with Mr. Taft's earnest intentions; for it was plain that Malvar was almost as much of a nuisance as Aguinaldo had been. On June 10 he directed a meticulous attack near Lipa, only a hundred miles south of Manila, which resulted in heavy U.S. casualties and a new proclamation: "Forward . . . All wars for independence have been obliged to suffer terrible tests." Guerilla commanders were much heartened, and it occurred to the harassed Americans that it might be necessary to ensnare General Malvar without too much delay. But he was elusive all year, nor could a single Tagalog be found to supply information as to his whereabouts. . . .

IV

On July 4, 1901, before Señor Cayetano Arellano, chief justice of the Supreme Court, Mr. Taft took oath as the first civilian governor of the Philippines. On that same date General Mac-Arthur sailed for the United States, having been replaced by Major General Adna Chaffee, a humorless officer just back from China where he had commanded U.S. forces during the Boxer Rebellion. Of the seventy-seven provinces in the islands, fifty-five were still under military rule and Taft was still battling his army commander tooth and nail. These differences were kept from the American and Philippine public, but they were no secret among Washington's inner circles; and Mr. Roosevelt unhappily wrote Chaffee, "I am deeply chagrined, to use the mildest possible term, over the trouble between yourself and Taft."

Governor Taft had begun to emerge as a contradictory

character—on one hand sympathetic to the Filipinos, on the other evincing signs of growing indifference. Not long after taking office, he dealt native aspirations a near-deathblow by proclaiming it a punishable crime to encourage, publicize, join, speak for, or act with the independence movement. Yet he seemed to understand and vaguely to sympathize with that movement. Despite his disquieting new words and deeds, the people genuinely liked him. When offered a post on the U. S. Supreme Court he refused it; he felt that he could do more good in Manila. He scoffed at the idea that the islanders were divided (except for the Moros) into mutually exclusive tribes. "The word 'tribes,'" he said, "gives an erroneous impression . . . There is a racial solidarity among them undoubtedly. They are homogeneous. I cannot tell the difference between an Ilocano and a Tagalog or a Visayan . . . To me all Filipinos are alike." But it was his job to help quell the insurrection, to institute American sovereignty, and he performed it with inhuman neutrality—so diligently, in fact, that one is not too surprised to learn that in later years (as secretary of war and president) he was to move from coolness to criticism to near-enmity toward the people he had once cherished.

Thus assimilation went on. Hundreds of American teachers arrived to conduct native schools. Toothbrushes and soap accompanied them—and tennis and football and baseball. Tagal shouts of "Kill the umpire" replaced other calls for blood. Sadly American newspapers reported, however, that the natives were inclined to change the holy rules of the sacred game, in that natives of better family and more distinguished military reputation refused to sully their dignity by running bases; they would only bat. Literacy soared, the death rate declined, smallpox and cholera were arrested, taxation dropped. True, one sixth of the population of Luzon had been wiped out by what General Bell confessed might be considered "in other countries . . . rather harsh measures," but it was all in the name of progress; and meanwhile the road-building program was moving along wonderfully well, hemp and sugar mills were bustling with business, and the guerilla war had been reduced to a sporadic, hopeless pitch—the sort which had once caused us to intervene in Cuba. "You never hear of any disturbances in Northern Luzon," said a Republican congressman just back from Manila, ". . . because there isn't anybody there to rebel . . . The good Lord in Heaven only knows the number of Filipinos that were put under ground. Our soldiers took no prisoners, they kept no records; they simply swept the country, and wherever and whenever they could get hold of a Filipino they killed him."

But as the summer of 1901 moved on, wet and broiling, acrid with anticlimax and blasted hopes, better things were in the air. The war was quite obviously in its final stages; whatever the sorrows of the past, a new day was dawning. In the United States what was left of the insurrection was relegated to the back pages of the newspapers. There, appropriately lost among the financial reports and the obituaries, it occasionally came to light when another flare-up of no consequence occurred in Mindanao or Samar. It was old hat now. "Teddy" was fishing, travelling, and writing speeches. The evening of September 6 saw him at Isla la Motte, Vermont, preparing to join his family in the Adirondacks.

That morning President McKinley was in Buffalo, New York, attending a public reception at the Temple of Music of the Pan-American Exposition. In frock coat, gray trousers and white waistcoat, he stood at the end of a long corridor, surrounded by associates and several secret-service men, and shook hands with citizens who filed past in a single line. One of them was a young man named Leon Czolgosz, whose right hand seemed to be wrapped in a white bandage. He reached out with his left. As the president grasped it, Czolgosz fired two quick shots which struck McKinley in the chest and abdomen. The assassin was smashed to the floor and jumped by a dozen men. Before they could tear him apart, the president muttered, "Don't let them hurt him." Held erect by his secretary, he said, "My wife—be careful, Cortelyou, how you tell her." An ambulance took him to an emergency hospital on the exposition grounds, where preparations for surgery were made. On September 12 gangrene set in. The following afternoon a guide handed Roosevelt a telegram. He knew what it contained before opening it. When he reached Buffalo next day the president was dead, and Elihu Root advised Roosevelt to waste no time taking the oath of office. In the same house where McKinley's body lay, "that damned cowboy," as Mark Hanna had termed him, became the twenty-fifth president of the United States. The news when flashed to the Philippines was received with apathy. Not half a hundred natives there had ever heard of the man.

14

END
AND
BEGINNING

L ATE IN THE EVENING OF SEPTEMBER 27, 1901, A GUN-
boat from the town of Basey on the island of Leyte
dropped anchor off Balangiga, a village at the southern tip of Samar, the exact spot where Ferdinand Magellan
had first sighted the Philippine Islands in March 1521, about
ninety miles from where he was to die a month later at the
hands of the natives. One of the ship's cutters was lowered
from davits. Tiny waves chuckled under her bow as Lieutenant Bumpus and four enlisted men were rowed toward the
shore, carrying with them a large sack of mail for Company
C of the 9th Infantry.

Balangiga was a peaceful little port garrisoned, like dozens
of others, by a U.S. army detachment; and Samar was like
many another island in the archipelago—its wild interior still
unpacified and unexplored by the military arm of the invader.
The guerilla leader there, General Vincente Lukban, was an
incorrigible last-ditch fighter; but his force was considered
too tenuous to be much of a threat to men of the 9th Infantry, one of the most hard-bitten regular regiments in the
American army. It had returned recently from China, where

it had helped capture Tientsin and storm the walls of Peking's Imperial City during the Boxèr Rebellion. Company C consisted of seventy-four veterans, most of whom had seen service not only in China but in Cuba and northern Luzon. It was led by Captain Thomas O'Connell, a West Pointer, and his second in command, Lieutenant E. C. Bumpus. Major Richard S. Griswold was attached as company surgeon.

For some weeks the outfit had been engaged in placid patrol duties and in cleaning up the accumulated debris of the town, with the forced assistance of a hundred male citizens. Of late eighty more natives had also been impressed into the chore; they came from the nearby hills and had been recommended by the town *presidente*. As it happened, they were Lukban's best bolomen. The Americans found them unusually industrious and good-natured.

The morning after Bumpus arrived, the men bounded excitedly out of bed at 0630 hours and into reveille formation. No mail had been received by them for four months. After it had been distributed, they went to breakfast at an outdoor kitchen about a hundred feet from their quarters, where the rifles were stacked. The native workmen were also up and about, under the eyes of three sentries. While the Americans were reading their letters, the Filipino chief of police strolled over to one of the guards, grabbed his rifle, and smashed him to his knees with the butt. Church bells began to clang; from the hills came the honk of conch shells; and the 180 workmen and other townsmen fell upon the Americans, not one of whom was armed except for the sentries, who were killed instantly.

The commissioned officers were caught in their quarters, a former convent opposite the enlisted men's area. In his pajamas O'Connell leaped from a second-story window and ran toward the barracks. He was boloed before arriving there. Major Griswold was stabbed to death in his room. Bumpus, who had a pile of mail in his lap, never got out of his chair. A boloman lopped off the front of his face from the bridge of the nose to the throat. Next he was shoved out the window into the square below, where his eyes were gouged out and his head smeared with jam to attract ants.

Meanwhile several hundred natives had stormed the mess tables. One of the first victims was the company first sergeant, whose skull was split open by an ax. Another man's head, when removed by a bolo, fell into his breakfast plate. Most troops were butchered before they could rise from the tables. The company cook threw boiling water and canned goods at the natives, then grabbed a meat cleaver and struggled toward the barracks. Others defended themselves with rocks, picks, baseball bats, and shovels. A huge sergeant named Markley reached the arms cache, where he snatched a Krag and began firing into the mob. He was joined by another soldier, bleeding from a dozen cuts, who helped hold off their assailants with a pistol.

Some Americans ran toward the hills. Others mistakenly tried to swim to safety. They were pursued in boats and boloed to death in the water. Within minutes, the streets and plaza of Balangiga were strewn with American bodies, brains, and intestines. A dozen men under Sergeant Markley held out in the barracks. All of them were wounded but continued to fire their hot rifles until the bolomen withdrew. Now the problem of these and sixteen other survivors was to escape across the narrow strait to Basey in outrigger canoes resting near the waterfront, several of which were hurriedly put out to sea. One soon filled with water and was tossed back to the shoreline by a light surf. Two of its occupants managed to escape, but the rest were killed in a silent, horrible melee on the sand. Another boat containing only two men also drifted back to the beach, where both were cut down by waiting Filipinos. The remaining canoes were paddled laboriously across to Leyte. When they arrived there next day only one American could speak coherently. They had had no water, the wounded were suffering and dripping blood which had attracted sharks, they had been warding off attacks by natives in boats, and two more had died en route. Of the company's original complement, forty-eight were killed or forever unaccounted for, twenty-two were wounded, and only four were unharmed.

Lukban congratulated the Balangigans by proclamation and urged others to imitate them. Several days later ten Americans were killed and six wounded in a similar uprising at Gandara. It was the bitter end to sweetness and light in the central islands. The massacres chilled America to the bone, and from her new president came an anguished cry to Chaffee to put an end to these deeds, to finish the insurrection speedily and with all necessary firmness. Orders couched in broad terms assigned General "Jake" Smith the job of pacifying Samar. His first move was to order all civilians out of the interior. When they came straggling into the coastal towns they were thrown, one and all, into stockades. "I want no prisoners," he said. "I wish you to kill and burn; the more you burn and kill the better it will please me." He directed that Samar be converted into "a howling wilderness." All persons who had not surrendered and were capable of carrying arms were to be shot.

Who was capable? asked Major Waller of the Marines. Anyone over ten years of age, replied Smith. Samar boys of ten could carry a rifle and swing a bolo, he insisted; they were just as dangerous as their elders. The major executed his orders more or less to the letter, and within six months Samar was as quiet as a cemetery.* It was now 1902 and active warfare, Mr. Root confessed to the House Committee on Military Affairs, was still going on in southern Luzon. "The process of settlement . . . is necessarily a slow one," he explained, but inevitably "the moral force of the American troops" was making itself felt. Moral or otherwise, the job was about done. General Lukban was captured in February. The Negro deserter, David Fagan, carrying a six-hundred-dollar

* Shortly after the end of the campaign both Waller and Smith were court-martialed and retired from the service.

price on his head, was discovered with two insurgents and
three native women enjoying a fish dinner on a beach in
Nueva Ecija. In short order his head was delivered in a
wicker basket to officers of the 34th Infantry by a Tagal deer-
hunter named Anastacio Bartolome.

Once more it became necessary to cool down the provinces
south of Manila—Batangas, Cavite, and Tabayas—where five
thousand guerillas under General Miguel Malvar had re-
gained control over the population and most local governments. This last Philippine campaign in the grand style was
led by Brigadier General J. Franklin Bell, a spectacular, ambitious youngster who only three years ago had been a cavalry lieutenant. In circular orders to all station commanders
he outlined a policy much like Smith's in Samar. There were
to be no more neutrals; inhabitants were to be classified either
as active (not passive) friends or enemies. The latter, regardless of age or sex, were to be killed or captured. Everyone had
to live within designated military zones and nowhere else.
The municipal police were disarmed. Outside the concentration zones all food supplies were to be confiscated or destroyed. An eight o'clock curfew went into effect. Any Filipino
found on the streets after that hour was to be shot on sight.
Whenever an American soldier was killed, a native prisoner
would be chosen by lot and executed. Native houses in the
vicinity of telegraph lines cut by the *insurrectos* would be
burned.

The program worked. It entailed, however, unforeseen by-
products. When one hundred thousand destitute natives
poured into the designated areas, Bell discovered that there
was not enough food for them; and epidemics broke out as
they invariably do under such circumstances. By the end of
the year, fifty-four thousand civilians had died in Batangas
alone.

Meanwhile Bell was personally leading four thousand
troops against Malvar, under the slogan "Remember Balangiga." Again one may turn away from the details of the cam-

paign. James H. Blount, at that time a lieutenant of volunteers
and later to become a judge in the islands, writes: "The
American soldier in officially sanctioned wrath is a thing so
ugly and dangerous that it would take a Kipling to describe
him"; and the punitive expedition conducted early in 1902
was a classic of its genre, resulting in the devastation of the
countryside and the total extirpation of guerilla resistance
there. For three months Malvar evaded capture. Chased
from valley to valley and over mountains by an enemy who
killed all domestic animals, burned the crops, summarily shot
all defiant natives who remained in the hinterland and were
aiding him, he fought on like a cornered lion. His troops were
sick, famished, and almost without cartridges. They and
their exhausted, middle-aged, bearded leader surrendered on
April 16.

That date marked the practical end of the insurrection,
although it was not officially terminated by edict of President
Roosevelt until July 4. Amnesty was granted to all who would
take the oath of allegiance to the United States. Everywhere
but in the Moro islands civil government replaced the military. The president thanked the army for having "ended the
great Insurrection which has raged throughout the Archipelago against the lawful sovereignty and just authority of the
United States . . . Bound themselves by the laws of war, our
soldiers were called upon to meet every device of unscrupu-
lous treachery and to contemplate without reprisal the inflic-
tion of barbarous cruelties upon their comrades . . ." He told
of the accomplishments of the army, its courage and resolution "accompanied by self-control, patience and magnanimity
. . . whose soldiers . . . love liberty and peace." In congress
Democrats had a field day with the proclamation; it was
called claptrap and an insult to the Philippine people. The
facts, they declared, spoke for themselves—we had struck
down an innocent people and stolen their land. Many had
been the legalisms and rationalizations designed to fit Monroe's statement—"With the existing colonies or dependencies

of any European power we . . . shall not interfere"; and the price of the transaction had been distressingly high; 4234 Americans lay buried there (scarcely any bodies were ever brought home), hundreds more later died in America of service-connected diseases, 2,818 had been wounded, and the dollar cost came to six hundred million. Inaccurately the Chicago *Record-Herald* jeered, "The war in the Philippines has cost the United States over $170,000,000 thus far. But think of the glory!"

On the Filipino side of the ledger the entry was much larger. Sixteen thousand rebels had been killed and their corpses actually counted by the Americans. The true total exceeded twenty thousand. About two hundred thousand civilians were dead of pestilence or disease. The carabao, upon which the population relied for transportation, agriculture, and meat, had been reduced to a tenth of their prewar number. Without them, rice, the staple food of the islands, could not be cultivated. An unyielding U.S. bureaucracy was in political and economic control. The islanders had been conquered in every sense of the word.

It would seem *de rigueur* to observe that Roosevelt's manifesto was greeted with jubilation, prayer and parades in the United States; but it was not. Newspaper treatment was skimpy, noncommittal, flat in tone. One feels that only common courtesy brought it to the front pages. Long since, the American public had virtually forgotten the insurrection, had thrust it out of mind, had relegated it to the dustbin of history.

II

Events trailed off in scraps of words and the occasional crackle of gunfire. . . .

General Funston returned home to a hero's welcome. In a New York speech he referred to Aguinaldo as a cold-blooded murderer and a would-be dictator. The Filipinos he described as "a drunken uncontrollable mob" with the minds of four-year-old children. He recommended that those who wrote "The Anti-Imperialist" be hanged for treason.

In reply Mark Twain ironically wrote "In Defense of General Funston" for the *North American Review*. Bring on the noose, he said; I am a traitor. Nor did he blame Funston for his words and deeds—the man was only a willing, efficient, and perfectly ignorant tool of the imperialists.

On September 25 Chaplain William McKinnon of the 1st Californians died in Manila of amoebic dysentery.

Congress passed the Philippine Organic Act, which put into law actions previously taken by the president and the Taft Commission, including Secretary Root's letter of instructions to the latter dated April 7, 1900. In addition to the legislative and judicial measures already in operation, it provided for two Filipino commissioners in Washington and (in certain instances) appeal to the U. S. Supreme Court.

In February 1903 Apolinario Mabini finally signed the oath of allegiance in Guam which paved the way for return to his native land. On the day he sailed he issued this statement to the press:

> After two long years of absence I am returning, so to speak, completely disoriented and, what is worse, almost overcome by disease and sufferings. Nevertheless, I hope, after some time of rest and study, still to be of some use, unless I have returned to the Islands for the sole purpose of dying.

He passed away in Manila three months later, at the age of thirty-eight.

In the United States senate Mr. Hoar delivered a parting shot against his adversaries:

> You chose war instead of peace. You chose force instead of conciliation . . . talked of the wealth of the Philippine Islands and about the advantage to our trade . . . declared in the Senate Chamber and on the hustings that the flag should never be hauled down . . .

You, my imperialistic friends, have had your ideals and sentimentalities. One is that the flag shall never be hauled down
where it has once floated. Another is that you will not talk or
reason with a people with arms in their hand. Another is that
sovereignty over an unwilling people may be bought with
gold. And another is that sovereignty may be got by force of
arms . . .

What has been the practical statesmanship which comes from
your ideals and sentimentalities? You have wasted six hundred millions of treasure. You have sacrificed nearly ten thousand American lives, the flower of our youth. You have
devastated provinces. You have slain uncounted thousands of
the people you desire to benefit. You have established reconcentration camps. Your generals are coming home from their
harvest, bringing their sheaves with them, in the shape of
other thousands of sick and wounded and insane . . .

Your practical statesmanship has succeeded in converting a
[grateful] people . . . into sullen and irreconcilable enemies,
possessed of a hatred which centuries cannot eradicate . . .

Other notes, other trivia . . . Near Pittsfield, Massachusetts, President Roosevelt was nearly killed in a traffic acci-
dent. Woodrow Wilson was named president of Princeton
University. In a seventy-horsepower racing car Henry Ford
established a world's record of fifty-nine miles per hour. Hans
Wagner of the Pittsburgh Pirates won the National League
batting title with an average of .355. Mark Twain composed
his vitriolic piece, "The Stupendous Procession," a description
of the floats in an imaginary parade dedicated to the twentieth century. Bringing up the rear, he suggested, might be an
ornate symbolism of "The American Flag":

Waving from a Float piled high with property—the whole
marked with Boodle. To wit:

1,200 Islands . . .

Filipino Independence.

Crowd of slaughtered patriots—called "rebels."

Filipino Republic—annihilated.

Crowd of deported patriots—called "rebels."

A Crowned Sultan—in business with the United States and officially-recognized member of the Firm . . .

Motto on the Flag—"To what base uses have I come at last."

The Pirate Flag. Inscribed: "Oh, you will get used to it, Brother. I had sentimental scruples at first myself."

Both in April and May 1903, troops under Captain John J. Pershing were sharply attacked by *amigos* still operating near Lake Lanao. In his official report for that year Elihu Root admitted that "the conduct of the Moros has been growing steadily more unsatisfactory."

There seemed to be, in truth, no end to the problems with the Mohammedans. Their wretched conduct could hardly be dignified by the term insurrection, for it was religious in character and had little to do with independence or political freedom; yet, whatever the motives, they remained a thorn in the side of American authority. On the island of Jolo, following several murders of U.S. soldiers, another ponderous campaign was fitted out in 1906. In the pitched battle which ensued the Americans took no prisoners and left no wounded. Six hundred natives were killed and the episode was noteworthy in that many were women and children who had "mingled with the warriors during the battle to such an extent that it was impossible to discriminate . . ." As late as 1916 a similar scene was enacted in Mindanao.

So the insurrection faded away in the manner of all such struggles, a minor sequel to a comic-opera war, lost in the clamor and shuffle of greater events; and the United States found herself in possession of an Asian archipelago which as a gift, under other circumstances, might well have been spurned. Would it prove, as outward-looking men hoped, a superlative base for economic operations in the Far East, fulfilling Seward's strident cry for domination of the Pacific and markets beyond the setting sun? Few Americans doubted that the nation's power and wealth were now to be enhanced; yet forebodings disturbed their dreams of glory. For better or worse America would never again be the same. "The jocund youth of our people now passes away never to return," wrote Admiral Mahan; "the cares and anxieties of manhood's years henceforth are ours." Yet responsibility was a cheap price to pay for progress, provided progress was indeed in the cards.

But what of the Filipinos—those of the original eight million who, having survived the war, faced the future in a ravaged land? How they and their country were henceforth to fare is another long story. At this writing one of their *insurrectos* is still alive in Kawit, Cavite Province, the town where he was born ninety years ago. His name is Emilio Aguinaldo.

BIBLIOGRAPHY

CERTAIN NEWSPAPERS, MAGAZINES, PAMPHLETS, REPRINTS OF speeches, and other transient materials used in the preparation of this narrative are not listed here, especially since in most cases they are cited in the text itself. Official documents consulted only for minor data have also been omitted. Those references which remain are, I believe, the fundamental primary and secondary sources having to do with the Insurrection, the most important being indicated by an asterisk (*). Each quotation, direct or paraphrased (even those as brief as a single word), each figure and factual statement, was derived from them. Yet I would be the last to claim that the book is "true" in the sense that a column of numbers can be summed up with unimpeachable accuracy. Depending upon the person at the easel, any shade of black, gray, or white can be mixed from a palette of documents, statistics, and memoirs.

Now that the story is ended it may be well for the author to state his evident bias concerning the Insurrection—one which, fortunately, few do not share sixty years after the event—namely, that the Spanish-American War which preceded it was unnecessary, that the Filipinos were indeed capable of self-rule, that in any event the problem was not ours, and that their forcible annexation was a moral wrong. Perhaps they were not capable of defense against other powers whose intentions in the far east at the time were, to say the least, suspicious; and in later years America did govern her new wards with astonishing decency; but it is fair to observe that these considerations only counterpoint the main theme.

Since with one exception all major participants in the episode are dead, my obligation to the following printed materials is total. Recent publication of Señor Aguinaldo's memoirs has permitted me to deal with several matters somewhat more confidently than would have been the case heretofore. But there exists only Funston's book and not another biography or autobiography of any U.S. general in the islands before or during the Insurrection; and for this and other reasons (stringent censorship on both sides, the loss and destruction during the war of many boxes and files of insurgent records, etc.) much of the story will never be known and can never be told.

AGUINALDO, EMILIO: *True Version of the Philippine Revolution.* Tarlac, 1899

——   *A Second Look at America.* New York, Robert Speller, 1957

ALEJANDRINO, JOSÉ: *The Price of Freedom.* Manila, 1949

ALGER, RUSSELL A.: *The Spanish-American War.* New York, Harper, 1901

"The Anti-Imperialist," June 3, 1899, and October 1, 1900

BAILEY, THOMAS A.: *The Man in the Street.* New York, Macmillan, 1948

——   *A Diplomatic History of the American People.* New York, Appleton-Century-Crofts (5th Ed.), 1955

BEALE, HOWARD: *Theodore Roosevelt and the Rise of America in World Power.* Baltimore, Johns Hopkins, 1957

BEARD, CHARLES A.: *The Idea of National Interest.* New York, Macmillan, 1934

——— AND MARY R.: *The Rise of American Civilization.* New York, Macmillan, 1946

BELLAIRS, EDGAR G.: *As It Is in the Philippines.* New York, Scribners, 1902

BEMIS, SAMUEL F.: *Diplomatic History of the United States.* New York, Holt, 1942

BERNSTEIN, DAVID: *The Philippine Story.* New York, Farrar, Straus, 1947

BLEYER, WILLARD G.: *Main Currents in the History of American Journalism.* New York, Houghton Mifflin, 1927

*BLOUNT, JAMES H.: *American Occupation of the Philippines.* New York, Putnam, 1913

BOWERS, CLAUDE G.: *Beveridge and the Progressive Era.* Cambridge, Houghton Mifflin, 1932

BRYAN, WILLIAM J.: *Memoirs.* Philadelphia, John C. Winston Co., 1925

——— AND OTHERS: *Republic or Empire; The Philippine Question.* Chicago, The Independence Co., 1899

CARLSON, OLIVER AND BATES, ERNEST S.: *Hearst: Lord of San Simeon.* New York, Viking, 1936

CHADWICK, FRENCH E.: *The Relations of the U.S. and Spain; Volumes 2 and 3; The Spanish-American War.* New York, Scribners, 1911

CHAMBERLIN, FREDERICK C.: *The Blow from Behind.* Boston, Lee and Shepard, 1903

——— *The Philippine Problem.* Boston, Little, Brown, 1913

COOLIDGE, ARCHIBALD C.: *The United States as a World Power.* New York, Macmillan, 1917

CRAIG, AUSTIN: *Lineage, Life and Labors of José Rizal.* Manila, Philippine Education Co., 1913

CUNNINGHAM, ALFRED: *The Chinese Soldier.* London, Low, 1902

CURTI, MERLE E.: *Bryan and World Peace*. Northampton, Mass., Smith College, 1931

——— *Peace or War; The American Struggle, 1636–1936*. New York, Norton, 1936

DAVIS, OSCAR F.: *Our Conquests in the Pacific*. New York, F. A. Stokes, 1899

DAWES, CHARLES G.: *A Journal of the McKinley Years*. Chicago, Lakeside Press, 1950

DENNETT, TYLER: *Americans in Eastern Asia*. New York, Macmillan, 1922

DEWEY, GEORGE W.: *Autobiography*. New York, Scribners, 1916

DULLES, FOSTER R.: *The Imperial Years*. New York, Crowell, 1956

*ELLIOTT, CHARLES B.: *The Philippines to the End of the Military Regime*. Indianapolis, Bobbs-Merrill, 1917

ELLIS, ELMER (Ed.): *Mr. Dooley at His Best*. New York, Scribners, 1938

FAULKNER, HAROLD U.: *Politics, Reform and Expansion, 1890–1900*. New York, Harper, 1959

FERNANDEZ, LEANDRO H.: *The Philippine Republic*. New York, Columbia University, 1926

FISKE, BRADLEY A.: *Wartime in Manila*. Boston, The Gorham Press, 1913

FONER, PHILIP S.: *Mark Twain: Social Critic*. New York, International Publishers, 1958

FORBES, W. CAMERON: *The Philippine Islands (Vol. 1)*. New York, Houghton Mifflin, 1928

FOREMAN, JOHN: *The Philippine Islands*. New York, Scribners, 1899

FREEMAN, NEEDOM H.: *A Soldier in the Philippines*. New York, F. T. Neely Co., 1901

FREIDEL, FRANK: *The Splendid Little War*. Boston, Little Brown, 1958

FUNSTON, FREDERICK: *Memories of Two Wars*. New York, Scribners, 1911

GRISWOLD, A. WHITNEY: *Far Eastern Policy of the United States.* New York, Harcourt, Brace, 1938

*GRUNDER, GANEL A. AND LIVEZEY, WILLIAM E.: *The Philippines and the United States.* Norman, Okla., University of Oklahoma, 1951

HALLE, LOUIS H.: *Dream and Reality.* New York, Harper, 1958

HALSTEAD, MURAT: *Aguinaldo and His Captor.* Cincinnati, Halstead Publishing Co., 1901

HAMLIN, C. H.: *The War Myth in United States History.* New York, Vanguard Press, 1927

HARRINGTON, FRED H.: *The Anti-Imperialist Movement.* Mississippi Valley Historical Review, September, 1935

HEALY, LAURIN H. AND KUTNER, LUIS: *The Admiral.* Chicago, Ziff-Davis, 1944

HERMAN, FREDERICK J.: *The Forty-Second Foot.* (n.p.) 1942

HOBSON, J. A.: *Imperialism.* London, Allen and Unwin, 1938

HOFSTADTER, RICHARD: "Manifest Destiny and the Philippines." (From *America in Crisis,* Daniel Aaron, ed., New York, Knopf, 1952)

——— *The American Political Tradition.* New York, Knopf, 1948

IRWIN, WILLIAM G.: "The First Fight with the Insurgents." *The Independent,* March 30, 1899

JOSEPHSON, MATTHEW: *The President Makers, 1896–1912.* New York, Harcourt, Brace, 1940

KALAW, MAXIMO M.: *The Case for the Filipinos.* New York, Century, 1916

*KALAW, TEODORO M.: *The Philippine Revolution.* Manila, Manila Book Co., 1925

KELLER, ALBERT G.: *Colonization.* New York, Ginn & Co., 1908

KENNAN, GEORGE F.: *American Diplomacy, 1900–1950.* University of Chicago, 1951

LATANE, JOHN H.: *America as a World Power, 1897–1907.* New York, Harper, 1907

LAUBACH, FRANK C.: *The People of the Philippines.* New York, Doran, 1925

*LEROY, JAMES A.: *The Americans in the Philippines* (2 Volumes). New York, Houghton Mifflin, 1914

Leslie's Official History of the Spanish-American War. Washington, War Records Office, 1899

LEUCHTENBURG, WILLIAM E.: "The Needless War with Spain." (From *Times of Trial,* Allan Nevins, Ed., New York, Knopf, 1958)

Literary Digest: "Aguinaldo's Version of the Philippine Troubles." February 3, 1900

LOLA, RAMON R.: "Aguinaldo." *The Independent,* September 22, 1898

MALCOLM, GEORGE A.: *The Commonwealth of the Philippines.* New York, Appleton-Century, 1936

MC ALEXANDER, ULYSSES G.: *History of the 13th Regiment of United States Infantry.* F. D. Gunn, 1905

MC DEVITT, V. EDMUND: *The First California's Chaplain.* Fresno, California, Academy Library Guild, 1956

*MILLET, FRANK D.: *Expedition to the Philippines.* New York, Harper, 1899

—— "The Filipino Leaders." *Harper's Weekly,* March 11, 1899

MILLIS, WALTER: *The Martial Spirit.* Literary Guild, 1931

MOON, PARKER T.: *Imperialism and World Politics.* New York, Macmillan, 1926

MORISON, SAMUEL E. AND COMMAGER, HENRY S.: *The Growth of the American Republic* (Vol. 2). New York, Oxford University, 1950

NEELY, FRANK T.: *Fighting in the Philippines.* New York, F. T. Neely Co., 1899

OLCOTT, CHARLES S.: *Life of William McKinley* (Vol. 2). New York, Houghton Mifflin, 1916

PALMER, FREDERICK: *With My Own Eyes.* Indianapolis, Bobbs-Merrill, 1932

PARKER, JAMES: *The Old Army*. Philadelphia, Dorrance, 1929

PENN, JULIUS A.: *A Narrative of the Campaign in Northern Luzon of the 2nd Battalion, 34th U.S. Volunteer Infantry*. Batavia, Ohio, 1933. (Privately circulated)

PERKINS, DEXTER: *A History of the Monroe Doctrine*. Boston, Little Brown, 1955

PRATT, JULIUS W.: *Expansionists of 1898*. New York, Peter Smith, 1951

―――― *America's Colonial Experiment*. New York, Prentice Hall, 1950

―――― "American Business and the Spanish-American War." *Hispanic-American Historical Review*, May, 1934

PRINGLE, HENRY F.: *Theodore Roosevelt*. New York, Harcourt, Brace, 1931

Public Opinion: "Aguinaldo as Insurgent Leader." August 11, 1898

―――― "The Manila Correspondents' Statements." July 27, 1899

RHODES, JAMES F.: *The McKinley and Roosevelt Administrations*. New York, Macmillan, 1923

*ROBINSON, ALBERT G.: *The Philippines, the War, and the People*. New York, Doubleday, Page, 1901

ROOSEVELT, THEODORE: *Letters* (*Vol. 2*). Cambridge, Harvard University, 1951

―――― *Selections from the Correspondence of Theodore Roosevelt and Henry Cabot Lodge* (*Vol. 1*). New York, Scribners, 1925

ROOSEVELT, THEODORE, JR.: *Colonial Policies of the United States*. Garden City, Doubleday, Doran, 1937

ROOT, ELIHU: *The Military and Colonial Policy of the United States*. Cambridge, Harvard University, 1916

RUSSELL, CHARLES E.: *The Outlook for the Philippines*. New York, Century, 1914

SAWYER, FREDERICK L.: *Sons of Gunboats*. Annapolis, U.S. Naval Institute, 1946

SCHRIFTGIESSER, KARL: *The Gentleman from Massachusetts: Henry Cabot Lodge.* Boston, Little, Brown, 1944

*SEXTON, WILLIAM T.: *Soldiers in the Sun.* Harrisburg, Pa., Military Service Publishing Co., 1939

SHERIDAN, RICHARD B.: *The Filipino Martyrs.* New York, John Lane, 1900

SORLEY, LEWIS S.: *History of the 14th U.S. Infantry.* Chicago, 1909. (Privately circulated)

SPIELMAN, WILLIAM C.: *William McKinley, Stalwart Republican.* New York, Exposition Press, 1954

STEVENS, WILLIAM O. AND WESTCOTT, ALLAN: *A History of Sea Power.* Garden City, Doubleday, Doran, 1935

STICKNEY, JOSEPH L.: *Life and Glorious Deeds of Admiral Dewey.* Chicago, Ayer, 1899

*STOREY, MOORFIELD AND LICHAUCO, MARCIAL P.: *The Conquest of the Philippines by the United States, 1898–1925.* New York, Putnam, 1926

———   *Marked Severities in the Philippines; Secretary Root's Record.* Boston, George Ellis, 1902

———   *The Moro Massacre.* (Undated letter)

SULLIVAN, MARK: *Our Times: The United States, 1900–1925; Vol. 1, "The Turn of the Century."* New York, Scribners, 1926

WALWORTH, ARTHUR: *School Histories at War.* Cambridge, Harvard University, 1938

WARBURG, JAMES P.: *The United States in a Changing World.* New York, Putnam, 1954

WATTERSON, HENRY: *History of the Spanish-American War.* 1898 (n.p.)

*WEINBERG, ALBERT K.: *Manifest Destiny.* Baltimore, Johns Hopkins, 1935

WELSH, HERBERT: *The Other Man's Country.* Philadelphia, Lippincott, 1900

WEST, RICHARD S., JR.: *Admirals of American Empire.* New York, Bobbs-Merrill, 1948

WHITE, WILLIAM A.: *The Autobiography of William Allen White.* New York, Macmillan, 1946

*WILCOX, MARRION (Ed.): *Harper's History of the War in the Philippines.* New York, Harper, 1900

WILDMAN, EDWIN: *Aguinaldo: A Narrative of Filipino Ambitions.* Boston, Lothrop, 1901

WILKERSON, MARCUS M.: *Public Opinion and the Spanish-American War.* Baton Rouge, University of Louisiana, 1932

WISAN, J. E.: *The Cuban Crisis as Reflected in the New York Press.* New York, Columbia University, 1934

*WORCESTER, DEAN C.: *The Philippines, Past and Present.* New York, Macmillan, 1930

*ZAIDE, GREGORIO F.: *The Philippine Revolution.* Manila, Modern Book Co., 1954

MISCELLANEOUS U.S. DOCUMENTS

*Adjutant General, U.S. Army; Correspondence Relating to the Philippine Islands May 3, 1898 to July 30, 1902. Washington, Government Printing Office, 1903

Bureau of Insular Affairs; Compilation of Philippine Insurgent Records. Washington, Government Printing Office, 1903

Bureau of Insular Affairs; Report of the United States Philippine Commission to the Secretary of War, for the Period from December 1, 1900, to October 15, 1901. Volumes 1 and 2. Washington, Government Printing Office, 1901

*Otis, General Elwell S.: Official Report to the Adjutant General, U.S. Army. Washington, Government Printing Office, 1899

Report of the Philippine Commission to the President. (The Schurman Report). Volumes 1 and 2, 1900; Volume 4, 1901. Washington, Government Printing Office

Report of the Taft Philippine Commission. Washington, Government Printing Office, 1901

HOUSE DOCUMENTS

*H.D. 2, Vol. 5, 56 Congress, 1st Session. Report of the War Department, Secretary

H.D. 2, Vol. 6, 56 Congress, 2nd Session. Report of the War Department, Lieutenant General Commanding

*H.D. 2, Vol. 7, 56 Congress, 2nd Session. Report of the War Department, Lieutenant General Commanding

H.D. 2, Vols. 5 and 6, 57 Congress, 1st Session. Report of the War Department, Lieutenant General Commanding

H.D. 2, Vol. 4, 57 Congress, 2nd Session. Report of the War Department, Secretary and Bureau Chiefs

SENATE DOCUMENTS

*S.D. 62, 55 Congress, 3rd Session

S.D. 169, 55 Congress, 3rd Session

S.D. 208, Volume 12, Miscellaneous, 56 Congress, 1st Session

S.D. 221, Vols. 17 to 24, 56 Congress, 1st Session. Conduct of the War Department in the War with Spain. (The Dodge Report)

S.D. 205, Vol. 15, 57 Congress, 1st Session. Charges of Cruelty in the Philippines

*S.D. 331, 3 Volumes, 57 Congress, 1st Session. Hearings before the Senate Committee on the Philippines

INDEX

Adams, Brooks, 335
Adams, Henry, 195, 272, 335
Ade, George, 187
Agoncillo, Felipe, 38, 229; deals with Wildman, 34–35; and McKinley, 161–62; and State Department, 211–12
Aguinaldo, Baldomero, 340
Aguinaldo, Crispulo, 286
Aguinaldo, Emilio, 36–37, 54, 98, 99, 110, 122–24, 137–39, 144, 161, 168–70, 178, 183, 190, 228, 232–33, 235, 238, 248, 256, 259, 266, 269, 272, 278, 293, 300–2, 315, 331, 335, 347, 349, 360, 364; and Biak-na-bato pact, 26; personality and background, 27ff.; and 1896 revolt, 28ff.; negotiates with de Rivera, 30–32; sails for Hong Kong, 32; dealings with Dewey and Wood, 46–47; with Bray and Pratt, 47–54; returns to Hong Kong, 50; and Wildman, 50–51; relations with Dewey after May 16, 64ff.; declares Philippine independence, 72; writes McKinley, 74–75; his difficulties with

U.S. officers, 100ff.; and Noriel's withdrawal, 103; demands surrender of Manila, 108; and German interference, 115; and Merritt, 120–21; warned to stay out of Manila, 125; and Anderson, 134–35; and church problem, 142; and first Filipino congress, 145–47; his 1898 policy toward U. S., 148; and ultimatum from Otis, 149–51; reacts to Paris Treaty, 175; late 1898 counter-proclamation, 200–1; before the outbreak, 203–6; and Luna's death, 247; and U.S. Democratic party, 252; his final peace overture, 257; and autumn 1899 flight, 280ff.; proclaims guerilla warfare, 288; appraised by MacArthur, 311; issues currency, 321–22; and General Order No. 202, 322; captured, 340–45; calls for peace, 345–46; his memoirs, 366
Alexandrino, José, 223, 278, 340
Alexandrino, Mascardo, 349
Alger, Russell A., backs intervention in Cuba, 41–42; on occupying the Philippines, 61; and War Depart-

Some other Oxford Paperbacks for readers interested in Central Asia,
China and South-East Asia, past and present

CAMBODIA

GEORGE COEDÈS
Angkor

MALCOLM MacDONALD
Angkor and the Khmers*

CENTRAL ASIA

PETER FLEMING
Bayonets to Lhasa

ANDRE GUIBAUT
Tibetan Venture

LADY MACARTNEY
An English Lady in Chinese
Turkestan

DIANA SHIPTON
The Antique Land

C.P. SKRINE AND
PAMELA NIGHTINGALE
Macartney at Kashgar*

ERIC TEICHMAN
Journey to Turkistan

ALBERT VON LE COQ
Buried Treasures of Chinese
Turkestan

AITCHEN K. WU
Turkistan Tumult

CHINA

All About Shanghai: A Standard
Guide

HAROLD ACTON
Peonies and Ponies

VICKI BAUM
Shanghai '37

ERNEST BRAMAH
Kai Lung's Golden Hours*

ERNEST BRAMAH
The Wallet of Kai Lung*

ANN BRIDGE
The Ginger Griffin

CHANG HSIN-HAI
The Fabulous Concubine*

CARL CROW
Handbook for China

PETER FLEMING
The Siege at Peking

MARY HOOKER
Behind the Scenes in Peking

NEALE HUNTER
Shanghai Journal*

REGINALD F. JOHNSTON
Twilight in the Forbidden City

GEORGE N. KATES
The Years that Were Fat

CORRINNE LAMB
The Chinese Festive Board

W. SOMERSET
MAUGHAM
On a Chinese Screen*

G.E. MORRISON
An Australian in China

DESMOND NEILL
Elegant Flower

PETER QUENNELL
Superficial Journey through
Tokyo and Peking

OSBERT SITWELL
Escape with Me! An Oriental
Sketch-book

J.A. TURNER
Kwang Tung or Five Years in
South China

HONG KONG AND
MACAU

AUSTIN COATES
City of Broken Promises

AUSTIN COATES
A Macao Narrative

AUSTIN COATES
Macao and the British, 1637–1842

AUSTIN COATES
Myself a Mandarin

AUSTIN COATES
The Road

The Hong Kong Guide 1893

INDONESIA

DAVID ATTENBOROUGH
Zoo Quest for a Dragon*

VICKI BAUM
A Tale from Bali*

'BENGAL CIVILIAN'
Rambles in Java and the Straits
in 1852

MIGUEL COVARRUBIAS
Island of Bali*

AUGUSTA DE WIT
Java: Facts and Fancies

JACQUES DUMARÇAY
Borobudur

JACQUES DUMARÇAY
The Temples of Java

ANNA FORBES
Unbeaten Tracks in Islands of the
Far East

GEOFFREY GORER
Bali and Angkor

JENNIFER LINDSAY
Javanese Gamelan

EDWIN M. LOEB
Sumatra: Its History and People

MOCHTAR LUBIS
The Outlaw and Other Stories

MOCHTAR LUBIS
Twilight in Djakarta

MADELON H. LULOFS
Coolie*

MADELON H. LULOFS
Rubber

COLIN McPHEE
A House in Bali*

ERIC MJÖBERG
Forest Life and Adventures in the
Malay Archipelago

H.W. PONDER
Java Pageant

HICKMAN POWELL
The Last Paradise

F.M. SCHNITGER
Forgotten Kingdoms in Sumatra

E.R. SCIDMORE
Java, The Garden of the East

MICHAEL SMITHIES
Yogyakarta: Cultural Heart of
Indonesia

LADISLAO SZÉKELY
Tropic Fever: The Adventures of
a Planter in Sumatra

EDWARD C. VAN NESS
AND SHITA
PRAWIROHARDJO
Javanese Wayang Kulit

HARRY WILCOX
Six Moons in Sulawesi

MALAYSIA

ODOARDO BECCARI
Wanderings in the Great
Forests of Borneo

ISABELLA L. BIRD
The Golden Chersonese: Travels
in Malaya in 1879

MARGARET BROOKE
THE RANEE OF
SARAWAK
My Life in Sarawak

SIR HUGH CLIFFORD
Saleh: A Prince of Malaya

HENRI FAUCONNIER
The Soul of Malaya

W.R. GEDDES
Nine Dayak Nights

C.W. HARRISON
Illustrated Guide to the Federated
Malay States (1923)

BARBARA HARRISSON
Orang-Utan

TOM HARRISSON
Borneo Jungle

TOM HARRISSON
World Within: A Borneo Story

CHARLES HOSE
The Field-Book of a Jungle-Wallah

CHARLES HOSE
Natural Man

W. SOMERSET
MAUGHAM
Ah King and Other Stories*

W. SOMERSET
MAUGHAM
The Casuarina Tree*

MARY McMINNIES
The Flying Fox*

ROBERT PAYNE
The White Rajahs of Sarawak

CARVETH WELLS
Six Years in the Malay Jungle

SINGAPORE

RUSSELL GRENFELL
Main Fleet to Singapore

R.W.E. HARPER AND
HARRY MILLER
Singapore Mutiny

MASANOBU TSUJI
Singapore 1941–1942

G.M. REITH
Handbook to Singapore (1907)

C.E. WURTZBURG
Raffles of the Eastern Isles

THAILAND

CARL BOCK
Temples and Elephants

REGINALD CAMPBELL
Teak-Wallah

ANNA LEONOWENS
The English Governess at the
Siamese Court

MALCOLM SMITH
A Physician at the Court of Siam

ERNEST YOUNG
The Kingdom of the Yellow Robe

* Titles marked with an asterisk have restricted rights.

Philippine Archipelago